UNDERSTANDING AND RESPONDING TO CHILD SEXUAL EXPLOITATION

The issue of child sexual exploitation (CSE) has received intense scrutiny in recent years, following a number of high profile legal cases, serious case reviews and inquiries. This has resulted in increasing expectations that those working in the field will know how to appropriately manage and respond to this form of abuse. Of course, this is no easy task given the widely acknowledged difficulties of identifying and responding to sexual abuse and the particular complexities associated with the gain dynamic within CSE and the predominantly older age of children affected by it.

This edited collection draws on the latest research evidence and academic thinking around CSE to consider issues of understanding and response. Written by researchers from 'The International Centre: Researching child sexual exploitation, violence and trafficking' at the University of Bedfordshire, Part I considers issues of understanding and conceptualisation. Part II considers the practical implications of some of this thinking, sharing learning from research and evaluation on prevention, identification and response.

Understanding and Responding to Child Sexual Exploitation presents critical learning for academics and students, and for those working in the fields of policy, practice and commissioning. It is relevant to a wide range of disciplines including social care, youth work, education, criminology, health and social policy.

Helen Beckett is Director of 'The International Centre: Researching child sexual exploitation, violence and trafficking' and a Reader in Child Protection and Children's Rights at the University of Bedfordshire, UK. She has twenty years' experience of undertaking and managing applied social research across academia and the voluntary and statutory sectors. She holds particular specialism in CSE and related adolescent safeguarding issues, and in ethics around engaging vulnerable individuals in sensitive research. Dr Beckett has published and presented widely on issues of sexual harm against children and regularly consults on research, policy and practice in this field.

Jenny Pearce (OBE) is Professor of Young People and Public Policy at the University of Bedfordshire, UK, where she was Founder of 'The International Centre: Researching child sexual exploitation, violence and trafficking'. She is a Visiting Professor at Goldsmiths College, London, UK, and is the Chair of the Local Safeguarding Children Board for the London tri-borough partnership (London boroughs of Hammersmith and Fulham, Westminster, and The Royal Borough of Kensington and Chelsea). She was Chair of the Academic Advisory Board for The Independent Inquiry into Child Sexual Abuse and continues to advise on reviews and inquiries into child sexual abuse.

UNDERSTANDING AND RESPONDING TO CHILD SEXUAL EXPLOITATION

Edited by Helen Beckett and Jenny Pearce

Routledge
Taylor & Francis Group

LONDON AND NEW YORK

First published 2018
by Routledge
2 Park Square, Milton Park, Abingdon, Oxon OX14 4RN

and by Routledge
711 Third Avenue, New York, NY 10017

Routledge is an imprint of the Taylor & Francis Group, an informa business

British Library Cataloguing in Publication Data
A catalogue record for this book is available from the British Library

Library of Congress Cataloging in Publication Data
Names: Beckett, Helen, editor. | Pearce, Jenny J., editor.
Title: Understanding and responding to child sexual exploitation / edited by Helen Beckett and Jenny Pearce.
Description: 1st Edition. | New York : Routledge, 2018. | Includes bibliographical references and index.
Identifiers: LCCN 2017038212 | ISBN 9781138293700 (hardback) | ISBN 9781138293724 (pbk.) | ISBN 9781315231945 (ebook)
Subjects: LCSH: Child sexual abuse—Investigation. | Sexually abused children—Services for.
Classification: LCC HV8079.C48 U5295 2018 | DDC 362.76—dc23
LC record available at https://lccn.loc.gov/2017038212

ISBN: 978-1-138-29370-0 (hbk)
ISBN: 978-1-138-29372-4 (pbk)
ISBN: 978-1-315-23194-5 (ebk)

Typeset in Bembo
by Swales & Willis Ltd, Exeter, Devon, UK

CONTENTS

ILLUSTRATIONS

Figures

Tables

CONTRIBUTORS

Elizabeth Ackerley is currently undertaking an ESRC funded 1+3 CASE studentship at the University of Manchester, UK, on 'Youth Activism in an Age of Austerity' partnered with RECLAIM, a youth leadership and social change organisation. Prior to this Elizabeth undertook an internship with the MsUnderstood Partnership between the University of Bedfordshire, Imkaan and Girls Against Gangs. She then worked from 2015–2017 as a Research Assistant at 'The International Centre: Researching child sexual exploitation, violence and trafficking' at the University of Bedfordshire, focussing on developing creative, meaningful and ethical ways of involving children and young people in research into sexual violence and related forms of harm.

Debra Allnock is a Senior Research Fellow at 'The International Centre: Researching child sexual exploitation, violence and trafficking' at the University of Bedfordshire, UK, where she leads on work around criminal justice responses to sexual abuse. She obtained her PhD in Policy Studies from the University of Bristol, UK, in 2015 and has developed a cumulative expertise in child sexual abuse and child protection over nearly 20 years of research in the United Kingdom. She previously worked for the National Evaluation of Sure Start, the National Society for the Prevention of Cruelty to Children and consulted for organisations such as UNICEF, Research in Practice and Victim Support.

Helen Beckett is Director of 'The International Centre: Researching child sexual exploitation, violence and trafficking' and a Reader in Child Protection and Children's Rights at the University of Bedfordshire, UK. She has twenty years' experience of undertaking and managing applied social research across academia and the voluntary and statutory sectors. She holds particular specialism in CSE and related adolescent safeguarding issues, and in ethics around engaging vulnerable individuals in sensitive research. Dr Beckett has published and presented widely on issues of sexual harm against children and regularly consults on research, policy and practice in this field.

Silvie Bovarnick is a Research Fellow at 'The International Centre: Researching child sexual exploitation, violence and trafficking' at the University of Bedfordshire, UK, where much of her work focuses on youth participatory approaches to researching sexual violence. Silvie holds a PhD in International Relations and has over 15 years of research experience, both internationally and in the UK, in the fields of human rights, gendered violence and child maltreatment. She undertook work on child trafficking and neglect when employed at the NPSCC and undertook a comprehensive national research programme on the health and mental health effects of violence and abuse when at the Department of Health.

Isabelle Brodie is a Senior Research Fellow in 'The International Centre: Researching child sexual exploitation, violence and trafficking', University of Bedfordshire, UK. Isabelle has worked for some 20 years as a researcher in the field of child welfare, working on a range of projects relating to children and young people in care, educational exclusion and child abuse. She currently leads the participation strand of The Alexi Project, a national evaluation of a hub-and-spoke model of child sexual exploitation services.

Kate D'Arcy has been working in education for many years as a youth worker, teacher and researcher. Her working practice has always been situated in the margins of education, supporting a variety of vulnerable and often disengaged children, young people and communities in a variety of settings. Kate continues to work to promote an agenda for change for marginalised individuals and groups, currently working on the participation of children and young people in relation to sexual violence. She has a particular interest and expertise in exploring race and ethnicity and ensuring active participation of marginalised children, young people and adults in research.

Carlene Firmin MBE is a Principal Research Fellow at 'The International Centre: Researching child sexual exploitation, violence and trafficking' at the University of Bedfordshire, UK, where she leads on peer-on-peer abuse and contextual approaches to safeguarding adolescents. Carlene has been researching young people's experiences of community and group-based violence for ten years, advocating for comprehensive approaches to safety in public places. A board member for NOTA and the Prison Reform Trust, Carlene has written on the issues of safeguarding and violence in *The Guardian* since 2010 and is widely published in the area of child welfare. In 2011 Carlene became the youngest black woman to receive an MBE for her seminal work on gang-affected young women in the UK.

Danielle Fritz worked as a Research Assistant with 'The International Centre: Researching child sexual exploitation, violence and trafficking' at the University of Bedfordshire, UK, from 2016–2017. She helped develop and launch the Contextual Safeguarding Network, a platform that brings UK-based practitioners together to share and generate knowledge on contextual approaches to safeguarding young people from violence and abuse. She also supported research on local authority responses to peer-on-peer abuse. Danielle currently works as an attorney at an immigration centre for women and children in San Francisco, California.

David Hancock worked for the London Borough of Camden for over ten years in Family Services and Social Work undertaking a variety of roles. David has spent the last two years working as a Child Sexual Exploitation (CSE) and Missing Analyst/Coordinator in which he provided the local authority and partner agencies problem profiles around CSE and missing children. David is experienced in both qualitative and quantitative research and evaluation. He has presented widely on CSE with particular focus around using social media to track/prevent/disrupt CSE.

Lia Latchford has ten years' experience of work in the ending violence against women and girls (VAWG) sector with expertise on issues affecting young black and 'minority ethnic' (BME) women and girls. She is currently the Development Co-ordinator at Imkaan, a second-tier black feminist organisation that represents a national network of frontline ending VAWG organisations that are led 'by and for' BME women and girls. Her work focuses on quality assurance, research and evaluation. She also co-leads Purple Drum, an Imkaan project committed to archiving and amplifying young black women's voices in policy, media and wider discourses.

Jenny Lloyd is a Research Fellow at 'The International Centre: Researching child sexual exploitation, violence and trafficking' at the University of Bedfordshire, UK. After completing her PhD in Human Geography at Newcastle University, UK, she joined 'The International Centre: Researching child sexual exploitation, violence and trafficking' working within the Contextual Safeguarding Team. Her research interests include peer-on-peer abuse, harmful sexual behaviour and serious youth violence. She is particularly interested in gender-based violence and the need for intersectional approaches to equality.

Jenny Pearce (OBE) is Professor of Young People and Public Policy at the University of Bedfordshire, UK, where she was Founder of 'The International Centre: Researching child sexual exploitation, violence and trafficking'. She is a Visiting Professor at Goldsmiths College, London, UK, and is the Chair of the Local Safeguarding Children Board for the London tri-borough partnership (London boroughs of Hammersmith and Fulham, Westminster, and The Royal Borough of Kensington and Chelsea). She was Chair of the Academic Advisory Board for The Independent Inquiry into Child Sexual Abuse and continues to advise on reviews and inquiries into child sexual abuse.

Roma Thomas is a Research Fellow at 'The International Centre: Researching child sexual exploitation, violence and trafficking' at the University of Bedfordshire, UK. She joined academe in 2012, having previously run her own consultancy business. Her research interests include young masculinities, emotional methodologies and family support. Roma's past work includes evaluative research such as the Barnardo's Families and Communities against Sexual Exploitation project and the Nightwatch project. She is Course Coordinator for a Master's programme in International Social Work and Social Development. Roma is currently completing her doctoral studies in young masculinities at the University of Sussex, UK.

Joanne Walker is a Research Assistant at 'The International Centre: Researching child sexual exploitation, violence and trafficking' at the University of Bedfordshire, UK. Since joining in 2015, she has worked across a range of projects including the production of CSE evidence reviews and guidance for policy and practice, using evidence to improve criminal justice responses to CSE and the gathering of empirical data on harmful sexual behaviour. Prior to joining the university, Joanne worked for a number of charity and statutory organisations monitoring, analysing and evaluating research, policy and practice pertaining to child sexual abuse.

Camille Warrington is a Senior Research Fellow at 'The International Centre: Researching child sexual exploitation, violence and trafficking' at the University of Bedfordshire, UK. In recent years her work has focused on adolescent experiences of sexual violence in the UK, and in particular their experiences of service responses including police, social care and third-sector support. Camille is particularly interested in how children's decision-making informs or is marginalised from these processes and the implications for children's safety. Her work involves developing a range of creative, participatory projects seeking to further meaningful dialogue between young people, policy makers and researchers.

ACKNOWLEDGEMENTS

As an applied research centre, we could not deliver the work we do without the active engagement of participants, advisors and dissemination partners. First and foremost, we wish to acknowledge all the children and young people who have participated in, and advised on, our work. We know the courage it takes to engage in research, particularly on sensitive issues, and we are so grateful for your willingness to engage with us and so articulately share your experiences and perspectives. It has been a pleasure and privilege learning from you. We would also like to acknowledge all the professionals who have supported these young people's engagement and/or participated in our work in their own right. Your willingness to work in partnership with us to improve children and young people's lives is appreciated and greatly enhances both the quality and relevance of our work. And to those who have funded our work over the years, sincere thanks for your investment and for supporting us to pursue our objective of increasing understanding and improving responses to sexual violence and abuse.

To the authors in this book, thank you for all your work. As editors, it is a pleasure to be able to showcase such quality work and innovative thinking and to work with such committed and excellent colleagues. To our other colleagues in 'The International Centre: Researching child sexual exploitation, violence and trafficking' at the University of Bedfordshire, we are immensely grateful for your contributions to the work that we draw on in this book and for your support in developing this volume. It is a genuine pleasure to work with such a fantastic and innovative team of researchers who are so passionate about bringing about change within this field.

Jenny would like to thank all of her friends for their continued support and encouragement of her work. In particular, she would like to thank her two daughters, Anne-Marie and Rosie, their partners, Eliot and Fordy, and her grandchild, Finley, all of whose energy for life abound. Her extended family and parents have been so important to engaging with life outside of work, for which she is really grateful. Finally, she would like to thank her partner, John Coleman, for standing alongside her and for never doubting her for one moment.

Helen would like to thank her husband, Alistair, for his unwavering support for her work and overall belief in her; this would not be possible without him. She would also like to thank her parents for all their investment over the years, and her friends who help keep balance in life.

ABBREVIATIONS

BME	Black and minority ethnic
CoE	Council of Europe
CSA	Child sexual abuse
CSAAS	Child sexual abuse accommodation syndrome
CSE	Child sexual exploitation
DfE	Department for Education
DOH	Department of Health
EU	European Union
IIOC	Indecent images of children
NI	Northern Ireland
OCC	Office of Children's Commissioner
PSHE	Personal social health and economic (education)
RSE	Relationships and sex education
SCA	Serious Crime Act
SVBAC	Sexual violence between and against children
UK	United Kingdom
UNCRC	United Nations Convention on the Rights of the Child
US	United States

INTRODUCTION

Helen Beckett and Jenny Pearce

The issue of child sexual exploitation (CSE) has received intense scrutiny within the United Kingdom (UK) in recent years, following a number of high profile legal cases, serious case reviews and inquiries. The associated media interest in such developments has also meant that its public profile has increased significantly. Whilst in the past few may have heard of the term 'child sexual exploitation', now its usage is deeply embedded across media, policy and practice discourse.

Whilst increasing awareness of any form of abuse is clearly to be welcomed, this increased attention on CSE has not been without its difficulties and challenges. As explored within Part I of this book, some of these difficulties and challenges relate to how CSE has been conceptualised and responded to in relation to other forms of sexual violence and abuse. Others emanate from our partial understanding around patterns of perpetration and victimisation and an unhelpful focus on particular forms of CSE over others. Challenges also stem from our inability to reconcile the concurrent presence of victimhood and gain, and to recognise how individual biographies and structural constraints interact in creating patterns of vulnerability and protection. Underpinning all of this is a continuing societal discomfort around accepting that CSE – or indeed any other form of sexual violence or abuse – can affect any child and, as such, is a problem that affects us all.

The evidence base around CSE has undoubtedly mushroomed in recent years with the publication of increasing numbers of research reports, evaluations, inquiries and serious case reviews. However, in spite of this, gaps in our knowledge remain; a critical example of this is the ongoing absence of accurate prevalence or pattern data. Challenges also exist in relation to interpretation and application of this increasing body of evidence – how do busy practitioners determine quality and relevance, and how can they navigate their way through what is now a substantial body of publications around CSE?

Whilst the debate around CSE has certainly developed over the last five to ten years, it is the editors' contention that it is now timely to move beyond discrete project evaluations or thematic research (valued as these are) and create space for a deeper, more holistic, assessment of the issue. This applies not only to its relative conceptualisation in relation to other forms of sexual violence and abuse, but also to our understanding of who such abuse affects, how it affects them and what we need to do about this. We need to engage with the 'big questions' of structural inequalities, societal norms, contextual contributors and inhibitors to abuse and the inter-connected nature of these. We also need to engage with the relationship between child development and sexuality, and how increasing capacity and protective responsibilities can be reconciled. Importantly, we need to do this in partnership with children and young people, whose voices must become more central to this debate.

Written by researchers from 'The International Centre: Researching child sexual exploitation, violence and trafficking' at the University of Bedfordshire, and drawing on the work of colleagues within the Centre and other researchers working in the field, this book attempts to begin some of these conversations.

There are two distinct, but related, parts to the book. Part I consists of four chapters that explore how we currently conceptualise and engage with CSE and other forms of sexual harm against children. As explored in more detail below, these chapters highlight the need for:

- better overall engagement with issues of sexual harm against children at both an individual and societal level;
- a more critical engagement with our current conceptualisations of different forms of sexual harm and the existing evidence base around this; and
- a more holistic understanding of the ways in which individual biographies and structural constraints interact.

Part II of the book explores the practical implications of these issues, sharing learning from a range of recent initiatives on prevention, identification and response. This includes consideration of:

- involving young people in preventative initiatives;
- the role of youth workers in prevention and identification;
- equipping those working in the night-time economy to identify potential harm;
- a contextual approach to problem profiling; and
- how to develop participatory practice in working with those affected by CSE.

Chapter overview

Part I: contemporary perspectives on understanding

In Chapter 1, Helen Beckett and Joanne Walker explore the current conceptualisation of sexual harm against children, with specific reference to the concept of CSE. They do so with a particular focus on the relationship between CSE and the wider concept of child sexual abuse (CSA), observing unclear definitional boundaries and confused interpretation in practice. Whilst recognising the gains that have been introduced through an increasing focus on CSE, the authors propose that the current conceptualisation of the term – and in particular its relative status to other forms of abuse – is neither reflective of reality nor fit for purpose as the basis of our model of response. Given the many bases on which children and young people's experiences of abuse vary, the authors argue that there is no rationale for prioritising exchange over other factors (as the basis for categorising experiences), particularly given how broadly exchange is currently defined. This approach, the authors conclude, suggests both a homogeneity within CSE cases – and an 'othering' from other CSA cases – that is not supported by the evidence base. The authors conclude that it is time to develop an alternative multi-faceted conceptualisation of CSA that recognises exchange as just one defining feature of an abusive experience, and as such, more accurately reflects our increased understanding of the realities of young people's experiences of abuse and the variations and complexities observable within this.

In Chapter 2 Jenny Pearce addresses the critical issue of how we as a society engage (or fail to engage) with the issue of sexual violence between and against children (SVBAC), exploring the ways in which this has been 'hidden' and/or 'othered' within society. She argues that practices of distancing and denial means that those who are affected are isolated and marginalised as 'different'. Indeed, SVBAC in these 'othered' families, communities or places is often described as 'normalised' there, further separating it from 'our' non-sexually violent lifestyles. Pearce argues that a denial of the extent and prevalence of SVBAC, an undue reliance on the child protection system for identification and response and the adoption of an outward facing rather than inwardly reflective lens results in limited rather than universal ownership of the problem. This, she argues, leaves the child carrying the burden of responsibility for the abuse they experience. Rather than talking of SVBAC as 'normalised' within specific communities, she argues for generic approaches where everyone engages with further understanding of, and scope to, prevent SVBAC.

Debra Allnock returns to the theme of similarities and differences between CSE and other forms of CSA in Chapter 3. Addressing this specifically through the lens of learning around disclosure, she explores the transferability of learning between the CSE and wider CSA field. Allnock highlights a range of gaps and inconsistences in the literature in relation to clarity around definitions of abuse and, specifically, whether cases of CSE (recognised to be a form of CSA within the UK) are included in these. She notes how the context of the abuse can impact upon propensity to disclose, highlighting the need for greater attention to issues of context within the existing body of literature. Whilst noting similarities between disclosure findings from the CSA and CSE bodies of literature, she also notes variation both in terms of the issues identified as relevant and the manifestation of these issues within those varying contexts. As such, she concludes that the current CSA literature only partially captures the challenges that exist in relation to disclosure of CSE. Noting also that the current CSE literature insufficiently engages with the theoretical foundations of disclosure studies, she argues the need for (a) cautious application of learning from one field to the other and (b) better integration of these currently discrete bodies of knowledge in the future.

Also considering the importance of context, Elizabeth Ackerley and Lia Latchford highlight the need to move to a more nuanced and holistic understanding of vulnerability to CSE and other forms of sexual violence in Chapter 4. They observe that whilst there has been recognition of vulnerabilities and structural constraints within the existing body of literature, this has tended to be singularly observed. As such they argue that much of the existing body of literature has inadequately accounted for the ways in which different aspects of young people's biographies and the multiple structural constraints within which they exist combine to cumulatively influence both their experiences of abuse and how others respond to this abuse. The authors propose that intersectionality theory offers a helpful lens for exploring these influences. Illustrating this with particular reference to the intersection between race and gender, they use both secondary data and practice examples to explore how the adoption of an intersectional approach could improve both research and practice understanding of young people's lived experiences of sexual violence.

Part II: contemporary perspectives on prevention and response

The second part of the book commences with an exploration of the contribution that young people can make to our preventative efforts around sexual violence. Exploring this with reference to the learning from 'Our Voices' (a pan-European participation project) in Chapter 5, Silvie Bovarnick and Kate D'Arcy consider both the arguments for and challenges associated with involving young people in delivering educative initiatives around sexual violence. Having outlined the need for such education in order to address ongoing stigma and silence around these issues, they explore how peer-led educative initiatives can offer benefits to both the young people delivering the work and those being educated. Whilst promoting the benefits of such initiatives, the authors also recognise that their practical implementation can involve challenges and difficulties. Drawing on the experiences of 'Our Voices' the authors identify what these challenges may be and the necessary infrastructure needed to address them.

Chapter 6 also considers issues of prevention, specifically in relation to the potential contribution that detached youth work can make to preventative and identification efforts. To explore this, Jenny Lloyd and Danielle Fritz draw on observations of detached youth work and interviews with young people and youth workers, collated as part of the contextual safeguarding programme of work at The International Centre. Whilst recognising that youth work is but one element of a holistic response to CSE, they note that it is one that is not yet fully utilised. Focusing particularly on the detached nature of their work, the authors explore how detached youth workers' presence within communities offers a unique and critical perspective on the harm that may be experienced in such communities and the contexts within which such harm occurs. They further argue that the physical presence of detached youth workers in communities and their relational working methods contribute to enhanced engagement with young people. They note how this can enable such workers to challenge potentially harmful attitudes and behaviours before they escalate, as well as enhancing the likelihood of young people approaching them for support.

Writing in Chapter 7, Roma Thomas explores what the adage 'CSE is everyone's business' means for those working in the night-time economy. Commencing with a précis of the development of the night-time economy, Thomas argues that responses to the movement of young people into these traditionally adult environments have frequently seen them problematised and/or made invisible. As such, their presence in such spaces has not been accompanied by the necessary consideration of their safety within such environments or acceptance of a responsibility to address this. Drawing on the findings of an evaluation of an awareness raising programme for the night-time economy, she explores the learning in relation to how we can enhance protective capacity amongst those working in this field. In doing so she considers the challenges inherent in such an endeavour and explores potential means of overcoming these.

Also emphasising the importance of understanding local contexts of harm, in Chapter 8 Carlene Firmin and David Hancock explore the benefits of adopting a contextual approach to problem profiling. Currently being used primarily to map trends and patterns of known cases of CSE, the authors explore how the contextual application of problem profiling can also highlight particular social contexts within which risk may be exacerbated and contribute to the potential identification and reduction of as yet unknown harm. Drawing on the findings of a seminar series held with analysts and data holders – and illustrating this with practice examples – the authors explore this extended use of problem profiling. They identify three key considerations necessary to facilitate this – agreed objectives, information sharing and dissemination of learning – exploring these as both distinct entities and inter-dependent concepts. The authors conclude that problem profiling also holds the potential to move beyond a deficit-based model to map, for example, protective peer networks or contexts in which young people can safely socialise and develop.

Returning to the issue of young people's participation explored in relation to preventative initiatives in Chapter 5, in Chapter 9 Camille Warrington and Isabelle Brodie explore its application in work with those who experienced CSE. The authors argue that embedding participation rights begins with good relationship-based practice, expressed through principles of voluntary engagement, two-way information and a strengths-based approach. They note that although individual practitioners may adhere to such principles within their work, organisational commitment is also required for participation to become truly embedded. This relates both to support for practitioners seeking to pursue participatory practice within their individual practice and to a wider commitment to valuing the collective voices of service users at a service-wide level. Whilst clearly promoting such an approach, the authors recognise the emerging nature of the evidence base around this, emphasising the need for a strengthened evidence base around which to build enhanced commitment and practice.

PART I
Contemporary perspectives on understanding

1

WORDS MATTER

Reconceptualising the conceptualisation of child sexual exploitation

Helen Beckett and Joanne Walker

Introduction

> Words matter because they affect how we conceptualise problems, prioritise issues, and forge responses. Inconsistent use of language and terms can lead to inconsistent laws and policy responses on the same issue. Despite the existence of legal definitions for a number of sexual crimes against children, there is still considerable confusion surrounding the use of different terminology related to the sexual exploitation and sexual abuse of children. Even where the same terms are used, there is quite often disagreement concerning their actual meaning, leading to use of the same words to refer to different actions or situations. This has created significant challenges for policy development and programming, development of legislation, and data collection, leading to flawed responses and limited and ineffective methods of measuring impact or setting targets.
>
> *(Inter-agency Working Group on Sexual Exploitation of Children, 2016, p. 1)*

Ever since the term 'child sexual exploitation' (CSE) entered policy and practice discourse, confusion around its meaning, application and relationship to the wider concepts of 'child sexual abuse' (CSA) and 'sexual violence' has abounded. This is true of its usage in both the UK and in a range of other international contexts, as reflected in the above quotation from the 2016 Luxembourg guidelines.

Recognition of this confusion, and discussion of both the practical and conceptual implications of this, is not new (Melrose, 2012, 2013; Pitts, 2013; Hallett, 2015; Coy, 2016). The introduction of new definitions of CSE in three of the four United Kingdom (UK) nations in 2016/17[1] – and the production of the new set of international terminology guidelines referenced above – does however shift the parameters and context of the debate somewhat. As such, it is timely to revisit the application and utility of the concept and its relationship to other forms of sexual violence and abuse.

The chapter draws on an evaluation of CSE policy frameworks across the four UK nations and a review of UK CSE literature conducted by the authors. It also draws on the authors' reflections on their delivery of CSE training programmes to a range of professionals across the UK over the last five years,[2] specifically participant engagement around issues of definitional confusion and practice challenges. The chapter considers international learning from and for UK developments with particular reference to the 2016 Luxembourg Terminology Guidelines referenced above.

We commence with a brief overview of the development of the concept of CSE within the UK. This is followed by an exploration of how CSE is currently defined across the four UK nations and the ongoing challenges in relation to its conceptualisation and interpretation. Core to this is consideration of the role of 'exchange' and the resultant conceptualisation of victims when they are the ones receiving something from the abusive act. Also critical is the lack of clarity as to the parameters of this exchange.

Having explored some of the key challenges in relation to the concept of CSE, we take a step back from the current policy position to consider the relative merits of continuing along the CSE trajectory or adopting an alternative conceptualisation of the forms of harm currently labelled CSE. Whilst evidenced primarily with reference to developments in the four UK nations, the issues raised hold wider significance for other jurisdictions also facing the conceptual and consequent operational confusion referenced above.

The journey to CSE

Although a relatively recent term, CSE is in no way a new phenomenon. Cases of what we would now term CSE have been recorded as far back as the 19th century (Brown and Barrett, 2002). As accounts of the historical development of the issue are well documented elsewhere (Brown and Barrett, 2002; Melrose, 2012; Hallett, 2015, 2017) they will not be rehearsed here. We will however briefly consider the recent history of the issue within the UK, specifically the move from the terminology of 'child prostitution' to that of 'CSE' witnessed since the turn of the 21st century, as this holds pertinent learning for where we are now in 2017.

In brief, the 1980s and 1990s saw increasing discomfort in child protection circles with the application of the term 'prostitution' to those under 18 years of age. Adopting the adage that 'if a child cannot consent to have sex, they cannot consent to sell it' campaigners, both within the UK and internationally, lobbied for recognition of what was then called 'child prostitution' as a form of child abuse rather than a criminal offence on the part of the child (Barrett, 1997; Inter-agency Working Group on Sexual Exploitation of Children, 2016).

A significant win for those campaigning for this change within the UK occurred at the turn of the century, when new government guidance (DOH, 2000, p. 12) recognised that children 'involved in prostitution should be treated primarily as the victims of abuse'. Further progress was observable in 2004 (Wales) and 2006 (England) which shifted the discourse from children 'involved in' prostitution to those abused through the same. Whilst still retaining the language of prostitution, this move further reframed a child's involvement in it as abusive rather than criminal. In doing so it redefined them primarily as victims rather than offenders, a development in line with international discourse on the issue at the time.[3] Relatedly it was the beginning of the movement away from a criminal justice response and towards a child protection response to those affected by the issue.

Interestingly, the guidance did retain the option to pursue a criminal justice response to those who would not accept help and were deemed to be persistent offenders. Whilst not couched as such, this was clearly predicated on a judgement-based understanding of victimhood that differentiated between 'deserving' and 'undeserving' victims. As explored below, this is a harmful binary distinction that continues today and has clearly contributed to the overlooking of harm in some cases of CSE, particularly those cases where a young person can be seen to be benefiting from and/or initiating the exchange.

Whilst the recognition of the abusive nature of child prostitution was welcomed, campaigning efforts continued to move away from the terminology of prostitution entirely and its association with an adult practice, and reframe the issue more clearly in child protection terms. 2008–2010 was a seminal time period in this regard, with the English and Welsh governments introducing statutory guidance that reframed the issue as one of 'child sexual exploitation' rather than as prostitution (All Wales Child Protection Procedures Review Group, 2008; DCSF, 2009; Welsh Assembly Government, 2010). The language of CSE has dominated discourse since and has now become deeply embedded within both practice and policy. This has not however been without complications or challenges, as explored below.

Current policy definitions of CSE and CSA in the UK

All four UK nations currently operate a definition of CSE that, although expressed in slightly different terminology, hold true to a number of core common components.[4] All purport that CSE is a form of child sexual abuse that can affect any child under the age of 18 years. Although less explicitly stated, also common to all four nations' policy positions is recognition that CSE:

- Is an umbrella term covering many different manifestations of abuse; both contact and non-contact;
- Can affect both males and females;
- Can be perpetrated by a range of abusers – male/female; adult/peer; any social class or ethnicity; operating alone, in groups or organised gangs.

Interestingly, all of the same things can be said of the broader definitions of CSA across the four UK nations. So, if CSE is a form of CSA, what is it that distinguishes CSE from other forms of CSA?

Although there are some differences between the four nations' CSE and CSA definitions around the degree to which power dynamics are referenced and, relatedly, whether the abuse is described as coerced or enticed, these are more semantics rather than substantive differences. The core substantive difference between definitions of CSE and broader definitions of CSA is the additional requirement in the former for some form of 'exchange', in which the victim and/or perpetrator 'receives something' in return for the sexual activity.

This exchange or receipt of something – the defining feature of CSE within current policy definitions – is variably defined across the four UK nations, with resultant differences in what is understood to constitute CSE within those jurisdictions. As explored below, the lack of clarity around the parameters of the exchange within this has also resulted in varying interpretations of what might fall within or outside of the conceptualisation. We explore this with reference to (a) victim gain and (b) perpetrator gain in turn below, the presence of either (or both) of which would constitute a case as CSE.

Victim gain: can a young person gain from their abuse?

Before considering the detail of what is defined as constituting victim gain for the purposes of CSE, it is worth commenting on the general concept of victim gain itself, given (a) its centrality to the definition of CSE and (b) the apparent discomfort that exists in some circles around this. Our experience of training professionals and supporting definition development clearly demonstrates that people can struggle with the concept that a child or young person may engage in sexual activity in return for something they need or want, and thus gain something as part of an abusive dynamic. A specific anxiety articulated to us in relation to this is that highlighting the gain for the child could conceal the abusive nature of the act. This concern – that professionals will not recognise it as abuse if the child is getting something they need or want from the situation – has led some to propose that recognition of such gain should be less central within, or indeed entirely removed from, the definition. This, we argue, is not a definitional issue. It is instead an educative one. Indeed, it is one that lies at the heart of the problem and a significant contributor to our failure to adequately identify and respond to some cases of CSE.

Core to these identification and response problems is our partial understanding of victimhood and our flawed perception of what constitutes a victim, together with a failure to adequately recognise the potential complexities of, and variations within, abusive situations. To expand, our understanding of, and responses to, CSE have historically been informed by the 'puppet on a string' model (Barnardo's, 2011), in which the child is perceived as having no say or choice in what happens to them, their actions and experiences being entirely manipulated by an abusive individual or group. Whilst this degree of external control is indeed present in some cases of CSE, we know that there are many other cases in which the axis of power and decision-making is much more subtle and complex (Melrose, 2010; Pearce, 2010; Beckett, 2011; Beckett et al., 2013; Pitts, 2013; Hallett, 2015; Beckett, Holmes and Walker, 2017). Practice evidence shows that the reality of many young people's experiences of CSE are not necessarily driven by threat or force, but may be driven more by need or want or, akin to many domestic violence situations, loyalty to or love for the perpetrator. Although also provided for within the definitions of CSE, these are the cases that we are less likely to recognise as abusive, and where the child/young person can be misconstrued as 'making active lifestyle choices' (Jago and Pearce, 2008; Griffiths, 2013; Pearce, 2013; Jay, 2014; Bedford, 2015; Research in Practice, 2015).

This dynamic of 'choice' or 'agency' – and the presence of victim gain often observed within CSE – complicated and uncomfortable as it may be, is not one that can be avoided or denied. Indeed it is the very presence of such gain that both distinguishes cases of CSE from other cases of sexual abuse and adds an additional layer of complexity in responding to such cases.[5]

What constitutes victim gain within CSE?

So, if we can resolve the ideological dilemmas addressed above and accept that one of the core dynamics of CSE is the fact that someone receives something in return for the sexual activity, and, critically, that this someone can be the victim, what are the definitional parameters of such gain?

All four UK nations,[6] and the new Luxembourg guidelines (Inter-agency Working Group on Sexual Exploitation of Children, 2016), define this gain quite broadly and allow for it to include both tangible gains, such as money or goods, and more intangible gains, such as protection, affection or status. Although less explicitly articulated in some of the definitions, the 'something received' by the victim is also generally accepted to include the avoidance of harm to them or others (for example, a child who engages in sexual activity in order to stop someone enacting a threat to abuse a sibling or physically harm a friend). Similarly, although not explicitly articulated in the UK definitions, this is also generally accepted to include the promise of something, as per the Luxembourg guidelines.

These broad parameters around 'victim gain' mean that the concept of CSE is a long way from – and much more expansive than – the origins of the issue; namely that of child prostitution. That conceptualisation, as set out in UK legislation,[7] is related only to tangible gain, specifically that which could be financially measured. Interestingly, as explored later in the chapter, legislation has remained aligned with the concept of tangible gain, resulting in a mismatch between policy and practice around CSE following terminology changes introduced under the Serious Crime Act (SCA) in 2015.

To elaborate on this a little further, it is interesting to look at the work of Melrose who, writing in 2013 on the introduction of CSE within policy discourse, purported that 'arguably this new language stretches the concept to the point of meaninglessness and in practice this means that distinguishing CSE from other forms of adolescent sexual activity has become increasingly difficult' (Melrose, 2013, p. 11). Five years on, we would argue that although some progress has been made in this regard, following work by the authors and others, the challenge of where CSE ends and other forms of CSA start – or indeed as Melrose notes, the difference between CSE and adolescent sexual activity – is still one that causes difficulties for both data capture and practice responses.

That is not to say that there are not exchange-based scenarios that are predicated on other forms of gain, such as perceived receipt of love or acquisition of status or protection. Indeed, the expansion of the concept came about in response to the identification of such cases in practice and has certainly been helpful in shedding light on their existence. The question is not, therefore, whether such cases exist or whether we need to respond to them, but rather whether labelling them as CSE is the best response?

We would propose that the general lack of clarity around what constitutes 'something the child needs or wants', together with the fact that many abused children receive gifts or treats from their abuser, continues to pose a practical problem in terms of delineating between CSE and other forms of CSA. Theoretically, one could conceivably argue that any child who receives something from their abuser is therefore experiencing CSE. Recognising this challenge, the new English guidance has attempted to offer some interpretative guidance around this, emphasising that cases should only be classed as CSE if the 'exchange' is the core dynamic at play, as opposed to incidental to the abuse (Department for Education [DfE], 2017a, p. 6; Beckett, Holmes and Walker, 2017, p. 8). Of course, what constitutes a core dynamic also remains open to individual interpretation.

What constitutes perpetrator gain within CSE?

Similar interpretive and implementation challenges arise when we consider the issue of perpetrator gain in CSE scenarios. Indeed, this is where more apparent differences present across the four UK definitions with those more recently constructed attempting to provide greater clarity as to the boundaries of perpetrator gain. The reason for this, as the authors and colleagues argued in their response to the consultation on the new English definition and in their support for the Scottish government to develop their new definition, was that the previous construction of the issue was so broad that it failed to represent any difference from the broader CSA definition.

To expand, an open-ended definition of what constitutes an exchange to the benefit of the perpetrator means that perpetrator sexual gratification alone can meet the exchange requirement for CSE. It is hard to imagine any case of CSA where the perpetrator does not gain something from the abuse. Indeed, in the absence of some form of benefit or the fulfilling of a need/desire, why would they abuse in the first place?

If the requirement of perpetrator sexual gratification is the only criteria that has to be met for abuse to be defined as CSE, then arguably all cases of sexual abuse could fit into this sub-category, thereby collapsing any distinguishable differences between the broader definition of sexual abuse and the sub-category of CSE. The obvious question then arises of why have two labels for the same thing; does this not create confusion rather than provide clarity? Both our policy review and our experience of training professionals in the field would strongly suggest this is indeed the case.

The new Scottish, England and Northern Irish, introduced in 2016 and 2017, have attempted to address some of these difficulties. They do this primarily by introducing additional clarifications as to what constitutes perpetrator gain (when they are the only one gaining from the exchange) retaining flexibility of interpretation as to the nature of the 'exchange' when it is the victim who is receiving something they need or want (as outlined above and in Figure 1.1 below).

All three definitions explicitly state that if the exchange is only to the benefit of the perpetrator, the gain must be more than sexual gratification for it to constitute CSE. Under the new English definition (adopted verbatim in Northern Ireland) if the exchange is only to the benefit of the perpetrator, what they gain must be financial (money, discharge of a debt or free/discounted goods or services) and/or increased status, for it to constitute CSE. If sexual gratification, or exercise of power and control is the only gain for the perpetrator (and there is no gain for the child/young person) this would not constitute CSE under the new definition.[8] This is not, of course, to say that it is not sexual harm that should be responded to, but rather

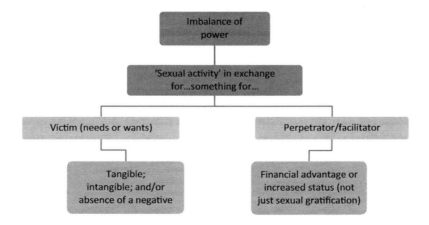

FIGURE 1.1 Interpreting the DfE CSE definition (Beckett, 2017)

than it should be done so under the more generic category of CSA rather than the sub-category of CSE. Such clarification is still outstanding in Wales,[9] and in many international contexts including the Luxembourg guidelines that retain a broad definition of what may constitute perpetrator gain (in exchange for something). This presents ongoing questions as to the utility of the concurrent use of two definitions (CSA and CSE) with little practical differentiation, but significant practice implications depending on which is utilised.

How helpful is the concept of CSE?

These definitional ambiguities lead us to the critical question as to whether the present conceptualisation of CSE – and its relative status to the wider field of CSA – is a helpful framework within which to pursue our efforts to holistically and comprehensively protect children and young people from abuse?

We would propose there are many reasons why it is not, as explored below. This is not to take away from the significant 'wins' that the introduction and development of the concept have brought thus far in terms of recognition of hitherto unrecognised forms of abuse. Rather it is to challenge us to think about how we could maintain these gains whilst moving to an alternative conceptualisation that more accurately reflects our increased understanding of the realities of young people's experiences of abuse and the variations and complexities observable within this, as explored below.

Returning to the premise with which we started this chapter, definitions and descriptors are more than words. They become living organisms through interpretation and implementation and, where inadequate clarification is provided, can result in variable responses depending on the interpretative lens through which they are being implemented, as explored below.

Operational variation

The definitional ambiguities outlined above in relation to CSE, specifically with reference to the parameters of what constitutes gain, have – and continue to – cause challenges in relation to data capture and service responses. For example, delivering training across the UK the authors and their colleagues have observed how a lack of clarity as to the boundaries of CSE – or any consistent direction on how to interpret this – have resulted in regional variations as to the allocation of cases via CSE/CSA service routes.[10] Driven by an understandable necessity to have a way to consistently determine which cases are dealt with by which route, areas have variably categorised according to their own classifications. Some have done so by age, with adolescents being directed to CSE services and younger children being directed via more traditional CSA routes. Others have done so by medium of abuse, with online versus offline contact abuse being used as the basis for categorisation. Yet others have done so by the victims' relationship to perpetrator, with familial cases being categorised as CSA and non-familial being categorised as CSE.

Interestingly, none of these differential categorisations have any basis in the actual definition of CSE, which allows for: abuse of any child under 18, abuse by those known or not known to the child and both on and offline abuse. Yet the operational implementation of such delineations holds serious practice implications in terms of both the statutory conceptualisation of and response to the abuse and the type of (often voluntary) specialist services likely to receive referrals (and therefore receive funding to work with such referrals).

It also holds significant implications for our ability to determine prevalence of CSE, with counts of CSE based on such variable categorisations, consequently both inaccurate (as per the actual definition) and incommensurable.

Similar issues result from an observable failure to adequately differentiate between risk and actuality of CSE. According to both the UK and international definitions, CSE only occurs when sexual activity actually takes place. Should a young person be propositioned to exchange sex for drugs, for example, but not actually do this, this would not constitute CSE as per the definition. Similarly if they are being groomed for abuse but no sexual activity has yet occurred, this would not constitute CSE either.[11] Yet such cases of 'risk of CSE' are often being recorded as 'CSE' without adequate differentiation from actual cases of CSE within recording mechanisms such as police CSE flags (used to record concerns about CSE) or referral patterns of agencies.

This is not simply limited to definitional debate; the implications of lack of definitional clarity and potential for variable interpretation filter through to identification and response. Many of the risk assessment procedures used to determine risk of CSE also fail to distinguish between risk and actuality, with some reviewed by the authors categorising evidenced cases of sexual activity in exchange for something as 'high risk' of CSE alongside those with heightened risk factors or recognised warning signs, but no known or even suspected abuse. Similarly – also reflecting inadequate understanding of current definitional parameters of CSE – some remain predicated on an outdated and incorrect understanding of CSE as something solely perpetrated by adults against children and/or in an offline environment.[12]

Disjuncture between legislation and policy

Unfortunately, the issue of clarifying what constitutes CSE has recently become even more complicated in England and Wales as a result of terminology changes introduced under the SCA 2015. This created a set of offences entitled 'sexual exploitation of children' which does not align with the policy definition of CSE (or vice-versa). To expand, the SCA replaced all references to 'child prostitution' and 'child pornography' within the Sexual Offences Act 2003 with the phrase 'sexual exploitation of a child'. The motive behind this stemmed from the campaign to move away from terminology of prostitution outlined above, to the language of sexual exploitation and the recognised association with abuse. However, the operationalisation of this change of language has proved problematic.

The crux of the problem lies in the fact that new language was simply imported onto existing legislation. Scant consideration appears to have been given to the relative breadth or specificity appropriate within policy and legislative contexts and the appropriateness of transferring 'terminology' across what are very different constructs. The behaviours to which these newly named offences of 'sexual exploitation of children' apply, remain exactly as was when entitled prostitution and pornography. As such, the SCA states that 'for the purposes of section 48 to 50, a person (B) is sexually exploited if:

- on at least one occasion and whether or not compelled to do so, B offers or provides sexual services to another person in return for payment or a promise of payment to B or a third person, or
- an indecent image of B is recorded

As illustrated in Figure 1.2 below, this has resulted in a clear mismatch between the policy and legislative definitions. The former (but not the latter) includes exchange for intangible gain. The latter includes indecent images with no requirement for exchange, the absence of which would exclude such cases from the policy definition.[13]

Hidden heterogeneity

Beyond the specific definitional and interpretative issues outlined above, which clearly need redress, we would contend that the very existence of a definition of CSE, as the only legislated sub-category of CSA, creates an unhelpful dichotomy between CSE and other forms of CSA. Such a dualistic differentiation may be taken to indicate a homogeneity of CSE experiences that we would argue the practice evidence does not support given the breadth of the current definition and the variable interpretation of this. It may also be taken to suggest that CSE cases are somehow 'other' from different forms of sexual abuse, again an assertion that we see as at odds with the evidence base. The wide range of CSE victims and CSE cases that we have met/reviewed in our research[14] and the work of others suggest that although they share the commonality of exchange, the nature of their abuse, the dynamics at play within this and the consequent considerations for response vary considerably.

For example, a case where the perpetrator is arranging the sexual assault of a child/young person and taking payment for this (where there is no apparent gain for the child), holds less in common with one where a young person engages in a sexual relationship with an older individual because they are seeking 'love' (also CSE), than it does a case of enforced rape by multiple individuals where there is no exchange present (not CSE but another form of CSA). We would suggest that the evidence base on both CSE and CSA more generally

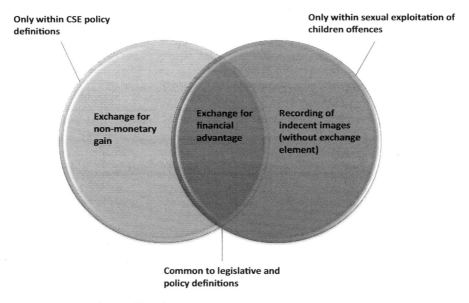

FIGURE 1.2   CSE: policy and legislation comparison (Beckett, 2015)

demonstrates that there are many different forms of CSA and 'exchange' is only one of many factors which unites or distinguishes these. As such, as we explore below, we propose it is now time to revisit the current conceptualisation of CSE and CSA and seek to develop a more nuanced construct that is more reflective of the diversity of children and young people's lived experiences.

Time to move beyond CSE?

Before setting forth our stall on why and how it may be time to move beyond the current usage of CSE, it is important to briefly pause to recognise the contribution that the introduction and development of the concept has made. There is no doubt that CSE as a concept has played a key role in driving forward recognition and understanding of those forms of CSA which were traditionally conceptualised as 'illegal behaviour' rather than safeguarding concerns. In particular, the concept of CSE has brought around a significant shift in understanding regarding the recognition that just because a child receives something they need or desire does not negate the abusive nature of the act. The dedicated work of many operating in the CSE field has also crucially drawn attention to the historically overlooked abuse of adolescents (as opposed to younger children), and raised awareness of the presence of CSA occurring outside of the familial home. Relatedly, it has highlighted the need for adaptation to our current system responses to such forms of abuse, which as widely recognised have been predicated on managing and minimising harm within the family environment (Bilston, 2006; Firmin, 2013; Hanson and Holmes, 2014; Research in Practice, 2015). Most critically, it has meant that many young people who may not have had their need for support and protection previously identified – and perpetrators who may therefore not have been known – are now on the radar of professionals working in the social care and criminal justice fields.

Nothing in what we propose is designed to undermine this contribution, but rather to challenge us to honestly ask: Is the dichotomous conceptualisation of CSE and other forms of CSA that we now find ourselves using truly serving the interests of children and young people?

We do not naively suggest that such change is without challenge. We recognise that CSE, as a concept, has gained considerable currency and familiarity in the mind of both professionals and public alike. However, we would argue that even this increased awareness (an apparently good thing on the surface) may serve to conspire against the identification of harm for some young people, given the partial understanding/misunderstandings that abound in relation to who CSE affects, who perpetrates it and the different forms it can take. The primary focus of media attention, for example, has led many to associate CSE as something perpetrated by groups of Asian men against white girls, which is, of course, one possible manifestation of the abuse. Yes, we are in a position where people recognise the term CSE, but if their understanding of what that means prioritises the experiences of some victims over others, is that recognition actually a helpful thing?

Similarly we recognise that funding is granted and services are provided on the basis of hard-fought recognition of CSE as a form of harm that needs to be addressed. However, we also observe a growing concern around access to support becoming based on an apparent hierarchy of harm in which investment in CSE services is prioritised over those which address other forms of sexual abuse, which are less in the public eye at this time (Allnock, Sneddon with Ackerley, 2015; Smith, Dogaru and Ellis, 2015). Surely a better commissioning criterion is one that avoids such (de)prioritisation of harm and allows for access to services based on assessment of need, irrespective of the label placed on the harm experienced.

A more holistic and integrated framework?

Whilst recognising the gains that have been introduced through an increasing focus on CSE, it is our proposition that the current conceptualisation of the term within the UK – and in particular its relative status to other forms of abuse – is neither reflective of reality nor fit for purpose as the basis of our model of response. Adopting the lens of the best interests of the child, we need to dispassionately identify both the strengths and weaknesses of our current system of conceptualisation, finding a way to harness the former and jettison the latter.

As outlined within this chapter, some attempts have been made to do this to date through clarifications as to the boundaries of CSE and what falls within and outwith this. This is certainly progress from the ambiguity that preceded, but it is the firm belief of the authors that tinkering around with the current dualistic system – differentiated only by the presence or absence of (a vaguely defined) exchange – will only allow us to go so far.

This is not to deny the importance of the presence of exchange in young people's experiences of CSE, but to recognise that there are other key factors that are also important in determining their experience of abuse and thus the appropriate response to this. Policy and practice already recognise that CSE can take many different forms, with similar recognition in relation to the wider concept of CSA. Research shows us that experiences of both CSE and CSA vary in terms of a large number of factors including:

- Who is perpetrating the abuse and their 'relationship' to the child;
- The nature of the power imbalance at play;
- Where the abuse occurs;
- The duration of the abuse;
- The type of sexual activity involved;
- The degree of force or threat utilised;
- Whether there are single or multiple victims or perpetrators;
- Whether the child or the perpetrator is the one gaining from the abuse, where exchange is part of the core dynamic.

(Beckett, 2011; Beckett et al., 2013; McNaughton et al., 2014; Hallett, 2015; Warrington et al., 2017; Kelly and Karsna, 2017)

Whilst understandable in relation to the narrower origins of the issue (abuse through prostitution, or as currently still conceptualised in some other countries 'the commercial sexual exploitation of children'),[15] prioritising exchange over these other factors as the basis for categorising experiences and determining responses holds little benefit given the current expansiveness of the concept within the UK. As noted above, it suggests both a homogeneity within CSE cases – and an 'othering' from other CSA cases, that is not supported by the evidence base.

We therefore contend that whilst the exchange dynamic is a critical factor to consider in conceptualising a child/young person's experience, it should not be the primary one on which to classify their experience or determine our response. Rather than have CSE as the only identified sub-category of CSA, we should recognise that there may be many different sub-categories of experience and seek to move towards a model that allows for a nuanced understanding of these and does not prioritise one over the other.

As well as reconsidering issues of sub-categorisation in relation to CSE, we would propose that there is also a need to provide further clarity around the parameters of the wider concept of CSA itself, which we would argue is both too broad and too blunt a definitional tool in its current form. It is beyond the scope of this chapter to explore the problems with the wider CSA definition in any depth but, using the English definition for illustrative purposes (DfE, 2015), some critical points that should be borne in mind in relation to this when revisiting issues of conceptualisation include:

- The inclusion of 'grooming a child in preparation for abuse' as a form of CSA, and associated questions around where the parameters of defining abuse should start if there is no actual requirement for sexual activity to take place;
- The absence of reference to victim/perpetrator power dynamics (no comparable requirement for a power imbalance, as per the CSE definition);
- The blanket application of the definition to all under 18s without reference to issues of competence or capacity;
- The inclusion of sexual activity that is 'enticed' rather than forced, specifically the relevance of this for young people who can legally consent to have sex and/or make informed choices;
- The wide range of sexual activity that is encompassed (kissing, for example) without reference to age-appropriate sexual development;
- Relatedly, the misalignment with sexual offending legislation which, categorising offences against children by age (under 13, under 16 and under 18) recognises that whilst all under 18s may be vulnerable to abuse, what constitutes such abuse varies according to context and competence.

Conclusion

Whilst recognising the important contribution that the focus on CSE has made to our understanding and responses to young people's experiences of sexual abuse, we propose that using 'exchange' as the sole determinant of conceptualisation (and thus response) is a blunt and inappropriate framework for an inherently complex problem. It creates an artificial distinction between CSE and other forms of CSA that denies the heterogeneity of individual victims' experiences and fails to take account of the many interacting axes on which such experiences vary.

Given our noted concerns with both the current CSE and CSA definitions, we conclude that it is time to move beyond a dualistic conceptualisation of CSE and other forms of CSA. We propose it is time to return to the drawing board and develop an alternative multi-faceted conceptualisation of CSA that recognises exchange as just one defining feature of an abusive experience. In considering this alongside other contextual factors, we can develop a more complex – yet in many ways more simple – model that more accurately reflects our increased understanding of the realities of children's and young people's experiences of abuse and the variations and complexities observable within this.

Notes

1 Scotland introduced a new definition in 2016, with England and Northern Ireland (NI) following in 2017.
2 The authors and their colleagues have delivered training on definitional issues and associated challenges, as part of their five-day accredited CSE course and bespoke training courses, to over 500 professionals over the last five years. This has included representation from social care, police, voluntary sector CSE workers, education, youth work and health.
3 Writing in 2005, the Subgroup Against the Sexual Exploitation of Children observed that 'these constructions ["child prostitution" and "child prostitute"] on their own, fail to make it clear that children cannot be expected to make an informed choice to prostitute themselves' (cited in Inter-agency Working Group on Sexual Exploitation of Children, 2016, p. 30).
4 The four UK definitions are contained within the following documents: Scottish Government (2016), Department of Health NI (2017), DfE (2017a) and Barnardo's on behalf of AWCPPRG (2013).
5 We recognise that not all CSE involves gain for the child and that perpetrator gain alone (however variably constituted within different definitions) can render a case as one of CSE.
6 See endnote 4.
7 Sexual Offences Act 2003; Sexual Offences NI Order 2008; the Protection of Children and Prevention of Sexual Offences (Scotland) Act 2005 and Sexual Offences (Scotland) Act 2009.
8 A similar clarification exists under the Scottish definition, but the Scottish definition less definitively states that the additional gain 'could be' financial advantage or status/power; allowing for the inclusion of other forms of gain beyond those specified.
9 A new Welsh definition is expected to be forthcoming in 2018.
10 It is too early, at the time of writing, to determine whether this will change in light of the clarifications introduced in the new definitions.
11 That is not to say such cases do not require a response.
12 Risk scores of test cases, conducted by the authors, differed dramatically depending on only the age of the perpetrator or whether the abuse was on/offline. Conversely factors that should hold greater sway in our assessment of risk, such as the age/capacity of the child, the power dynamics at play within potentially abusive context, the strength of protective structures and the nature of the risk posed by others (rather than the vulnerability of the child) fail to feature strongly enough (if at all) in some risk assessments and subsequent response plans.
13 Clarification approaches made to the authors, through our policing programme of work, have demonstrated consequent confusion in some police forces as to what now constitutes CSE, specifically whether or not indecent images (in the absence of any exchange) should be recorded as such. Flagging this mismatch between policy and legislation during the development of the new definition and guidance in England, the authors identified a need for a clear steer to be given to police forces in relation to whether their mandated requirement to record CSE cases should be based on cases falling within the policy or legislative definition. A resultant clarification was included in the new CSE guidance document stating that police forces should 'flag all police recorded offences that meet the policy definition of child sexual exploitation. This will include those that fall under the offences of child sexual exploitation but also those falling under other sexual offences that are being perpetrated within the context of child sexual exploitation' (DfE, 2017b, p. 14).
14 See www.beds.ac.uk/ic/publications for an overview of publications.
15 Although NI retains a category of commercial sexual exploitation of children within its child protection guidelines, this does not align with other countries' interpretation of the concept; nor is it clear how it differs from their category of CSE.

References

All Wales Child Protection Procedures Review Group (2008) *All Wales child protection procedures*. Wales: All Wales Child Protection Procedures Group.
Allnock, D., Sneddon, H. with Ackerley, E. (2015) *Mapping therapeutic services for sexual abuse in the UK in 2015*. Luton: University of Bedfordshire.

Barnardo's (2011) *Puppet on a string: the urgent need to cut children free from sexual exploitation*. Barkingside: Barnardo's.

Barnardo's on behalf of the All Wales Child Protection Procedures Review Group AWCPPRG (2013) *All Wales protocol: safeguarding and promoting the welfare of children who are at risk of abuse through sexual exploitation*. Wales: All Wales Child Protection Procedures Group.

Barrett, D. (ed.) (1997) *Child prostitution in Britain: dilemmas and practical responses*. London: The Children's Society.

Beckett, H. (2011) *Not a world away: the sexual exploitation of children and young people in Northern Ireland*. Belfast: Barnardo's NI.

Beckett, H., Brodie, I., Factor, F., Melrose, M., Pearce, J., Pitts, J., Shuker, L. and Warrington, C. (2013) *'It's wrong but you get used to it': A qualitative study of gang-associated sexual violence and exploitation*. Luton: University of Bedfordshire.

Beckett, H., Holmes, D. and Walker, J. (2017) *Child sexual exploitation: definition and guide for professionals*. Luton: University of Bedfordshire.

Bedford, A. (2015) *Serious case review into child sexual exploitation in Oxfordshire: from the experiences of Children A, B, C, D, E, and F [overview]*. Oxfordshire: Oxfordshire Safeguarding Children Board.

Bilston, B. (2006) 'A history of child protection'. *Open University Open Learn* website. The Open University: Department of Health and Social Care.

Brown, A. and Barrett, D. (2002) *Knowledge of evil: child prostitution and child sexual abuse in twentieth century England*. Devon: Willan Publishing.

Coy, M. (2016) 'Joining the dots on sexual exploitation of children and women: a way forward for UK policy responses'. *Critical Social Policy*, 36(4), pp. 1–20.

Department for Children, Schools and Families (DCSF) (2009) *Safeguarding children and young people from sexual exploitation: supplementary guidance to working together to safeguard children*. London: Department for Children, Schools and Families.

Department for Education (DfE) (2017a) *Child sexual exploitation: definition and a guide for practitioners, local leaders and decision makers working to protect children from child sexual exploitation*. London: Department for Education.

Department for Education (DfE) (2017b) *Child sexual exploitation. annexes to 'definition and a guide for practitioners, local leaders and decision makers working to protect children from child sexual exploitation'*. London: Department for Education.

Department of Health (DoH) (2000) *Safeguarding children involved in prostitution: supplementary guidance to working together to safeguard children*. London: Crown Copyright.

Department of Health NI (2017) *Co-operating to safeguard children and young people in Northern Ireland*. Northern Ireland: Department of Health NI.

Firmin, C. (2013) 'Something old or something new: do pre-existing conceptualisations of abuse enable a sufficient response to abuse in young people's relationships and peer groups?' in Melrose, M. and Pearce, J. (eds.) *Critical perspectives on child sexual exploitation and related trafficking*. Palgrave Connect. pp. 38–51.

Griffiths, S. (2013) *The overview report of the serious case review in respect of young people 1, 2, 3, 4, 5 and 6*. Rochdale: Rochdale Borough Safeguarding Children Board.

Hallett, S. (2015) '"An uncomfortable comfortableness": "care", child protection and child sexual exploitation'. *British Journal of Social Work*, 46(7), pp. 2137–2152.

Hallett, S. (2017) *Making sense of child sexual exploitation: exchange, abuse and young people*. Bristol: Policy Press.

Hanson, E. and Holmes, D. (2014) *Evidence scope: that difficult age: developing a more effective response to risks in adolescence*. Dartington: Research in Practice.

Home Office (HO) (2003) *The Sexual Offences Act 2003, c.42*. London: The Stationary Office. Available at: www.legislation.gov.uk/ukpga/2003/42 (Accessed: 28 July 2017).

Home Office (HO) (2015) *The Serious Crime Act 2015 c. 9*. London: The Stationary Office. Available at: www.legislation.gov.uk/ukpga/2015/9/pdfs/ukpga_20150009_en.pdf (Accessed: 28 July 2017).

Inter-agency Working Group on Sexual Exploitation of Children (2016) *Terminology guidelines for the protection of children from sexual exploitation and abuse.* Luxembourg: ECPAT International.

Jago, S. and Pearce, J. (2008) *Gathering evidence of the sexual exploitation of children and young people: a scoping exercise.* Luton: University of Bedfordshire.

Jay, A. (2014) *Independent inquiry into child sexual exploitation in Rotherham: 1997–2013.* Rotherham: Rotherham Metropolitan Borough Council.

Kelly, L. and Karsna, K. (2017) *Measuring the scale and changing nature of child sexual abuse and child sexual exploitation: scoping report.* London: Centre of Expertise on Child Sexual Abuse.

McNaughton Nicholls, C., Cockbain, E., Brayley, H., Harvey, S., Fox, C., Paskell, C., Ashby, M., Gibson, K. and Jago, N. (2014) *Research on the sexual exploitation of boys and young men: a UK scoping study. Summary of findings.* London: Barnardo's, NatCen and UCL.

Melrose, M. (2010) 'What's love got to do with it? Theorising young people's involvement in prostitution'. *Youth and Policy*, 104, pp. 12–31.

Melrose, M. (2012) 'Twenty-first century party people: young people and sexual exploitation in the new millennium'. *Child Abuse Review*, 22(3), pp. 155–168.

Melrose, M. (2013) 'Young people and sexual exploitation: a critical discourse analysis' in Melrose, M. and Pearce, J. (eds.) *Critical perspectives on child sexual exploitation and related trafficking.* London: Palgrave Macmillan. pp. 9–22.

Northern Ireland Office (2008) *The Sexual Offences NI Order 2008, (S.I.2008/1769 (N.I.2).* UK: The Stationary Office Limited. Available at: www.legislation.gov.uk/nisi/2008/1769/contents (Accessed: 28 July 2017).

Pearce, J. J. (2010) 'Safeguarding young people from sexual exploitation and from being trafficked: tensions within contemporary policy and practice'. *Youth and Policy*, 104, pp. 1–11.

Pearce, J. J. (2013) 'A social model of "abused consent"' in Melrose, M. and Pearce, J. (eds.) *Critical perspectives on child sexual exploitation and related trafficking.* London: Palgrave Macmillan. pp. 52–68.

Pitts, J. (2013) 'Drifting into trouble: sexual exploitation and gang affiliation' in Melrose, M. and Pearce, J. (eds.) *Critical perspectives on child sexual exploitation and related trafficking.* London: Palgrave Macmillan. pp. 23–37.

Research in Practice (2015) *Working effectively to address child sexual exploitation: an evidence scope.* Dartington: Research in Practice.

Scottish Government (2016) *Child sexual exploitation: definition and practitioner briefing paper.* Edinburgh: Scottish Government.

Scottish Parliament (2005) *The Protection of Children and Prevention of Sexual Offences (Scotland) Act 2005, asp 9.* Norwich: The Stationery Office. Available at: http://webarchive.nationalarchives.gov.uk/20100402231328/http://www.opsi.gov.uk/legislation/scotland/acts2005/asp_20050009_en_1 (Accessed: 28 July 2017).

Scottish Parliament (2009) *The Sexual Offences (Scotland) Act 2009, asp 9.* Edinburgh: Parliamentary Copyright. Available at: www.legislation.gov.uk/asp/2009/9/pdfs/asp_20090009_en.pdf (Accessed: 28 July 2017).

Smith, N., Dogaru, C. and Ellis, F. (2015) *Hear me. Believe me. Respect me. A survey of adult survivors of child sexual abuse and their experiences of support services.* Ipswich: University Campus Suffolk.

Warrington, C. with Beckett, H., Ackerley, E., Walker, M. and Allnock, D. (2017) *Making noise: children's voices for positive change after sexual abuse.* Luton: University of Bedfordshire.

Welsh Assembly Government (2010) *Safeguarding children and young people from sexual exploitation. Supplementary guidance to safeguarding children: working together under the Children Act 2004.* Cardiff: Welsh Assembly Government. *et al.*

2

PRIVATE/PUBLIC BODIES

'Normalised prevention' of sexual violence against children

Jenny Pearce

Introduction

Recent years, and the presence of some high-profile cases, have seen an increasing focus on sexual violence between and against children (SVBAC). Whilst this is to be welcomed, there remains a tendency within mainstream society to view SVBAC as something that impacts on 'others' and not something that happens in 'our' homes, 'our' communities or 'our' neighbourhoods.

This chapter explores how societal denial around SVBAC, an undue reliance on the child protection system for identification and response and an outward facing (rather than inwardly reflective) lens results in limited rather than universal ownership of the problems. This, I argue, means that those who are affected are isolated and marginalised as 'different'. Indeed, SVBAC in these 'othered' families, communities or places is often described as 'normalised' there, further separating it from 'our' non-sexually violent lifestyles. This is something that needs to be addressed. Rather than talking of SVBAC as 'normalised' within specific communities, we need to move towards generic approaches where everyone engages with understanding, preventing and responding to SVBAC.

The chapter begins with an exploration of the meaning of SVBAC and what is known about its prevalence. I then explore the ways in which SVBAC can be denied and how it is perceived to be 'hidden' within a child protection system and/or within 'other' communities or families where violence is seen as 'normal'. I explore how recent scandals, such as the abuse perpetrated by Jimmy Savile and football coaches, and increasing awareness of abuse online is challenging this othering and bringing child sexual abuse (CSA) closer into the reality of everyone's lives. I argue that whilst this welcome focus has created a stronger awareness and ownership of improving identification of SVBAC, we need a gender and trauma informed public health response that addresses the issue at primary, secondary and tertiary levels.

Defining sexual violence

Sexual violence is defined by the World Health Organisation (WHO) as:

Any sexual act or attempt to obtain a sexual act – including unwanted sexual comments or advances or acts to traffic a person for sexual exploitation – directed against a person using coercion by any person regardless of their relationship to the victim, in any setting.

(WHO, 2002, p. 149)

The United Kingdom (UK) defines CSA and child sexual exploitation (CSE) as follows:

[CSA] involves forcing or enticing a child or young person to take part in sexual activities, not necessarily involving a high level of violence, whether or not the child is aware of what is happening.

(DfE, 2015, p. 93)[1]

[CSE] is a form of child sexual abuse. It occurs where an individual or group takes advantage of an imbalance of power to coerce, manipulate or deceive a child or young person under the age of 18 into sexual activity (a) in exchange for something the victim needs or wants, and/or (b) the financial advantage or increased status of the perpetrator or facilitator. The victim may have been sexually exploited even if the sexual activity appears consensual. Child sexual exploitation does not always involve physical contact; it can also occur through the use of technology.

(DfE, 2017, p. 5)

In line with the United Nations Convention on the Rights of the Child (UNCRC), a child is defined as under the age of 18 years. Relatedly, the range of different legislations to protect children in the UK from sexual violence include recognition that a child under 13 does not, under any circumstances have the legal capacity to consent to any form of sexual activity; that sexual activity with and between children under 16 is illegal; that all children up to the age of 18 should be protected from certain forms of online and offline sexual violence and abuse; and that sex without consent is an offence irrespective of the age of the individual (Sexual Offences Act 2003, Serious Crime Act 2015).

Looking at the definitions of CSA and CSE provided above, it is clear that both are forms of sexual violence against children. Whilst the boundaries between the different definitions are blurred (see Chapter 1 for a discussion of this), essentially the use of sex as a means of exerting power over others is at the core of all definitions of sexual violence, abuse and exploitation against children. Although traditionally conceptualised as a form of violence perpetrated against children by adults, research clearly shows that all forms of SVBAC can be perpetrated by children as well as by adults, hence the inclusion of 'between' children alongside 'against' children in this chapter's discussion (Firmin, 2013, 2015; Barter, 2015; Barter and Stanley, 2016).

The prevalence of SVBAC

Radford *et al.* (2011), in their UK-wide study of child maltreatment, found that 11 per cent of 18–24 year olds reported they had experienced contact sexual abuse when under the age of 18 years.

The most recent Office for National Statistics (2016) data shows that 7 per cent of the UK population surveyed noted one or more sexual assaults during childhood and the Council of Europe (2017) draws on research from across Europe to note that one in five children in Europe are affected by sexual violence.

Specifically considering sexual violence perpetrated by peers, Radford *et al.* (2011), for example, noted that two-thirds of the childhood contact sexual abuse reported by 18–24 year olds in their study was perpetrated by someone under the age of 18 years. Beckett, Holmes and Walker (2017) also note that between one-quarter and one-half of CSE cases involve some degree of peer perpetration, whilst Barter *et al.* (2009) observe that 31 per cent of girls and 16 per cent of boys in their research into teenage intimate relationships reported some form of sexual partner violence.

As noted by researchers in this area, data around SVBAC is inevitably under reporting, as issues such as fear, lack of awareness and concerns about shame and stigmatisation mean that many children do not directly disclose their abuse (Warrington *et al.*, 2017). The same can be said in relation to adults reporting abuse experienced as children. Although we know that all forms of sexual violence can impact on children across gender, class and ethnicity boundaries, the data that we have to illustrate this is poor. Beyond the issues around self-initiated disclosure outlined above (as explored in Chapter 4), these difficulties stem from: misunderstandings about children's capacity to 'consent' to sexual activity (Pearce, 2013); denial or 'wilful ignorance' of the problem (Jay, 2014); undue reliance on disclosure (Cossar *et al.*, 2013; Cossar, Brandon and Jordan, 2016); and enhanced identification and reporting difficulties in certain communities (Gohir, 2013; Bernard and Harris, 2016).

Difficulties also stem from the various different forms of reporting and recording by the general public and professional agencies (Radford *et al.*, 2017, Kelly and Karsna, 2017). It has long been established that record keeping of UK data pertaining to SVBAC varies between professions, including health services, education, police and children's services. It is also known that the translation of these recordings into public databases and public awareness is slow and disjointed. Knowledge invariably remains within specific professional discourses and rarely comes into public consciousness (Corby, Shemmings and Wilkins, 2012; Parton, 2014). This clearly holds implications for public awareness, understanding and ownership.

Despite these challenges, what is known about the prevalence of SVBAC has been sufficient to raise international concern, with it now the focus of a number of major international efforts to prevent violence against children, including the 'Know Violence in Childhood' and the 'End Violence against Children' initiatives. Within the UK, it is also now widely accepted that SVBAC does exist. What remains in dispute is who it affects and therefore whose problem it is? The absence of clear and comprehensive data to substantiate this – and inadequate public discourse around the issue – keeps SVBAC hidden from view and results in limited rather than universal ownership of the problem.

Hidden from view: abuse within 'othered' communities

I began this chapter by saying that there is a tendency within mainstream society to view SVBAC as something that impacts on 'others' rather than something that happens in 'our' homes, 'our' communities or 'our' neighbourhoods. This offers a way for the general society to distance itself from SVBAC; to see it as happening in an 'other' space; a separate, invariably impoverished or deprived 'outside' community or individual. Whilst not negating the destructive impact of adverse childhood experiences, of drug and alcohol misuse problems, of multiple disadvantage and of deprivation on the behaviour of individuals and groups, all too often it is the 'damaged' individual or those living in what might be seen as deprived or under-resourced communities who are considered to be the source and sole owners of SVBAC. Whilst it is helpful to identify concern about vulnerabilities to SVBAC, I worry if this can lead to thinking of it as being dependent upon these vulnerabilities (both personal individual vulnerabilities and environmental and structural vulnerabilities) and thereby disguise the fact that it can affect any child or young person.

Take, for example, our construction of SVBAC in gang-affected communities. Such communities, where the informal economy and associated social norms may include sexual violence as a form of reprisal, retaliation and revenge, are often considered to be typified by SVBAC, to the degree that its existence has become normalised (Beckett *et al.*, 2013; Barter *et al.*, 2009; Barter, 2015; Barter and Stanley, 2016). As such, they can be portrayed by those outside as something distinctly 'other', something different from and incomparable to experiences within our own communities. Despite recognition of the levels of sexual violence within gang-affected communities, there is strong awareness amongst many of those affected that the sexual violence is wrong and unwelcome and not 'normal'. There is also recognition that their experiences do not exist in a vacuum; that they are not alone in being responsible for creating this wrong (Pitts, 2008). Many young people in Beckett *et al.*'s (2013) research into gang-associated sexual violence, for example, whilst acknowledging the harm within their communities, also highlighted that this was not unique to their situation but rather an intense reflection of what happened elsewhere in society:

> It's just like society, innit?. . . Cos like a lot of people from other areas, like more classier areas than round here say, 'Oh, the girls don't have no respect for themselves' blah, blah, but that's just how girls get treated. That's how girls get treated in the workplace. That's how girls get treated on the streets.
>
> *(18-year-old young woman, in Beckett* et al.*, 2013, p. 24)*

> I think there's such a big thing about gangs, gangs, if you get involved with someone in a gang this is going to happen, this is going to happen, and I think yes, you are more at risk, but I think the problem's much wider, yeah.
>
> *(21-year-old young woman in Beckett* et al.*, 2013, p. 24)*

As argued by Beckett *et al.* (2013, p. 17), attitudes towards sexual violence within gang-affected neighbourhoods that may be perceived to be 'normalised' in those settings cannot be 'divorced from experiences of sexual violence or exploitation within the wider adolescent population'. They argue that separating gang-affected neighbourhoods as radically different and separate from broader society attitudes 'would both inappropriately demonise young people within gang environments and detract attention away from the very real risk experienced by other young people outside of these environments' (Beckett *et al.*, 2013, p. 24).

A similar pattern of 'othering' can be seen in recent discourse around CSE. Recent media debate has concerned itself with the extent of abuse perpetrated by men of Pakistani origin, who are exploiting vulnerable white young women within communities where poverty and deprivation, resource limitations and inadequate child protection training and capacity can implode to condone bad professional practice and turn a blind eye to abuse (Jay, 2014). Without negating the significant concern of racist and sexist attitudes of some (including Pakistani) communities and the need to consider issues of proportionality, it could be argued that public attention to and awareness of CSE did actually catch the public eye specifically because it was 'othered'. It was not in 'our' community; it was 'over there' in deprived communities where an 'other', a Pakistani man, is abusing a white girl (Cockbain, 2013). This does not negate the fact that such abuse is intolerable and should be prosecuted against, but it does question whether it is more comfortable to be able to place the gaze outside the dominant white community?[2]

Adopting a gendered lens

Despite the media focus on ethnicity, the overarching, and often under or never, reported evidence from this data is that 93.97 per cent of the known perpetrators are male and 88.15 per cent of victims are female (Bailey, 2017). Similar figures of gender imbalance are evident from data on CSA and sexual violence between children (Barter and Stanley, 2016; Beckett, Holmes and Walker, 2017; Radford et al., 2017). This is something that pervades all aspects of girls and women's lives, including school environments where most girls spend substantial amounts of their day, and an issue that is not yet being taken seriously enough. Evidence submitted to the 2016 House of Commons Women and Equalities Committee Inquiry into sexual harassment and sexual violence in schools, for example, noted a problem with sexual harassment being dismissed as 'just teasing' or by a 'boys will be boys' culture (Richardson, 2016). It similarly noted the acceptance of a 'lad culture' where both teachers and pupils may not identify or report sexual violence or bullying (Sundaram, 2016) and where normalisation of sexual harassment and abuse makes reporting less likely. These messages are echoed in a range of research work including that undertaken by Coy et al. (2013) and Barter (2015).

A focus on ethnicity – or indeed other factors – can overshadow the need for recognition of this gender imbalance, one that is significantly impacted by assumptions about sexuality and sexual orientation (Firmin, Warrington and Pearce, 2016). It could be argued that it is easier and more comfortable to focus the gaze out into 'other' communities than into the blatant, but uncomfortable, fact that this is a gendered problem and one that all men need to own, in full partnership with women, for change to be effected. The key message is that public awareness and understanding of child abuse, and its gendered nature, needs to improve. The question to be considered is whether a direct challenge by men, in partnership with women, to this 'lad culture' might also challenge its 'normalisation'?

To displace our fears and anxieties of SVBAC onto 'others' – and to avoid meaningful engagement with the social constructs and norms that facilitate its continuation – fails children. It fails them because it locates SVBAC within another place, a place away from everyday life rather than acknowledging that it can be part of anyone's everyday life. The dominant message that I want to draw from above is that whilst there is rhetoric about the normalisation of SVBAC, this normalisation is 'othered': diverting attention from the way that it is, one way or another, through direct experience or latent fear and anxiety, embedded in all of our lives.

Hidden from view: sexual abuse and the child protection system

Andrew Cooper (2014) explores how a similar process of 'othering' works in relation to our perspectives on the child protection system. Writing about what he calls the 'dual role' of the child protection system, he argues that one publically acknowledged role is to protect children from abuse. The second, less recognised, role is to carry society's anxiety about the horrors of child abuse. This means that the general public are content to be relieved of the need to be aware of child abuse, including CSA, because they understand it as being managed by a separate, slightly distanced (away from the everyday life) child protection system. This is despite a drive in 2004 to improve generic awareness of the need for safeguarding every child and for all institutions working with children to be aware of their duty to safeguard children from abuse (Children Act, 2004).

Cooper (2014) argues that when the child protection system appears to be functioning well, with no scandals escaping into the general public consciousness, there remains an apparent blissful freedom from anxiety about child abuse. When accounts of failures of the child protection system to detect and manage abuse slip out into the general consciousness, however, there is a public outcry about the failure of a child protection system to protect children. This leads to calls for action; usually for an inquiry or review.

Inquiries and serious case reviews, if conducted as learning reviews, can offer lessons for all involved. However, Preston-Shoot (2017) explores some important concerns about the scope and reach of serious case reviews, noting concerns that others may sit back whilst the work of the review or inquiry is taking place and that the reflection and learning remains contained within limited circles. Not undermining the value of such inquiries and reviews to identify poor and inadequate practice, Cooper (2014) further argues that this response continues to locate the problem of abuse as the property and ownership of specialist 'professionals' rather than a societal issue.

In line with Munro (2011), Cooper (2014) argues for the importance of us all engaging with a 'tragic perspective' on child maltreatment. When he talks of a 'tragic perspective', he means everyone being prepared to recognise the pain, trauma and sadness that is caused by abuse, and the significant impact that this has on all of our children, families and communities. He encourages an engagement with, rather than rejection of the deep complexities that are associated with such abuse. His worry is that this pain is projected upon and invested in the child protection system, rather than acknowledged as the property and responsibility of us all. Indeed, he, with Munro, talks of the importance of countering any idealisations of the capacity of the formal child protection system to always and absolutely protect children.

Parton (2014) expresses similar thoughts when he talks about the 'politics of outrage': the vocal media and public concern that arise when children are thought to be failed by the child protection system. He argues that whilst some of this outrage is directed at sexual offenders, it is also specifically directed at the professionals and managers 'responsible for the case and the operation of the child protection system itself' (Parton, 2014, p. 11). Parton argues that the outrage and subsequent political focus is 'not concerned with how to address the problems of child maltreatment in society but how to improve child protection systems' (Ibid.). This does not negate the need to improve the child protection systems' identification and response to child abuse. It is more to say that seeing the problem of child abuse as only a problem for the child protection system leaves the rest of society absolved from responsibility for it, and fails to address the reasons for its occurrence.

In respect to SVBAC, this argument is compounded by the specifically private and personal, yet confused and conflicted attitudes towards children and sex. As noted by article 19 of the UNCRC, children should be able to grow into adulthood and into their own, self-determined sexual identity without pressure, intrusion and/or abuse. Yet, whilst we recognise the ability to consent to sexual activity at 16 years of age within law, we struggle to meaningfully engage with sexuality in adolescence or create spaces where young people can safely explore what constitutes healthy or unhealthy sexual encounters.

This societal failure to engage in issues of sexual development and sexuality sends a message that these issues are not for the public domain and should remain private and personal. This has obvious implications for children and young people's perceptions of society's potential receptiveness to reporting of experiences of SVABC. Exploring the impacts of abuse on the development of a child's sexuality, Moore and Rosenthal (2006) and Fisher *et al.* (2017), reflect on the significance of societal responses. Moore and Rosenthal (2006) conclude that managing safe passage through the stages of sexual development is not helped in a climate of secrecy, of fear and anxiety within schools, health services and some families and communities who are unable to recognise or talk about sex, sexual relationships and the possibility that some of these might be abusive.

Bringing SVBAC into the public domain

Recent events, where these secrets, fears and anxieties have been exposed, bring attention to Parton's phrase 'the politics of outrage' in relation to SVBAC. In the revelations of the extent of CSA perpetrated by Jimmy Savile, the societal pain and outrage was compounded by the fact that everyone, not only the professionals, were taken in by Jimmy Savile. The affected children could not be 'othered'; they were not from a different, deprived or disadvantaged background. They included a range of children from all backgrounds who were taking part in TV programmes, ill in hospitals, involved in sports events and/or engaging with educational and charitable activities.

As work on domestic and intimate violence has exploded the myth that violence against women is perpetrated by 'strangers', so too did the Jimmy Savile scandal explode the myth that CSA occurs only in dysfunctional families and communities. I explore the impact of this 'othering' more below. For here, it is important to note that suddenly CSA was seen to affect us all, making it harder to ignore and harder to locate blame on the child protection system alone. The media and the general public themselves failed: failed to recognise the abuse, disclose the abuse and, ultimately, failed to challenge or convict the offender.

The disclosure of sexual abuse of footballers by their own club managers, trainers and mentors has also brought into question the role of the general public in identifying and challenging the sexual abuse of children (Taylor, 2017). As with the Jimmy Savile case, the public outrage could not only look outwards towards a failing child protection system or an impoverished 'other' community, but had to look inwards to its own local clubs, local members of sporting and media communities who were part of the general public's own everyday lives.

Similarly, recent concern about the scale and nature of sexual abuse perpetrated online heightens awareness of the potential for any child to be affected in any home (Davidson and Gottschalk, 2011; Bailey, 2017). It brings the concern about sexual abuse into every family, irrespective of social class, education, ethnicity or ability. This includes abuse through online grooming, online sharing of indecent images, sexually abusive communication in teen chat rooms and via social networking, and sexual abuse through online recreational activities such as 'gaming'. Recent research into the arrests of (predominantly) men downloading indecent images of children (IIOC) has indicated shock and disbelief that family men, fathers and those holding professional and/or high-skilled posts, could be managing a secret life, downloading or, in some cases, creating IIOC. Suddenly it is my husband, my partner, my father who is arrested (Philpot, 2008; Stubley, 2015).

As the scale of sexual abuse of children within religious, educational, military, sport and other institutions and settings becomes exposed (with the recognition that children can be victims, perpetrators or both) there is increasing momentum for a stronger public acknowledgment that SVBAC cannot be denied or passed off as the territory of some 'other' community to be managed only by a child protection system. Illustrative of this change, as reported by a journalist in *The Times* newspaper on 24 June 2017, is the actions of the new Head Teacher of the elite private Gordonstoun Junior School, openly inviting ex pupils to come forward and report any incidents of abuse, including sexual abuse, experienced whilst in the school's care (Linklater, 2017, p. 12). This is a welcome move for two reasons. It openly acknowledges that rather than turning a blind eye and saying 'not in my establishment', a leading private school can be brave enough to be proactive, albeit about cases from the past, and acknowledge the existence of sexual abuse within its own grounds and try to respond sensitively. Secondly, it openly acknowledges that abuse can take place against and between 'privileged' groups of children.

Also illustrative of change in a positive direction is the incorporation of a statutory requirement for sex and relationship education to be included in personal, social, health and economic (PSHE) education. However, this alone will not address the issues raised above. It is a broad curriculum which can be taught in one-off sessions and need not fully engage with the realities of SVBAC. It is not enforced within all schools (private schools and some others can determine their own curriculum) and it is not a whole school approach; the only approach that evidence suggests can impact on children's development (Bovarnick and Scott, 2017; Bovarnick, McNeish and Pearce, 2017).

The need to recognise society's role in tackling SVBAC is not identified here as an argument in order to be politically correct or to excuse practitioner bad practice, wilful ignorance or denial, some of which does exist and needs to be addressed. Neither is it presented to create a state of paralysing anxiety about CSA in everybody's everyday life. The potential risk that a child could perpetrate sexual offences or be a victim or both are dangers that specifically impact on the internal, private world, and are therefore more difficult to own or admit to and more difficult for society to discuss. Adults have to feel 'OK' about talking about sexual relationships and 'OK' about explaining that sometimes a developing child may have particular vulnerabilities to being recipients or perpetrators of dangerous sexual practices (Hackett, 2014).

Private and public bodies

Taking these arguments further, Shuker and I developed a diagram to illustrate the relationship between the hidden works of child protection agencies (society's protector from child abuse, as argued by Cooper [2014] above) and the related hidden experience of sexual violence within the child's body. We looked at this as a relationship between private and public bodies. To expand, whilst society projects its fears about sexual abuse (in all its forms) onto the child protection system, isolating it as a bounded and contained problem for professionals to manage, so too does the child isolate their experience of abuse in a closed off part of themselves, containing it as their property that they have to manage.

This diagram tries to illustrate that the majority of the social body and the child's body (the yellow areas) that are the most visible, are assumed to be free of sexual violence. When and if sexual violence happens, the child contains it in a part of themselves, trying to separate it from the rest of their body, as society also does through the 'othering' explored above.

Mirroring the societal location of responsibility and blame in the child protection system, existing discourses and responses can mean that the child assumes responsibility for the existence of CSA and blame for its continuation (Warrington *et al.*, 2017). Warrington and colleagues' research with children who have disclosed sexual abuse note that post disclosure they suddenly leave a world where others had assumed them to be abuse free (the 'normal' world). They become the 'othered' victim. Their apparently hitherto 'normal' family or peer groups may be broken up and displaced, and from here on their perceived identity is dominated by 'victimhood' (Warrington *et al.*, 2017).

This is not to argue that children and society at large should continue to turn away from the existence of abuse. On the contrary, it is to argue the opposite. We wanted to suggest through development of our diagrammatic representation that there is a direct relationship between society imagining itself as free from sexual abuse and child victims feeling that they need to keep their abuse secret and hidden. It is this that needs to be understood to help

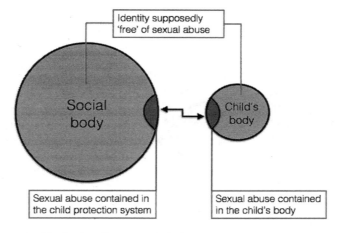

FIGURE 2.1 Private/public bodies (Pearce and Shuker, 2016)

support those affected by such abuse and to make the 'disclosure' of abuse less fearful and less open to resulting labelling and stigmatisation.

The whole process of 'disclosure' and telling, which research notes is fraught with difficulties (Cossar *et al.*, 2013; Warrington *et al.*, 2017), could be made easier through collective ownership of the problem. It can take on average 7.8 years before a child who has experienced CSA will start to tell of their experiences, and children may try to tell someone, in one way or another, an average of four times before it is heard, accepted or believed. The younger a child at the age that abuse starts, the longer the delay to disclosure (Allnock and Miller, 2013).

Whilst recognising that the barriers to disclosure are multi-faceted, the argument is that if sexual abuse against children were not such a taboo, but was sensibly integrated into lessons for life for children and into preventative education (both for potential victimhood and perpetration), there may be less need for children impacted by such abuse to hide it away and feel that it cannot be spoken of.

Returning to the diagram for a moment, it can be seen that if and when the abuse is identified, or children disclose its existence, the part of the child that had been 'holding' the abuse communicates with the child protection system. Two things happen here. Society at large (the school, the community) can continue to turn away from the knowledge of the abuse because they understand the child protection system to be managing it (as explained by Cooper (2014) above). Secondly, the child responds to this societal denial by continuing to hide the impact of the abuse they experienced. This is an unhealthy state of affairs as it prohibits an integrated awareness and ownership of the existence of CSA and continues to place the onus on the affected child. Shuker and I argue that if SVBAC was not so stigmatised, feared, split off and denied – if it were owned as the responsibility of everyone, not only the child protection system – affected children might feel less isolated (Pearce and Shuker, forthcoming).

Conclusion

Where does this leave us? There are important questions that need to be further explored and addressed, including:

- Can a public health approach to understanding and addressing SVBAC help to mainstream the issue, extending the ethos of safeguarding into public and private sector providers and relieving the child protection system from being the one and only 'container' of anxiety and response?
- Could our awareness of the gendered nature of sexual violence be improved, enhancing male ownership of the problem and developing the existing Violence Against Women and Girls Strategy to more overtly include a strategic approach to a government led 'men against sexual violence' strategy?
- How can PSHE or 'whole school' approaches better engage with supporting identification of children affected by sexual violence, overtly recognising its link with sexual bullying, with online and offline abuse awareness and with individual and group wellbeing?

- Can mental health and other service providers improve responses to affected children, helping to relieve them of the emotional burden of blame, responsibility, shame and stigma? Can trauma informed approaches to those who are directly impacted be improved, so that the significance of the sexualised trauma is understood, and the relevance of trauma bonds (Carnes, 2010) and secondary trauma is integrated into specialist service support?

Addressing such questions could take us further along the path we need to take, but the baseline of meaningful and sustainable change is recognition that SVBAC is not 'another's problem' but is instead everyone's business. This means normalising the prevention of sexual violence against and between children, rather than normalising its very existence as elsewhere, somewhere 'other' or away from our everyday life. It means taking the intentions of 'safeguarding' as advocated in the UK Children Act 2004 seriously rather than minimising it to a professional discourse of child protection. It means embracing lessons from public health approaches that address population risk by engaging with and resourcing primary prevention interventions.

Notes

1 English definition provided as illustrative of the UK-wide approach.
2 Research reviews of data on CSE cases tell us that 59 per cent of CSE cases are perpetrated by white offenders (Bailey, 2017; Kelly and Karsna, 2017). Data from a review of CSE cases available to the police in England and Wales from November 2014 to October 2015 notes that whilst 12 per cent of known offenders were noted to be of Asian origin, only 2 per cent of known victims were noted to be of Asian origin. This raises questions, as noted by Gohir (2013), about the visibility of black and minority ethic victims and of their accessibility to services.

References

Allnock, D. and Miller, P. (2013) *No one noticed, no one heard: A study of disclosure of abuse in childhood*. London: NSPCC. Available at: www.nspcc.org.uk/globalassets/documents/research-reports/no-one-noticed-no-one-heard-report.pdf.

Bailey, S. (2017) *Unite against child sexual exploitation*. Available at: https://news.npcc.police.uk/releases/cc-simon-bailey-blog-unite-against-child-sexual-exploitation.

Barter, C., McCarry, M., Berridge, D. and Evans, K. (2009) *Partner exploitation and violence in teenage intimate relationships*. London: NSPCC. Available at: www.nspcc.org.uk/globalassets/documents/research-reports/partner-exploitation-violence-teenage-intimate-relationships-report.pdf.

Barter, C. (2015) *Safeguarding teenage intimate relationships (STIR): Connecting online and offline contexts and risks*, Briefing Paper 4: Young People's Views on Intervention and Prevention for Interpersonal Violence and Abuse in Young People's Relationships. Available at: http://stiritup.eu/wp-content/uploads/2015/02/STIR-Briefing-Paper-21.pdf.

Barter, C. and Stanley, N. (2016) 'Inter-personal violence and abuse in adolescent intimate relationships: mental health impact and implications for practice'. *International Review of Psychiatry*, 14 Sep 2016, pp. 485–503.

Beckett, H., Brodie, I., Factor, F., Melrose, M., Pearce, J., Pitts, J., Shuker, L. and Warrington, C. (2013) *'It's wrong but you get used to it': A qualitative study of gang-associated sexual violence and exploitation*. Luton: University of Bedfordshire.

Beckett, H., Holmes, D. and Walker, J. (2017) *Child sexual exploitation: definition and guide for professionals*. Luton: University of Bedfordshire.

Bernard, C. and Harris, P. (2016) 'Introduction' in Bernard, C. and Harris, P., *Safeguarding Black children: Good practice in child protection.* London and Philadelphia: Jessica Kingsley.

Bovarnick, S. and Scott, S. (2017) *Child sexual exploitation – prevention education: A rapid evidence assessment.* Luton: University of Bedfordshire. Available at: www.beds.ac.uk/__data/assets/pdf_file/0004/540490/FINAL-REA-1.pdf.

Bovarnick, S., McNeish, D. and Pearce, J. (2017) *Child sexual exploitation – outreach work: A rapid evidence assessment.* Luton: University of Bedfordshire. Available at: www.beds.ac.uk/__data/assets/pdf_file/0005/540491/FINAL-REA-21.pdf.

Carnes, P. (2010) The betrayal bond: Breaking free of exploitive relationships. Deerfield Beach, Florida: Health Communications.

Cockbain, E. (2013) 'Grooming and the "Asian sex gang predator": The construction of a racial crime threat'. *Race and Class*, 54(4), pp. 22–32.

Cooper, A. (2014) 'A short psychosocial history of British child abuse and protection: Case studies in problems of mourning in the public sphere'. *Journal of Social Work Practice*, 28(3), pp. 271–285.

Corby, B., Shemmings, D. and Wilkins, D. (2012) *Child abuse: An evidence base for confident practice.* Open University Press.

Cossar, J., Brandon, M., Bailey, S., Belderson, P., Biggart, L. and Sharpe, D. (2013) '"It takes a lot to build trust". Recognition and telling: Developing earlier routes to help for children and young people'. Norwich and Cambridge: Centre for Research on Children & Families, University of East Anglia and Anglia Ruskin University.

Cossar, J., Brandon, M., Jordan, P. (2016) '"You've got to trust her and she's got to trust you": Children's views on participation in the child protection system'. *Child and Family Social Work*, 21(1), pp. 103–112.

Council of Europe (2017) One in five campaign. Available at: www.coe.int/t/dg3/children/1in5/OurCampaign/material_en.asp.

Coy, M., Kelly, L., Elvines, F., Garner, M. and Kanyeredzi, A. (2013) *'Sex without consent, I suppose that is rape': How young people in England understand sexual consent.* A report commissioned for the Office of the Children's Commissioner's Inquiry into Child Sexual Exploitation in Gangs and Groups Office of the children's commissioner for England and London Metropolitan University.

Davidson, J. and Gottschalk, P. (2011) 'Characteristics of the Internet for criminal child sexual abuse by online groomers'. *Criminal Justice Studies*, 24(1), pp. 23–36.

Department for Education (DfE) (2015) *Working together to safeguard children.* London: Department for Education. Available at: www.gov.uk/government/publications/working-together-to-safeguard-children--2.

Department for Education (DfE) (2017) Child sexual exploitation: Definition and a guide for practitioners, local leaders and decision makers working to protect children from child sexual exploitation. London: Department for Education.

Firmin, C. (2013) 'Something old or something new: Do pre-existing conceptualisations of abuse enable a sufficient response to abuse in young people's relationships and peer groups?' in Melrose, M. and Pearce, J. (eds.) *Critical perspectives on child sexual exploitation and related trafficking.* Basingstoke: Palgrave Macmillan. pp. 38–51.

Firmin, C. (2015) 'Peer on peer abuse: Safeguarding implications of contextualising abuse between young people within social fields'. *Professional Doctorate Thesis.* Luton: University of Bedfordshire.

Firmin, C., Warrington, C. and Pearce, J. (2016) 'Sexual exploitation and its impact on developing sexualities and sexual relationships: The need for contextual social work interventions'. *British Journal of Social Work*, early view.

Fisher, C., Goldsmith, A., Hurcombe, R. and Soares, C. (2017) *The impact of child sexual abuse: A rapid evidence assessment.* London: The Independent Inquiry into Child Sexual Abuse.

Gohir, S. (2013) Unheard voices: The sexual exploitation of Asian girls and young women. Birmingham, UK: Muslim Women's Network.

Hackett, S. (2014) Children and young people with harmful sexual behaviours. Dartington: Research in Practice.

Home Office (HO) (2003) *The Sexual Offences Act 2003, c.42*. London: The Stationary Office.

Home Office (HC) (2004) *The Children Act 2004*. London: The Stationary Office. www.legislation. gov.uk/ukpga/2004/31/contents.

Home Office (HO) (2015) *Serious Crime Act 2015 c. 9*. London: The Stationary Office.

Jay, A. (2014) Independent inquiry into child sexual exploitation in Rotherham (1997–2013).

Kelly, L. and Karsna, K. (2017) *Measuring the scale and changing nature of child sexual abuse and child sexual exploitation*. Available at: www.csacentre.org.uk/research-publications/scale-and-nature-of-child-sexual-abuse-and-exploitation-report/scoping-report/.

Linklater, M. (2017) 'Gordonstoun asks former pupils if they were abused'. *The Times*, June 24 2017, p. 12.

Moore, S. and Rosenthal, D. (2006) *Sexuality in adolescence: Current trends*. London: Routledge.

Munro, E. (2011) The Munro review of child protection. Final report: A child-centred system. London: The Stationery Office.

Office for National Statistics (2016) Abuse during childhood: Findings from the Crime Survey for England and Wales, year ending March 2016. www.ons.gov.uk/peoplepopulationandcommunity/crimeandjustice/articles/abuseduringchildhood/findingsfromtheyearendingmarch2016crimesurveyforenglandandwales.

Parton, N. (2014) *The politics of child protection: Contemporary developments and future directions*. Basingstoke: Palgrave Macmillan.

Pearce, J. (2013) 'A social model of "abused consent"', in Melrose, M. and Pearce, J. (eds.) *Critical perspectives on child sexual exploitation and related trafficking*. Basingstoke: Palgrave Macmillan.

Pearce, J. and Shuker, L. (2016) *Public and private bodies: The politics of child sexual abuse*. University of Bedfordshire: The International Centre. https://uniofbedscse.com/2016/12/06/public-and-private-bodies-the-politics-of-child-sexual-abuse/.

Philpot, T. (2008). *Understanding child abuse: The partners of child sex offenders tell their stories*. London: Routledge.

Pitts, J. (2008) *Reluctant gangsters: The changing face of youth crime*. London: Routledge.

Preston-Shoot, M. (2017) 'What is really wrong with serious case reviews?' *Child Abuse Review*. Published online in Wiley Online Library (wileyonlinelibrary.com). DOI: 10.1002/car.2487.

Radford, L., Corral, S., Bradley, C., Fisher, H., Bassett, C., Howat, N. and Collishaw, S. (2011) *Child abuse and neglect in the UK today*. NSPCC: London.

Radford, L., Richardson Foster, H., Barter, C. and Stanley, N. (2017) Rapid evidence assessment: What can be learnt from other jurisdictions about preventing and responding to child sexual abuse. Preston: University of Central Lancashire.

Richardson, A. (2016) in Women and Equalities Committee, *Sexual harassment and sexual violence in schools inquiry*. SVS0094, paragraph 6. www.parliament.uk/business/committees/committees-a-z/commons-select/women-and-equalities-committee/inquiries/parliament-2015/inquiry1/.

Sundaram, V. (2016) in Women and Equalities Committee, *Sexual harassment and sexual violence in schools inquiry*. SVS0042, paragraph 6. www.parliament.uk/business/committees/committees-a-z/commons-select/women-and-equalities-committee/inquiries/parliament-2015/inquiry1/.

Stubley, A. (2015) He's a family man, but this is a dark side of him that I didn't know about. The lived experience of Internet offenders' partners. *Unpublished doctoral dissertation*. Middlesborough: Teesside University.

Taylor, D. (2017) 'The football child abuse scandal just keeps on growing'. *The Observer*, 2 April 2017.

Warrington, C. with Beckett, H., Ackerley, E., Walker, M. and Allnock, D. (2017) *Making noise: Children's voices for positive change after sexual abuse*. Luton: University of Bedfordshire.

World Health Organization (2002) '*World report on violence and health*' Chapter 6. Geneva: World Health Organizations.

3

DISCLOSURE OF CSE AND OTHER FORMS OF CHILD SEXUAL ABUSE

Is an integrated evidence base required?

Debra Allnock

Introduction

Efforts to tackle child sexual exploitation (CSE) and other forms of child sexual abuse (CSA) are often frustrated by the secretive and hidden nature of the abuse and associated difficulties in disclosure and identification. 'Disclosure' has consequently emerged as a critical sub-field of interest within research on CSA and a significant body of literature has emerged around the prevalence and patterns of, and barriers to, children's disclosure (for reviews, see London *et al.*, 2005; 2008; Alaggia, Collin-Vézina and Lateef, 2017). In the simplest terms, 'disclosure' refers to the act of making something new or unknown, known: in this case, the act of a child or young person making their abuse known to others. However, decades of research in the field of CSA disclosure emphasises that disclosure is better understood as a process involving many different ways of making abuse known rather than a 'one-off' act that is verbal and direct in nature (Alaggia, 2004).

This recognition has been instrumental in shifting attitudes about victims of CSA by promoting a better understanding of the challenges encountered in seeking help following these experiences. However, as Alaggia and colleagues (2017) observe, there remain a number of key weaknesses within this body of knowledge: methodological concerns limit the generalisability of the studies; more is known about barriers to disclosure than about what facilitates it; and there is inadequate attention paid to understanding how disclosure is influenced by structural, social and cultural contexts across the life course.

Importantly, I would further argue that the CSA disclosure field has yet to effectively engage with different contexts of CSA, including the variety of ways in which CSE (as a form of CSA) manifests. This is not unique to the disclosure sub-field. Prevalence studies and research investigating risk and protective factors of CSA have also yet to successfully integrate consideration of CSE (Radford *et al.*, 2011; Finkelhor *et al.*, 2014). In fact, the literature on CSE disclosure appears to be developing uncomfortably alongside the literature on CSA rather than being effectively integrated into, or adopted by, the CSA disclosure field.

This phenomenon, I argue, is associated with the historical conceptualisation of CSE as 'child prostitution', which has resulted in a separate, parallel body of literature developing alongside that on CSA which is more commonly aligned with child protection/maltreatment within familial settings (Melrose, 2013). The more recent shifting of CSE into the realm of child welfare and child protection has not yet resulted in its seamless integration into the CSA literature.

This holds important implications for understanding the ways in which young people disclose different types of CSE experiences and the barriers they face, given the nature of exchange as a key characteristic of this form of sexual abuse (see Chapter 1). If CSE scholars and practitioners draw on the broad generalised CSA disclosure literature, this may be misleading for circumstances of CSE. This in turn will impact on how effectively they are able to contextualise and inform their work in supporting sexually exploited children and young people.

In this chapter, I will draw attention to these challenges with the following questions guiding the discussion:

1. How have theoretical approaches to CSA disclosure developed and what can these approaches tell us (or not) about disclosure in different CSA contexts, specifically CSE contexts?
2. What are the limitations to the CSA disclosure research literature and how does this impact on what can be known about disclosure of CSE?
3. How far does context really matter in relation to disclosure of sexual abuse?
4. Given the answers to the first three questions, how far do findings emerging from the 'CSA' disclosure literature assist us in making sense of disclosure in different contexts of CSA, particularly CSE?

The concluding section of the chapter will offer recommendations on moving the evidence base on CSA disclosure forward, suggesting the need to both integrate CSE in its variety of forms into the broader CSA disclosure field and develop a stronger, theoretically-informed evidence base on disclosure in the CSE field.

Barriers to CSA disclosure: theories rooted in abuse within the family

Tracing the historical development of theoretical approaches to CSA disclosure is instructive in understanding the basis of current knowledge in this area. In this section, I argue that the theoretical traditions which have shaped the field of CSA disclosure – and particularly theories that seek to explain non-disclosure – are firmly rooted in an understanding of sexual abuse as something occurring to younger children within the family. As such, their relevance to other forms of sexual abuse, including that perpetrated outside of the family home (as CSE often is) and against older children, is questionable. As indeed is the degree to which they can explain how 'exchange' – a critical component of CSE – intersects with and influences disclosures.

One of the earliest and most substantial theoretical influences on the field of disclosure is Roland Summit's Child Sexual Abuse Accommodation Syndrome (CSAAS) (Summit, 1983). Based on clinical observations, Summit proposed that in response to CSA, certain psychological factors (for example, shame, embarrassment, guilt, allegiance to the perpetrator) result in delayed disclosure, denial and recantation of abuse. Whilst Summit proposed the CSAAS theory to be used as a clinical tool to understand the behaviour of a child who has been sexually abused, it became hugely influential in forensic interview practices internationally, and Summit himself has argued that it has often been *mis*used as a diagnostic rather than a therapeutic tool (Summit, 1993).

The influence of the CSAAS in contemporary studies of disclosure can be observed in reviews of the literature seeking to establish whether the CSAAS can be supported by evidence (London *et al.*, 2005; 2008). Whilst the CSAAS offered important possibilities for understanding why some children do not disclose, it is constrained in terms of a variety of contexts of abuse. The CSAAS, for example, is largely focussed on abuse perpetrated by adults, and more specifically by fathers or other adult male relatives.[1] Mothers are only referred to as unwitting facilitators or enablers of intra-familial CSA. The CSAAS does not consider how disclosure may be influenced within other social fields or when the abuse is perpetrated by siblings, peers or strangers. Additionally, the CSAAS lacks attention to exchange where, for example, a young person may have exchanged sex (apparently willingly or not) for something they need or want or situations that reflect what traditionally was understood as 'child prostitution' (now CSE).

Other 'stage-based' disclosure models emerged in direct response to Summit's work (Sorenson and Snow, 1991; Paine and Hansen, 2002) as did alternative theories such as social exchange (Leonard, 1996) and social cognitive (Bussey and Grimbeek, 1995) theories. Leonard, for example, applied principles of cost and rewards to the CSAAS, demonstrating that children's disclosure patterns – secrecy, helplessness, entrapment, delayed disclosure and retraction of disclosures – reflects the least unprofitable of the limited options child victims perceive are available. Bussey and Grimbeek (1995, p. 186) draw on Bandura's social-cognitive theory to explain how 'the course of disclosure will vary according to children's cognitive capabilities, social experience, and the particular situation in which they find themselves'.

Whilst these theories may offer interesting perspectives for contexts of CSE, all of them have in common a focus on familial contexts of abuse and a neglect of contexts of victim-perpetrator exchange. The latter – the victim-perpetrator exchange context – is excluded most likely because 'child prostitution' was conceptualised as something 'other' than CSA at that time. It was understood within criminal justice rather than child welfare frameworks.

Despite the continued influence of the CSAAS model as seen by the attention it has garnered by other researchers and theorists, theoretical perspectives on disclosure have moved forward and notable attempts to understand the wider barriers to disclosure that may impact on a child's willingness to tell have emerged. The most influential framework in the contemporary literature is the ecological model, first applied to the child maltreatment field more generally by Belsky (1980).

Belsky (1980, p. 330) proposed the use of the ecological model as a foundation for integrating multiple yet separate and divergent strands of thinking about the aetiology of child maltreatment, conceptualising child maltreatment as 'a social psychological phenomenon that is multiply determined by forces at work in the individual (ontogenic development), and the family (the microsystem), as well as in the community (the exosystem) and the culture (the macrosystem) in which both the individual and the family are embedded'. Researchers have now borrowed and applied this framework to investigate the barriers and facilitators to disclosure of CSA. They have used it to understand how disclosure is multiply determined by a complex set of factors related to the child's characteristics, family environment, community influences and cultural and societal attitudes (Alaggia, 2010; Brazelton, 2015; Collin-Vézina et al., 2015).

Although Alaggia, Collin-Vézina and Lateef (2017, p. 18) quite rightly argue that 'knowledge on CSA disclosure has steadily been advancing toward a holistic understanding of the complex interplay of individual, familial, contextual and cultural factors', I would counter that this is only true in respect of certain forms of CSA and the field would benefit from directly addressing the broad array of contexts within which children are sexually abused.

Limitations to the literature

Contemporary scholars and practitioners with an interest in CSE today rely on general CSA disclosure literature to inform their understanding of disclosure patterns among victims of CSE (see Brayley, Cockbain and Gibson, 2014). This is because the evidence base on CSE has only expanded in recent years, and there are no prior studies specifically designed to investigate disclosure of CSE on which to draw. Whilst findings on CSE disclosure are emerging, these remain fairly limited because they:

- derive from studies which are not about disclosure per se;
- are not theoretically informed in the same way as the sub-field of CSA disclosure (for example, explicit application of an ecological or other framework);
- derive, in some cases, from interviews with professionals rather than victims themselves (McNaughton Nicholls, Harvey and Paskell, 2014; Franklin, Raws and Smeaton, 2015);
- are based on practice evidence (Palmer, 2015) which, whilst useful, lacks theoretical and empirical grounding;
- are not yet published in the peer-reviewed academic domain (for exceptions, see Beckett and Schubotz, 2014; Hallett, 2015).

Whilst the general CSA literature on disclosure is helpful for those working in the field of CSE, it is important that they are aware of the limitations of this, both in relation to the general basis of the evidence and in relation to its application to CSE. Below, I highlight five particular methodological problems that beset the CSA disclosure literature at present.

Firstly, it is striking that few of the studies on disclosure of CSA explicitly clarify the definition of CSA used in the study. Definitions are important in research because they articulate the boundaries of what is being measured, influencing who and what is included and excluded. It is also notable that only two contemporary studies of CSA disclosure mention the phrase 'sexual exploitation' (Priebe and Svedin, 2008) or acknowledge 'consensual' exchange (Kellogg, 2017).

Secondly, inclusion criteria in CSA disclosure studies have very likely excluded at least some forms of CSE. There is, for example, a set of studies which examine disclosure in relation to unwanted or non-consensual sexual contact (Ussher and Dewberry, 1995; Arata, 1998; Fergusson, Lynskey and Horwood, 1996; Hanson et al., 1999; Tang, 2002; Kogan, 2004; Collings, Griffiths and Kumalo, 2005; Mossige et al., 2007; Priebe and Svedin, 2008). This is particularly problematic when considering disclosure in some contexts of CSE where young people might consider their experiences as 'consensual'. This demonstrates how inclusion and exclusion criteria are defined and understood in individual national contexts may differ considerably in how they are defined and understood in other national contexts. Therefore, transferability of findings can be problematic.

Thirdly, disclosure studies often have broad or vague inclusion criteria. These studies often take a broadly inclusive approach by omitting inclusion definitions of CSA, allowing potential study recruits to self-identify as having experienced sexual abuse (see, for example, Crisma *et al.*, 2004; Jonzon and Lindblad, 2004; Schönbucher *et al.*, 2012; Easton, Saltzman and Willis, 2014; Collin-Vézina *et al.*, 2015; Gagnier and Collin-Vézina, 2016). This is not an unusual approach in qualitative studies of CSA where researchers are interested in understanding the sense that individuals make of their experiences as opposed to measuring 'incidences' or 'facts'. However, the omission of clear definitions for self-report participants is likely to mean that young people who experience CSE or sexual abuse by peers, and may not see it as abusive, will not self-define as victims of abuse and therefore not take part in the study. Indeed, it is generally problematic to know on what basis participants of these studies self-identify as victims at all.

Fourthly, disclosure studies often lack clarity about recruitment sources. There are a series of studies which draw on clinical samples from specialist services which assess children where there are concerns about sexual abuse (McElvaney, Greene and Hogan, 2013; McElvaney and Culhane, 2017) or in agencies/with professionals that undertake forensic interviews (Hershkowitz, Horowitz and Lamb, 2005; Hershkowitz, Lanes and Lamb, 2007; Schaeffer, Leventhal and Gotsegen Asnes, 2011). The studies lack clarity about the types of CSA cases that are referred to these settings, raising questions about the nature of the samples. Not all CSA services are equipped or trained to assess and respond to CSE, as a recent mapping study of therapeutic services for CSA (including CSE specialist services) in the UK found (Allnock, Sneddon and Ackerley, 2015). Depending upon how nations conceptualise CSE, victims may be diverted to non-child protective services (such as juvenile/youth services) and therefore not comprise referrals into CSA assessment centres. Unless referral criteria are made explicit in these research studies, it is may not be possible to ascertain whether CSE victims form part of the study samples.

Fifthly, disclosure studies have limited focus on abuse context. The CSA disclosure literature does provide insight into certain characteristics of CSA to assess whether these are associated with a greater or lesser likelihood for disclosing. Age, gender and victim-perpetrator relationship have all been found to exert some influence on disclosure. Some studies have found that younger children are less likely than older children to disclose abuse or delay for longer periods of time (Jonzon and Linblad, 2004; Collings, Griffiths and Kumalo, 2005; Easton, 2013; Collin-Vézina *et al.*, 2015). Females are consistently found to report CSA at higher rates than males (Paine and Hansen, 2002; Alaggia, Collin-Vézina and Lateef, 2017). Finally, the closer the victim and perpetrator relationship, the less likely the victim is to disclose (Paine and Hansen, 2002). Whilst useful, these variables are inadequate for capturing contexts of CSE. Perpetrator identity (intra- versus extra-familial or adult versus peer) is an inadequate marker for CSE as family members can groom, facilitate and perpetrate abuse for financial or other reward and peers can commit rape and assaults that do not stem from an exchange of something for sex. The *critical* characteristic of CSE – exchange – is not yet measured in these studies, which undermines what can be known about these contexts.

So does context matter?

The theoretical and research limitations described above only matter if there is agreement that context matters in relation to disclosure patterns. What we know about CSE suggests that context does matter. Internationally, CSE is increasingly recognised as a form of CSA, evidenced in various national legislative and/or policy directives (see Cameron *et al.*, 2015). There has been a concerted shift away from a discourse of 'child prostitution' to a discourse of 'child sexual exploitation', recognising children as victims of abuse (Melrose, 2013).

At the same time that CSE is understood to be a form of CSA, there is also policy recognition that CSE can be defined by particular characteristics that set it apart from other forms of CSA, implying that there are important practice implications for this (Pearce, 2009; Beckett, Homes and Walker, 2017). Indeed, Cole *et al.* (2016) found important differences between the impacts of abuse on sexually exploited young people and young people sexually abused (but not exploited), suggesting a need for tailored practice responses and support. Below, I set out three distinguishing features of CSE that underscore the importance of understanding context in relation to disclosure.

First, a distinguishing feature of CSE that underscores the importance of context for disclosure is the concept of *exchange* (United Nations Secretariat, 2003; Beckett, Holmes and Walker, 2017). The full definition of CSE as set out in English guidance emphasises that whilst all forms of CSA may occur for the sexual gratification of the perpetrator, CSE is defined as occurring in the context of exchange where either the victim and/or the perpetrator(s) gain something else from the exploitation (Greijer and Doek, 2016; Beckett, Holmes and Walker, 2017). In relation to disclosure, gain by the perpetrator may be crucial because they may threaten or coerce a young person so they do not lose out on what they are benefitting from (for example, money or status). Gain by the victim is also crucial because victims may not disclose if they fear they will lose access to the benefit they are receiving (for example, drugs, alcohol, money or love). This additional layer of complexity that is part of a CSE context is likely to have important implications for young people's disclosure patterns.

A second feature of CSE that highlights the importance of context in relation to disclosure is the intersection of age/developmental stage of victims and the associated professional responses to identification and response to CSE. Whilst it is recognised that CSE (or grooming for exploitation) may occur to any child regardless of age, the existing evidence tells us that CSE is most often identified at older ages than other forms of CSA, typically in the adolescent years (Kramer and Berg, 2003; Cobbina and Oselin, 2011; Dodsworth, 2014; Children's Commissioner for England, 2015; Smith, Dogaru and Ellis, 2015; Beckett, Holmes and Walker, 2017). Theories of child development highlight the developmental tasks that all adolescents face, such as a general movement towards independence, future interests, sexuality, ethics and self-direction, and, of course, there are a range of physical changes that occur (Erikson, 1993; McPherson, Smith-Lovin and Cook, 2001). These general developmental challenges have the potential to profoundly influence the nature and pattern of young people's capacity to disclose abuse and seek help. Young people who are seeking greater independence may inadvertently isolate themselves from, or be isolated by, safe adults, reducing accessibility of help. Young people may withhold disclosure if they believe they can handle their problems on their own in the context of expanding independence and self-direction. If wanting to be seen and treated as an 'adult' or 'grown up', young people may not seek help in order to preserve this status. Adding to these general developmental challenges, traumatic experiences of CSE can disrupt and have profound physical, emotional and social impacts on young people (Cole *et al.*, 2016; Sawyer and Bagley, 2017). In turn, these impacts may decrease young people's capacity to both recognise abuse and seek help. Further, we know that young people may cope with trauma through self-harm and substance abuse which, though considered to be maladaptive coping, may in the immediate term help young people to protect themselves from trauma through 'psychological escape', inhibiting recognition of abuse (Oaksford and Frude, 2003).

It is, however, the intersection of adolescence and professional response in the context of CSE that particularly compounds the difficulties young people face in seeking help. More generally, professional responses to abuse of adolescents lag well behind responses to younger children (Rees *et al.*, 2010). Poor professional understanding of and responses to CSE remain particularly pernicious (Sidebotham *et al.*, 2016). Professionals across the spectrum have struggled to reconcile young people's status as 'victim' with their parallel 'agency'. This dynamic is one of the more complex aspects of CSE which can, and has, resulted in outsiders 'blaming the victim', misinterpreting young people's limited 'choices' as unproblematic consent. Worrying professional attitudes and responses to young people who are perceived to have made an 'active choice' to be in exploitative relationships have been unearthed in a number of public inquiries in the United Kingdom in recent years (Griffiths, 2013; Jay, 2014). These types of attitudes act as powerful barriers to young people's help-seeking.

A third consideration in understanding the unique challenges of disclosure in relation to CSE is the context of peer perpetration. Whilst peer perpetration is not unique to CSE, estimates show that between one-quarter and one-half of identified CSE cases involve some degree of peer perpetration (Beckett, Holmes and Walker, 2017). Such abuse is likely to be experienced differently from abuse perpetrated by an adult, particularly when occurring within the young person's social circles. Young people's experiences of peer abuse will be influenced by the nature of the environments within which they spend their time. These not only provide a potential context for abuse; they embody strong social norms as to the acceptability, or lack thereof, of such behaviours. This will in turn influence potential recognition of the abuse, likelihood of, and capacity to, disclose and potential barriers to this. As Firmin (2011, p. 46) notes, 'if abusive relationships between young people take place in exploitative social fields, it seems unhelpful and unrealistic to define them, or attempt to intervene in them, without considering the power imbalances that exist between young people and the social fields they are navigating'.

What does the CSA disclosure literature tell us about disclosure of CSE?

This final section considers what we actually know about the barriers to CSA disclosure and whether these findings also emerge in the CSE literature. Alternately, are there themes in the CSE literature that are not appearing in the CSA disclosure research? If there are common themes, this is helpful for practitioners in transferring learning and practice across broadly shared experiences of sexual violence. If differences exist, however, it is important to consider how these two sources of evidence can be integrated to provide a more holistic picture of disclosure across a range of different contexts.

Whilst most of these broad themes can be found across both sources of evidence, it is crucial to note that the themes often manifest differently in CSA disclosure research and CSE research. This difference appears to be dependent upon context of abuse (namely, the type and nature of the abuse and the social context within which it occurs) and in relation to the developmental stage of the young person. The remaining part of this chapter considers some of these differences using an ecological framework. Not all themes will be covered given the limitations of space, but examples are used to demonstrate both subtle and more obvious differences.

Child-related barriers

Child-related barriers are those which arise from developmental characteristics of the child and/or emotional turmoil experienced by the child as a result of the abuse. Within these, the following themes appear in both the CSA disclosure literature and the emerging CSE findings on disclosure:

- Emotional impacts of abuse;
- Demographic characteristics of children;
- Developmental barriers;
- Coping mechanisms.

Three further themes within 'child-level barriers' – 'substance misuse', 'loss' and 'criminality/delinquency' – appear only in the CSE literature, not yet articulated within the broader CSA disclosure field. This section will consider the themes of 'emotional impacts' and 'developmental characteristics' that appear in both the CSE and CSA literature as well as the three themes that appear only in the CSE literature (substance misuse, loss and criminality/delinquency).

The CSA disclosure literature consistently identifies emotional impact as a key barrier to disclosure (Alaggia, Collin-Vézina and Lateef, 2017). Shame, guilt and embarrassment are often associated with children's belief that they were somehow 'complicit' in the abuse (Hershkowitz, Lanes and Lamb, 2007). Collin-Vézina et al. (2015, p. 128) refer to this as 'internalized victim-blaming'. These emotional impacts are well established in the CSE literature also (Beckett, 2011; Jago et al., 2011; Gohir, 2013; Hartill, 2014; McNaughton Nicholls, Harvey and Paskell, 2014; Hallett, 2015). However, societal attitudes towards adolescents (often seen as responsible for their abuse) and poor social understanding of CSE add additional, and often explicit, layers of blame onto victims of CSE which are deeply internalised (Beckett and Warrington, 2015). Whilst no more important than the shame and guilt felt by victims of other forms of abuse, the particular intersection between adolescence, professional responses and 'internalized victim-blaming' have been inadequately explored in the CSA literature. In addition, particular forms/modes of CSE highlight additional, and enduring, sources of shame and embarrassment that may differ for children experiencing other forms of abuse. For example, shame arising from online sexual exploitation can prevent young people from seeking help because of the longevity of their images and anxieties that other people will see the abuse (Palmer, 2015).

Developmental barriers also emerge in both sources of evidence. The CSA literature tells us that children and young people have been prevented from disclosing their abuse because they had not recognised their experiences as 'abusive', 'wrong' or 'criminal' and thought that these experiences were 'normal' (Ungar *et al.*, 2009; Allnock and Miller, 2013; Cossar *et al.*, 2013; Collin-Vézina *et al.*, 2015). This theme manifests in particular ways in line with age and developmental stage of the child at the time of abuse. In examples of CSA experienced by younger children, for example, 'normalisation' of abuse occurs because children are young, have small social circles and therefore lack wider reference points with which to compare their own experiences, or they may not even possess the vocabulary to name the experience as abusive (Ungar *et al.*, 2009; Allnock and Miller, 2013; Collin-Vézina *et al.*, 2015). Aligned to this, the CSA literature further identifies that disclosure is facilitated by age. This may be because, as children get older, their social circles begin to widen, allowing them to make different kinds of appraisals of their experience in relation to their peers, what they are learning in school or seeing on the television (Allnock and Miller, 2013; Cossar *et al.*, 2013).

The CSE literature also identifies recognition and understanding as problematic for disclosure, but in somewhat different ways. In contrast to 'normalisation' in other CSA contexts where children's knowledge may be limited by their isolation, 'normalisation' in certain contexts of CSE occurs within widened social and youth sub-culture networks, such as in peer groups (Shepherd and Lewis, 2016), gang contexts (Beckett *et al.*, 2013) and online (McNaughton Nicholls, Harvey and Paskell, 2014; Palmer, 2015). Some commentators highlight the wider sexualisation of adolescent girls which then serves to normalise harmful intimate relationships (Coy, 2009; Wood, Barter and Berridge, 2011). These wider contexts of so-called normalised sexual violence around the child/young person can serve to frame for young people what is acceptable in intimate and sexual relationships. They can also influence young people to 'reconcile' sexual violence as the currency for meeting their needs (Beckett *et al.*, 2013; Hallett, 2015).

Additionally, within some CSE contexts where young people (at least apparently and initially) 'choose' or 'consent' to abusive relationships or contexts, disclosure can be prevented because these young people do not identify as victims per se. Thus, whilst the broader CSA literature suggests that with age and development comes an increased recognition and understanding of abuse (potentially leading to increased disclosure), the CSE literature points out that adolescence, especially within particular contexts/sub-cultures tied to the adolescent period or 'relationship-based' CSE contexts, can actually prohibit the recognition of abuse.

There are, importantly, three themes that emerge in the CSE literature but have not yet appeared in the broader CSA literature. These are substance misuse, loss and criminality/delinquency. Substance abuse is deeply tied to contexts of CSE, identified as a key vulnerability for exploitation (Jago *et al.*, 2011; Beckett, Holmes and Walker, 2017). In some contexts of CSE, it can function either as the 'need' that a young person satisfies directly through the exchange of sex or alternatively may be used by CSE perpetrators to groom young people and prepare them for abuse and exploitation (Beckett, 2011; Beckett and Schubotz, 2014; Shepherd and Lewis, 2016). Loss is most often cited in relation to the loss of a perceived relationship (Firmin, 2011). This is explicitly identified in Franklin, Raws and Smeaton, (2015) whose work examining experiences of CSE amongst disabled young people, highlights anxieties disabled young people may have in securing future intimate relationships. Loss of a relationship, however abusive, was also identified as a barrier to disclosure of abuse occurring within intimate relationships (Beckett, 2011; Wood, Barter and Berridge, 2011).

Finally, young people's own criminality or delinquency as a barrier to disclosure is identified specifically within the CSE literature. It is highly relevant to CSE contexts in which sexually exploited young people are themselves involved in/linked with criminal activity that may be linked to their exploitation (Cockbain and Brayley, 2012; Beckett *et al.*, 2013; Shepherd and Lewis, 2016) or more generally display criminal or delinquent behaviours (Kramer and Berg, 2003). Young people can have anxieties that they will get in trouble for these co-presenting behaviours if they disclose their CSE experiences as well.

Relational barriers

Relational barriers are those which arise from the nature or characteristics of a relationship or set of relationships which can be actual or perceived. Within this category, the following five broad themes have appeared in both the CSA/E literature:

- Victim–perpetrator relationship and perpetrator silencing strategies;
- Professional responses;
- Familial responses and needs;
- Peer relationships;
- Intimate relationships.

Sometimes, the actual or perceived nature of a particular relationship or set of relationships can prevent disclosure and help-seeking. Professional responses and peer relationships will be used here as examples of how barriers manifest differently in different contexts of abuse.

The CSA literature has found that both actual and anticipated reactions to abuse disclosure can reduce children's likelihood of reporting abuse to professionals (Alaggia, 2010; Allnock and Miller, 2013; Cossar *et al.*, 2013; Collin-Vézina *et al.*, 2015; Warrington *et al.*, 2017). Some professional responses have been experienced as negative, including the failure of professionals to inform children what will happen following a disclosure, inadequate procedures being followed or the involvement of family members who might themselves be abusive or react poorly to the disclosure. Children have reported that they felt they were not believed or that their experiences were minimised by professionals (Crisma *et al.*, 2004). Concerns about confidentiality and 'losing control' of information can hinder children from disclosing (Ungar *et al.*, 2009; Warrington *et al.*, 2017). Findings from CSA studies also suggest that underlying experiences of abuse are often not recognised by professionals who respond only to obvious 'symptoms', failing to ask or explore with children and young people about other things that may be troubling them and that, in fact, children want to be 'noticed' and 'asked' (Crisma *et al.*, 2004; Allnock and Miller, 2013; Cossar *et al.*, 2013).

Professionals can sometimes act in biased and discriminatory ways to children's disclosures, hindering full engagement with professional support (Alaggia, 2010). It is interesting that biased and discriminatory responses tend to be reported more frequently in relation to abuse disclosed in the adolescent period (Alaggia, 2010), a theme that emerges very clearly in studies of CSE also (Beckett and Warrington, 2015; Beckett *et al.*, 2016). Whilst actual negative reactions from professionals to a disclosure can hinder future disclosures, anticipated or perceived negative reactions or responses from professionals can also prevent disclosure from occurring in the first place. Children and young people worry, for example, that professionals will intervene by removing them from their families if they disclose (Crisma *et al.*, 2004) and they can feel anxious about being judged, or indeed believed, which can lead to non-disclosure (Allnock and Miller, 2013).

These are all common themes emerging in the CSE literature, pointing to harmful barriers across professional practice. There are, however, additional professional responses that CSE victims encounter that do not emerge so clearly in the CSA disclosure literature. Professionals have struggled to recognise that adolescents have rights to protection, especially when it may appear they are making 'choices' to remain in apparently abusive relationships. The evidence tells us that professionals have historically been much better at responding to particular kinds of abuse (for example, that which occurs in the family home) and better at responding to young children whom they see as 'innocent' victims. In a wider social context where 'childhood' and 'adolescence' are constructed as separate developmental stages (as opposed to viewing all individuals under the age of 18 as a child with rights to protection), professionals have faced very real challenges in managing responses to young people whose behaviours may appear challenging. Victims of CSE can also lose confidence in seeking help because they are aware of the absence of convictions for similar cases and they have said they lack faith that services can protect them, particularly in complex CSE cases such as gang contexts (Beckett *et al.*, 2013). Professionals can fail to recognise CSE of boys because they are only able to attribute particular contexts and behaviours to the CSE of girls. This failure to acknowledge that boys can be victims of CSE can be a powerful inhibitor of disclosure amongst boys (Cockbain, Brayley and Ashby, 2014).

Peer relationships have been cited as barriers to disclosure in both the CSA and CSE literature. CSA studies, for example, find that children may not disclose because they want to be seen and treated by peers as 'normal', anxious that if identified as a victim of abuse they would be stigmatised (Allnock and Miller, 2013). Boys specifically have reported worrying that they will be seen by their peers as gay if their abuse was revealed (Allnock and Miller, 2013). These barriers have been reported in CSE studies also (McNaughton Nicholls, Harvey and Paskell, 2014), although additional dynamics emerge relating to abuse that occurs within peer social circles. CSE is sometimes so prevalent among peer groups that friends of victims may be experiencing similar abuse and exploitation. By disclosing, this can involve a friend who does not want to be helped, but also, crucially, a young person may be silenced by peer group pressure which can come in the form of threats, bullying and social isolation. These contexts of peer-normalised exploitation are a feature that has only been identified in CSE contexts (Beckett *et al.*, 2013).

Social barriers

Social barriers are those which arise from broader societal responses to or messages about sexual abuse that may prevent disclosure. Within this, three broad themes emerge across both sources of evidence:

- Education;
- Stigmatisation of sexual abuse;
- Societal messages about homosexuality.

All of these themes are evident in both the CSA disclosure literature and the CSE literature, but the specific dynamics within CSE contexts are not fully drawn out in the broader CSA research.

Historically, CSA has carried with it considerable stigma, often identified in CSA disclosure research as a crucial barrier to children and young people's help-seeking (Alaggia, 2010). While awareness has significantly increased, it is clear that victims and survivors continue to feel the burden of that stigma (NSPCC, 2013). While professional responses to CSA continue to garner criticism (CCE, 2015; Warrington *et al.*, 2017), there has been improvement in child protection processes relating to abuse within the family environment and there is far more awareness of CSA politically, socially and across professional contexts. This awareness can be observed in the increased reporting of sexual abuse that is both 'recent' and 'historical' (Kelly and Karsna, 2017). CSE, while now quite high on the political agenda, only recently emerged in the social and political consciousness. As a result, awareness, understanding and responses to CSE are only beginning to increase and evolve. Despite increased awareness, 'victim-blaming' continues to be a powerful discourse used with adolescents who are perceived to be 'choosing' and 'initiating' abusive relationships.

This victim-blaming discourse certainly existed historically for victims of other forms of CSA, but our understanding and awareness of the abuse of young children has advanced over more than 30 years, resulting in a broad societal consensus that the CSA of young children is repugnant (Lindland and Kendall-Taylor, 2013). This repugnance has been slow to extend to the sexual exploitation of adolescents and, despite the increasing awareness of CSE globally, 'victim-blaming' still occurs by professionals in positions of power and protection who are ignorant of the dynamics of CSE (Beckett and Warrington, 2015).

Conclusion

CSE is a form of CSA. Yet, the intersection of exchange, consent/choice, developmental stage and the associated professional responses which characterise CSE make such contexts distinct from other forms of CSA. Highlighting this distinction is in no way meant to minimise the challenges to disclosure faced by victims of CSA in other contexts. It is instead meant to draw attention to the distinctive factors which influence disclosure patterns amongst CSE victims in unique ways. Researchers and practitioners in the field of CSE are, at present, reliant on the CSA disclosure literature to inform their work because of an absence of equivalent, systematic and theoretically-informed literature based on research that is explicit in its inclusion of victims of CSE and acknowledgement of how exploitative contexts are distinct. Until CSA disclosure researchers make explicit acknowledgment of where and how CSE is positioned within their study designs, the disclosure sub-field remains insufficient and partial in terms of its relevance to the variety of forms of child sexual exploitation.

Future research in the CSA disclosure sub-field should, therefore: explicitly define CSA and simultaneously clarify the position of CSE within the research (are CSE contexts included, and if so, how are they analysed/treated); advance methods for measuring contexts of sexual abuse (if participants who have been sexually exploited are to be included); and clarify sample sources. It would be helpful if CSA disclosure researchers could also begin to engage in comparative research (as Cole *et al.* (2016) has done) by explicitly seeking to compare disclosure among samples of sexually exploited young people and young people who have experienced other forms of sexual abuse (without the presence of exchange). CSE researchers can also begin to build a more theoretically sound evidence base that robustly articulates the distinctive patterns of disclosure in exploitative contexts and applies relevant theory (for example, the ecological framework) or develops a new theory built on the lived experiences of CSE victims.

Practitioners working to support young people to disclose can find useful information in the CSA disclosure literature. Caution is advised, however. The lack of attention to CSE contexts in this literature may be misdirecting practitioners' efforts in identifying effective approaches to supporting disclosure. Practitioners drawing on this literature may wish to carefully examine the evidence in light of the experiences of young people they are observing in practice to assist in navigating this evidence base. The best interventions will inevitably be those that target what is most meaningful to young people.

Note

1 Summit (1983) argues: 'Virtually no child is prepared for the possibility of molestation by a trusted adult' (p. 181) and 'The child cannot safely conceptualize that a parent might be ruthless and self-serving; such a conclusion is tantamount to abandonment and annihilation' (p. 185) and, finally, 'Children often describe their first experiences as waking up to find their father (or stepfather, or mother's live-in companion) exploring their bodies with hands or mouth' (p. 183).

References

Alaggia, R. (2004) 'Many ways of telling: Expanding conceptualisations of child sexual abuse disclosure'. *Child Abuse and Neglect*, 28(11), pp. 1213–1217.

Alaggia, R. (2010) 'An ecological analysis of child sexual abuse disclosure: Considerations for child and adolescent mental health'. *Journal of the Canadian Academy of Child and Adolescent Psychiatry*, 19(1), pp. 32–39.

Alaggia, R., Collin-Vézina, D. and Lateef, R. (2017) 'Facilitators and barriers to child sexual abuse (CSA) disclosures: A research update (2000–2016)'. *Trauma, Violence and Abuse*, pp. 1–24.

Allnock, D. and Miller, P. (2013) *'No one noticed, no one heard': A study of disclosures of childhood abuse*. London: The NSPCC. Available at: www.nspcc.org.uk/globalassets/documents/research-reports/no-one-noticed-no-one-heard-report.pdf (Accessed 25 July 2017).

Allnock, D., Sneddon, H. and Ackerley, E. (2015) *Mapping therapeutic services for sexual abuse in the UK in 2015*. Luton: The University of Bedfordshire. Available at: www.beds.ac.uk/__data/assets/pdf_file/0004/504283/mapping-therapeutic-services-sexual-abuse-uk-2015.pdf (Accessed 25 July 2017).

Arata, C. M. (1998) 'To tell or not to tell: Current functioning of child sexual abuse survivors who disclosed their victimization'. *Child Maltreatment*, 3(1), pp. 63–71.

Beckett, H., Holmes, D. and Walker, J. (2017) *Child sexual exploitation: Definition and guide. Extended Text*. Luton: University of Bedfordshire. Available at: www.beds.ac.uk/__data/assets/pdf_file/0009/536175/UOB-RIP-CSE-GuidanceFeb2017.pdf (Accessed 25 July, 2017).

Beckett, H. (2011) *Not a world away*. Belfast: Barnardo's Northern Ireland. Available at: www.barnardos.org.uk/13932_not_a_world_away_full_report.pdf (Accessed 25 July 2017).

Beckett, H., Brodie, I., Factor, F., Melrose, M., Pearce, J., Pitts, J., Shuker, L. and Warrington, C. (2013) *'It's wrong but you get used to it': A qualitative study of gang-associated sexual violence towards, and exploitation of, young people in England*. Luton: The University of Bedfordshire and London: The Children's Commissioner's Office. Available at: www.beds.ac.uk/__data/assets/pdf_file/0005/293234/Gangs-Report-final.pdf (Accessed 25 July 2017).

Beckett, H. and Schubotz, D. (2014) 'Young people's self-reported experiences of sexual exploitation and sexual violence: A view from Northern Ireland'. *Journal of Youth Studies*, 17(4), pp. 430–445.

Beckett, H. and Warrington, C. (2015) *Making justice work: Experiences of criminal justice for children and young people affected by sexual exploitation as victims and witnesses*. Luton: The University of Bedfordshire. Available at: www.beds.ac.uk/__data/assets/pdf_file/0011/461639/MakingJusticeWorkFullReport.pdf (Accessed 25 July 2017).

Beckett, H., Warrington, C., Ackerley, E. and Allnock, D. (2016) *Children's voices research report: Children and young people's perspectives on the police's role in safeguarding: a report for Her Majesty's Inspectorate of*

Constabularies. Luton: The University of Bedfordshire and London: HMIC. Available at: www. beds.ac.uk/__data/assets/pdf_file/0011/496136/HMIC-UoB-Report-FINAL.pdf (Accessed 25 July 2017).

Belsky, J. (1980) 'Child maltreatment: An ecological integration'. *American Psychologist*, 35(4), pp. 330–335.

Brayley, H., Cockbain, E. and Gibson, K. (2014) *Rapid evidence assessment: The sexual exploitation of boys and young men*. UCL and Barnardo's. Available at: www.natcen.ac.uk/media/539627/16144-su-cse-rapid-evidence-report-v4.pdf (Accessed 25 July, 2017).

Brazelton, J. (2015) 'The secret storm: Exploring the disclosure process of African American women survivors of child sexual abuse across the life course'. *Traumatology*, 21(3), pp. 181–187.

Bussey, K. and Grimbeek, E. (1995) 'Disclosure processes: Issues for child sexual abuse victims', in Rotenbert, K. (ed.) *Disclosure processes in children and adolescents*. Cambridge: Cambridge University Press.

Cameron, G., Mendez Sayer, E., Thompson, L. and Wilson, S. (2015) *Child sexual exploitation: A study of international comparisons*. Nottingham: The Virtual Staff College. Available at: www.opm.co.uk/wp-content/uploads/2015/07/CSE-Main-Report-Final.pdf (Accessed 25 July 2017).

Children's Commissioner for England (CCE) (2015) *Protecting children from harm*. London: CCE. Available at: www.childrenscommissioner.gov.uk/publication/protecting-children-from-harm/ (Accessed 25 July 2017).

Cobbina, J. and Oselin, S. (2011) 'It's not only for the money: An analysis of adolescent versus adult entry into street prostitution'. *Sociological Inquiry*, 81(3), pp. 310–332.

Cockbain, E. and Brayley, H. (2012) 'Child sexual exploitation and youth offending: A research note'. *European Journal of Criminology*, 9(6), pp. 689–700.

Cockbain, E., Brayley, H. and Ashby, M. (2014) *Not just a girl thing: A large-scale comparison of male and female users of child sexual exploitation services in the UK*. Barnardo's, London. Available at: http://assets. mesmac.co.uk/images/Not-just-a-girl-thing.pdf?mtime=20160108191711 (Accessed 25 July 2017).

Cole, J., Sprang, G., Lee, R. and Cohen, J. (2016) 'The trauma of commercial sexual exploitation of youth: A comparison of CSE victim to sexual abuse victims in a clinical sample'. *Journal of Interpersonal Violence*, 31(1), pp. 122–146.

Collin-Vézina, D., De La Sablonnière-Griffin, M., Palmer, A. and Milne, A. (2015) 'A preliminary mapping of individual, relational, and social factors that impede disclosure of child sexual abuse'. *Child Abuse and Neglect*, 43, pp. 123–134.

Collings, S., Griffiths, S. and Kumalo, M. (2005) 'Patterns of disclosure in child sexual abuse'. *South African Journal of Psychology*, 35(2), pp. 270–285.

Cossar, J., Brandon, M., Bailey, S., Belderson, P. and Biggart, L. (2013) *'It takes a lot to build trust'. Recognition and telling: Developing earlier routes to help for children and young people*. Available at: www. childrenscommissioner.gov.uk/publications/it-takes-lot-build-trust-recognition-and-telling-developing-earlier-routes-help (Accessed 25 July 2017).

Coy, M. (2009) 'Milkshakes, lady lumps and growing up to want boobies: How the sexualisation of popular culture limits girls' horizons'. *Child Abuse Review*, 18(6), pp. 372–383.

Crisma, M., Bascelli, E., Paci, D. and Romito, P. (2004) 'Adolescents who experienced sexual abuse: Fears, needs and impediments to disclosure'. *Child Abuse and Neglect*, 28(10), pp. 1035–1048.

Dodsworth, J. (2014) 'Sexual exploitation, selling and swapping sex: Victimhood and agency'. *Child Abuse Review*, 23(3), pp. 185–199.

Easton, S. (2013) 'Disclosure of child sexual abuse among adult male survivors'. *Journal of Clinical Social Work*, 41, pp. 344–355.

Easton, S., Saltzman, L. and Willis, D. (2014) '"Would you tell under circumstances like that?" Barriers to disclosure of child sexual abuse for me'. *Psychology of Men and Masculinity*, 15(4), pp. 460–469.

Erikson, E. H. (1993) *Childhood and Society*. (2nd ed.). New York: Norton.

Fergusson, D., Lynskey, M. and Horwood, J. (1996) 'Child sexual abuse and psychiatric disorder in young adulthood: I. Prevalence of sexual abuse and factors associated with sexual abuse'. *Journal of the American Academy of Child and Adolescent Psychiatry*, 34(10), pp. 1355–1364.

Finkelhor, D., Shattuck, A., Turner, H. and Hamby, S. (2014) 'The lifetime prevalence of child sexual abuse and sexual assault assessed in late adolescence'. *Journal of Adolescent Health*, 55(3), pp. 329–333.

Firmin, C. (2011) *'This is it. This is my life': Female voice in violence final report*. London: ROTA. Available at: www.rota.org.uk/content/rota-march-2011-female-voice-violence-project-final-report-it-my-life (Accessed 17 July 2017).

Franklin, A., Raws, P. and Smeaton, E. (2015) *Unprotected, overprotected: Meeting the needs of young people with learning disabilities who experience, or are at risk of, sexual exploitation*. Essex: Barnardo's. Available at: www.bild.org.uk/resources/unprotected-overprotected/ (Accessed 25 July 2017).

Gagnier, C. and Collin-Vézina, D. (2016) 'The disclosure experiences of male child sexual abuse survivors'. *Journal of Child Sexual Abuse*, 25(2), pp. 221–214.

Gohir, S. (2013) *Unheard voices: The sexual exploitation of Asian girls and young women*. Birmingham: The Muslim Women's Network UK. Available at: www.mwnuk.co.uk/resourcesDetail.php?id=97 (Accessed 25 July 2017).

Greijer, S. and Doek, J. (2016) *Terminology guidelines for the protection of children from sexual exploitation and abuse*. ECPAT International with ECPAT Luxembourg.

Griffiths, S. (2013) *The overview report of the serious case review in respect of young people 1, 2, 3, 4, 5 and 6*. Rochdale: Rochdale Borough Safeguarding Children Board. Available at: www.scie-socialcareonline.org.uk/the-overview-report-of-the-serious-case-review-in-respect-of-young-people-1-2-3-4-5-and-6/r/a11G0000002z190IAA (Accessed 25 July 2017).

Hallett, S. (2015) 'An uncomfortable comfortableness': 'Care', child protection and sexual exploitation'. *The British Journal of Social Work*, 46(7), pp. 2137–2152.

Hanson, R., Resnick, H., Saunders, B., Kilpatrick, D and Best, C. (1999) 'Factors related to the reporting of childhood rape'. *Child Abuse and Neglect*, 23(6), pp. 559–569.

Hartill, M. (2014) 'Exploring narratives of boyhood sexual subjection in male sport'. *Sociology of Sport Journal*, 31(1), pp. 23–43.

Hershkowitz, I., Horowitz, D. and Lamb, M. (2005) 'Trends in children's disclosure of abuse in Israel: A national study'. *Child Abuse and Neglect*, 29(11), pp. 1203–1214.

Hershkowitz, I., Lanes, O. and Lamb, M. (2007) 'Exploring the disclosure of child sexual abuse with alleged victims and their parents'. *Child Abuse and Neglect*, 31(2), pp. 111–123.

Jago, S., Arocha, L., Brodie, I., Melrose, M., Pearce, J. and Warrington, C. (2011) *What's going on to safeguard children and young people from sexual exploitation?* Luton: The University of Bedfordshire. Available at: www.beds.ac.uk/__data/assets/pdf_file/0004/121873/wgoreport2011-121011.pdf (Accessed 25 July 2017).

Jay, A. (2014) *Independent inquiry into child sexual exploitation in Rotherham: 1997–2013*. Rotherham: Rotherham Metropolitan Borough Council. Available at: www.rotherham.gov.uk/downloads/file/1407/independent_inquiry_cse_in_rotherham (Accessed 25 July 2017).

Jonzon, E. and Lindblad, F. (2004) 'Disclosure, reactions and social support: Findings from a sample of adult victims of child sexual abuse'. *Child Maltreatment*, 9(2), pp. 190–200.

Kellogg, N. (2017) '"Why didn't you tell?": Helping families and children weather the process following a sexual abuse disclosure', in Teti, D. (ed.) *Parenting and family processes in child maltreatment and intervention*. Switzerland: Springer.

Kogan, S. (2004) 'Disclosing unwanted sexual experiences: Results from a national sample of adolescent women'. *Child Abuse and Neglect*, 28(2), pp. 147–165.

Kramer, L. and Berg, E. (2003) 'A survival analysis of timing of entry into prostitution: The differential impact of race, educational level and childhood/adolescent risk factors'. *Sociological Inquiry*, 73(4), pp. 511–528.

Leonard, E. D. (1996) 'A social exchange explanation for the Child Sexual Abuse Accommodation Syndrome'. *Journal of Interpersonal Violence*, 11(1), pp. 107–117.

Lindland, E. and Kendall-Taylor, N. (2013) *Mapping the gaps between expert and public understandings of child maltreatment in the UK*. Washington, DC: The Frameworks Institute. Available at: http://frameworksinstitute.org/pubs/mtg/childmaltreatment/index.html (Accessed 25 July 2017).

London, K., Bruck, M., Ceci, S. J. and Shuman, D. (2005) 'Children's disclosure of sexual abuse: What does the research tell us about the ways that children tell?' *Psychology, Public Policy, the Law*, 11, pp. 194–226.

London, K., Bruck, M., Wright, D. and Ceci, S. (2008) 'Review of the contemporary literature on how children report sexual abuse to others: Findings, methodological issues, and implications for forensic interviewers'. *Memory*, 16(1), pp. 29–47.

McElvaney, R., Greene, S. and Hogan, D. (2013) 'To tell or not to tell? Factors influencing young people's informal disclosures of child sexual abuse'. *Journal of Interpersonal Violence*, 29(5), pp. 928–947.

McElvaney, R. and Culhane, M. (2017) 'A retrospective analysis of children's assessment reports: What helps children tell?'. *Child Abuse Review*, 26(2), pp. 103–115.

McNaughton Nicholls, C., Harvey, S. and Paskell, C. (2014) *Gendered perceptions: What professionals say about the sexual exploitation of boys and young men in the UK*. UCL and Barnardo's. Available at: http://socialwelfare.bl.uk/subject-areas/services-client-groups/children-young-people/barnardos/16666616145_cse_interview_with_professionals_v5.pdf (Accessed 25 July 2017).

McPherson, M., Smith-Lovin, L. and Cook, J. (2001) 'Birds of a feather: Homophily in social networks'. *Annual Review of Sociology*, 27, pp. 415–444.

Melrose, M. (2013) 'Twenty-first century party people: Young people and sexual exploitation in the new millennium'. *Child Abuse Review*, 22(3), pp. 155–168.

Mossige, S., Ainsaar, M. and Svedin, C. G. (eds). (2007) *The Baltic Sea regional study on adolescents' sexuality*. NOVA Report 18/07. Oslo, Norway: Norwegian Social Research. Available at: www.nova.no/asset/2812/1/2812_1.pdf (Accessed 25 July 2017).

NSPCC (2013) *'Would they actually have believed me?' A focus group exploration of the underreporting of crimes by Jimmy Savile*. London: NSPCC. Available at: www.nspcc.org.uk/globalassets/documents/research-reports/would-they-actually-believed-me-savile-report.pdf (Accessed 25 July 2017).

Oaksford, K. and Frude, N. (2003) 'The process of coping following child sexual abuse: A qualitative study'. *Journal of Child Sexual Abuse*, 12(2), pp. 41–72.

Paine, M. and Hansen, D. (2002) 'Factors influencing children to self-disclose abuse'. *Faculty Publications, Department of Psychology*, Paper 59. http://digitalcommons.unl.edu/psychfacpub/59.

Palmer, T. (2015) *Digital dangers: The impact of technology on the sexual abuse and exploitation of children and young people*. Essex: Barnardo's. Available at: www.barnardos.org.uk/onlineshop/pdf/digital_dangers_report.pdf (Accessed 25 July 2017).

Pearce, J. (2009) *Young people and sexual exploitation: It's not hidden, you just aren't looking*. London: Routledge.

Priebe, G. and Svedin, C. (2008) 'Child sexual abuse is largely hidden from the adult society. An epidemiological study of adolescents' disclosures'. *Child Abuse & Neglect*, 32(12), pp. 1095–2008.

Radford, L., Corral, S., Bradley, C., Fisher, H., Collishaw, S., Bassett, C. and Howat, N. (2011) *Child abuse and neglect in the UK today*. London: NSPCC. Available at: www.nspcc.org.uk/childstudy (Accessed 25 July 2017).

Rees, G., Gorin, S., Jobe, A., Stein, M., Medforth, R. and Goswami, H. (2010) *Safeguarding young people: Responding to young people aged 11 to 17 who are maltreated*. London: The Children's Society. Available at: www.childrenssociety.org.uk/sites/default/files/tcs/research_docs/Safeguarding%20Young%20People%20-%20Responding%20to%20Young%20People%20aged%2011%20to%2017%20who%20are%20maltreated_0.pdf (Accessed 25 July 2017).

Sawyer, A. and Bagley, C. (2017) 'Child sexual abuse and adolescent and adult adjustment: A review of British and world evidence, with implications for social work and mental health and school counselling'. *Advances in Applied Sociology*, 7(1), pp. 1–15.

Schaeffer, P., Leventhal, J. and Gottsegen Asnes, A. (2011) 'Children's disclosures of child sexual abuse: Learning from direct inquiry'. *Child Abuse and Neglect*, 35, pp. 343–352.

Schönbucher, V., Maier, T., Mohler-Kuo, M., Schnyder, U. and Landolt, M. (2012) 'Disclosure of child sexual abuse by adolescents: A qualitative in-depth study'. *Journal of Interpersonal Violence*, 27(17), pp. 3468–3513.

Shepherd, W. and Lewis, B. (2016) *Working with children who are victims or at risk of sexual exploitation: Barnardo's model of practice*. Essex: Barnardo's. Available at: www.barnardos.org.uk/cse_barnardo_s_model_of_practice.pdf (Accessed 25 July 2017).

Sidebotham, P., Brandon, M., Bailey, S., Belderson, P., Dodsworth, J., Garstang, J. et al. (2016) *Pathways to harm, pathways to protection: a triennial analysis of serious case reviews 2011–2016*. London: Department for Education. Available at: www.gov.uk/government/uploads/system/uploads/attachment_data/file/533826/Triennial_Analysis_of_SCRs_2011-2014_-__Pathways_to_harm_and_protection.pdf (Accessed 25 July 2017).

Smith, N., Dogaru, C. and Ellis, F. (2015) *Hear me. Believe me. Respect me. A survey of adult survivors of child sexual abuse and their experiences of support services*. University Campus Suffolk and Survivors in Transition. Available at: http://cdn.basw.co.uk/upload/basw_122305-1.pdf (Accessed 25 July 2017).

Sorenson, T., and Snow, B. (1991) 'How children tell: The process of disclosure in child sexual abuse'. *Child Welfare*, 70(1), pp. 3–15.

Summit, R. (1983) 'The child sexual abuse accommodation syndrome'. *Child Abuse and Neglect*, 7(2), pp. 177–193.

Summit, R. (1993) 'Abuse of the Child Sexual Abuse Accommodation Syndrome'. *Journal of Child Sexual Abuse*, 1(4), pp. 153–164.

Tang, C. S. (2002) 'Childhood experiences of sexual abuse among Hong Kong Chinese college students'. *Child Abuse and Neglect*, 26(1), pp. 23–37.

Ungar, M., Tutty, L., McConnell, S., Barter, K. and Fairholm, J. (2009) 'What Canadian youth tell us about disclosing abuse'. *Child Abuse and Neglect*, 33(10), pp. 699–708.

United Nations Secretariat (2003) *Secretary-General's bulletin on special measures for protection for sexual exploitation and abuse*. Geneva: United Nations. Available at: www.unhcr.org/uk/protection/operations/405ac6614/secretary-generals-bulletin-special-measures-protection-sexual-exploitation.html (Accessed 25 July 2017).

Ussher, J. and Dewberry, C. (1995) 'The nature and long-term effects of childhood sexual abuse: A survey of adult women survivors in Britain'. *British Journal of Clinical Psychology*, 34(2), pp. 177–192.

Warrington, C. with Beckett, H., Ackerley, E., Walker, M. and Allnock, D. (2017) *Making noise: Children's voices for positive change after sexual abuse*. Luton: University of Bedfordshire.

Wood, M., Barter, C. and Berridge, D. (2011) *'Standing on my own two feet': Disadvantaged teenagers, intimate partner violence and coercive control*. London: NSPCC. Available at: www.nspcc.org.uk/globalassets/documents/research-reports/standing-own-two-feet-report.pdf (Accessed 25 July 2017).

4

APPLYING AN INTERSECTIONAL LENS TO SEXUAL VIOLENCE RESEARCH AND PRACTICE

Elizabeth Ackerley and Lia Latchford

Introduction

Research into child sexual exploitation (CSE) and other forms of sexual violence[1] has surged over the last few years, providing a growing evidence base for policy and practice to draw on when responding to these forms of harm (Barter *et al.*, 2009; Pearce, 2009; Beckett, 2011; Beckett *et al.*, 2013; Melrose and Pearce, 2013; Firmin, 2015; Firmin *et al.*, 2016). Within this growing evidence base, however, there is increasing recognition that less attention has been paid to some minoritised groups of young people (Ward and Patel, 2006; Beckett, 2011; Jago *et al.*, 2011; Gohir, 2013; Brayley, Cockbain and Gibson, 2014; McNaughton Nicholls *et al.*, 2014; Franklin, Raws and Smeaton, 2015; Fox, 2016).

Furthermore, while research identifies a range of issues that may increase vulnerability to sexual violence – such as looked after status, 'race'[2], class, sexuality or disability – significantly less attention has been paid to how these issues can intersect. One young person may embody multiple identities and be impacted by a range of inequalities simultaneously, which is likely to compound vulnerability to sexual violence, likelihood of identification by professionals and the accessibility and quality of service response they receive (Fox, 2016). It is critical that we find a way to adequately consider these complexities, if we are to holistically understand children and young people's experiences of harm and what they need in terms of a response to these.

This chapter is a theoretical think piece setting forth intersectionality theory as a helpful approach to dealing with these dilemmas. Intersectionality theory can help us think about and respond to the multiply-influenced experiences of children and young people affected by sexual violence within a wider context of structural inequality. We bring together intersectionality theory, current research into young people's experiences and perspectives, and reflections on practice to consider:

- the impact of intersecting inequalities on vulnerability to, experiences of, and responses post sexual violence;

- the importance of understanding children and young people's whole experiences of harm, and treatment in services, research, policy and society;
- how taking an intersectional lens to research and practice allows us to interrogate power imbalances and develop nuanced understandings around vulnerability;
- the importance of space, voice and representation of young people impacted by multiple inequalities.

The chapter concludes by considering how intersectional thinking and practice could help address current gaps in research and services, to better support all children and young people affected by CSE and other forms of sexual violence.

Methodology

The findings presented in this chapter are drawn from a cumulative body of evidence developed by The International Centre and other colleagues researching and practicing in the field of sexual violence against children and young people. The chapter is underpinned by The International Centre's approach to research, which is focused around four key principles; one of which is the prioritisation and promotion of children and young people's voices. This is in recognition of children's fundamental right to have a say on matters that affect their lives (United Nations Convention on the Rights of the Child, Article 12) and the acknowledgment that consideration of their perspectives significantly increases our capacity to effectively respond to and safeguard children and young people (Berelowitz et al., 2013; Cossar et al., 2013; Beckett and Warrington, 2015). Therefore, where possible, quotes will be used to illustrate the experiences and perspectives of children and young people themselves.

Another key principle of The International Centre's work is the strong link between research and practice. In line with this principle, we draw on evidence generated by Imkaan, a recent practice partner of The International Centre. Imkaan is a UK-based black feminist organisation that represents a national network of frontline, dedicated and specialist 'ending violence against women and girls' organisations that are led 'by and for' black and 'minority ethnic'[3] (BME) women and girls. Imkaan takes an intersectional approach to the work as a way of understanding and articulating BME women and girls' experiences of violence and access to safety, support, space and justice (Larasi with Jones, 2017).

What is intersectionality and how can it inform thinking about CSE?

The term intersectionality came out of, and is rooted in, the experiences of black women. It followed critical contributions made by African American women, scholars and activists, such as Angela Davis, the Combahee River Collective and Audre Lorde (Collins, 2000), who worked to challenge the marginalisation and oppression of black women within society. The specific term intersectionality was coined by Kimberlé Crenshaw in 1989, within her black feminist critique of American anti-discrimination law. It provided a way of articulating the specific and overlapping experiences of oppression faced by black women. Crenshaw found that the American legal system did not recognise the specific discrimination that black women experienced based on their 'race' and gender, and as a result did not provide justice for black women. Crenshaw (1991, p. 1243) later used the term to demonstrate the ways in which 'intersecting patterns of racism and sexism' resulted in policy, services, feminist and anti-racist movements failing to recognise or address the specific needs of black women who experience violence.

Intersectionality is therefore a useful framework from which to analyse historical and contemporary power relations, and the impact of power on those who are constructed as 'different' in multiple ways or at multiple intersections.[4] As Collins (2000, p. 18) explains:

> Intersectional paradigms remind us that oppression cannot be reduced to one fundamental type, and that oppressions work together in producing injustice.

Following the development of the theory, several pieces of research have studied everyday practices to explore how intersecting oppressions are subjectively lived (Lewis, 1985, 2000; hooks,[5] 1994) and to reflect on the ways in which intersecting oppressions are at the same time subjective and structural (Brah and Phoenix, 2004). Such studies demonstrate that black women experience oppression at an individual, subjective level, and that their experiences are also occurring within a wider context of structural inequality.

The use of intersectionality theory has now expanded and been adopted by social justice projects within civil rights, feminist and lesbian, gay, bisexual, transgender and queer (LGBTQ) movements to articulate a multiplicity of intersecting oppressions across the protected characteristics – including those based on class, age, sexuality, disability, religion and belief (Lewis, 2013). Whilst we consider how these characteristics impact on young people's experiences of sexual violence, in keeping with the origins of the approach we acknowledge the importance of centring discussions about intersectionality on black women and girls. As such, we primarily focus on the intersection between 'race' and gender, with a specific focus on the experiences of BME young people, within this chapter.

Intersectionality theory and sexual violence

Intersectionality theory can be used to provoke thought about how different children and young people experience discrimination, violence and abuse, including CSE. Often, violence against minoritised groups is viewed and responded to in ways that problematise those groups, rather than situating their experiences of violence within a context of structural inequality (Larasi with Jones, 2017). While there is increasing recognition within policy and practice of the impacts that structural inequality and different forms of discrimination have on young people's lives, this is often looked at in a siloed way. An understanding and active consideration of intersectionality in relation to sexual violence could contribute to a better awareness of the complex dynamics faced by young people navigating multiple systems of inequality. In turn, for researchers and practitioners, this would provide a more nuanced understanding of young people's experiences of violence, access to support and access to justice within such systems of inequality.

Thinking intersectionally requires active engagement to reflect on both the oppression young people may face at a subjective, individual level, and also the context of structural inequalities in which these oppressions operate. Developing intersectional approaches to research and practice requires an in-depth consideration of the systemic power imbalances that are at play and how these impact on young people's lived experiences. We look first at how experiences of sexual violence occur at the intersection of 'race' and gender, reporting on findings generated by Purple Drum; the team at Imkaan committed to archiving and amplifying young BME women's voices. We then look at how a context of structural inequality impacts on young people's likelihood, or not, to disclose sexual violence, their subsequent access to services and young people's experiences of responses from professionals and services within this context.

Experiences of sexual violence

There is currently limited research available on BME women and girls' experiences of sexual violence. This makes it difficult to assess the nature of such violence and its impact on BME women and girls' wellbeing, the ways in which they disclose violence and the responses they receive. The research that does exist, however, demonstrates that BME women and girls are impacted by multiple forms of sexual violence including rape and sexual assault, child sexual abuse, sexual exploitation and harassment (Imkaan and University of Warwick, 2015).

Further, much of the media coverage surrounding CSE in particular has focused on the experiences of white girls as victims, with less attention paid to victims of different ethnic backgrounds (Cockbain, 2013; Gohir, 2013).[6] This focus means that certain victims' experiences and voices are silenced, and their needs under-recognised (Gohir, 2013). This under-representation of young BME people's voices can be seen within wider discourse and research on sexual violence, and in the media more generally. As illustrated below, this impacts on young BME women's feelings about coming forward about sexual harassment.

Recognising and responding to this under-representation, Purple Drum has delivered several participatory programmes to ensure that the specificity of young BME women's experiences is acknowledged and addressed in policy and research. In 2016, Purple Drum conducted qualitative interviews with BME young women to explore their experiences of racialised sexual harassment in public spaces. Their responses outline the ways in which racism, sexism and age intersect to shape experiences of sexual harassment. Young women, featured in the resultant video, described incidents of harassment against them where racism and sexism were experienced simultaneously within an age-specific context. This included the impact of racialised sexist stereotypes and assumptions about young BME women, for example:

> My experiences are different as a black woman than they are for my white friends . . . I should be up for it, or that I am fair game, or that I shouldn't care if my body is touched in a specific way.
>
> *(Imkaan and EVAW, 2016)*

Young BME women also described the ways in which racist comments or threats formed part of the sexual harassment against them. Their experiences included:

> The next thing you know, he starts making monkey noises at me . . . so, you go from objectifying me, from me being like this sexual thing to you, and then when you get rejected, you think it's ok for you to then . . . shout racist taunts.
>
> *(Imkaan and EVAW, 2016)*

> After me ignoring them, that's when it turns racial. So that's when it might be 'you black this' or 'you black that, how dare you ignore me?'
>
> *(Imkaan and EVAW, 2016)*

> Being called 'a black whore' because you wouldn't give your number away to some guy . . . who's harassing you the entire time, whose only approach to you by the way was to grab your body, bits of my body, without consent.
>
> *(Imkaan and EVAW, 2016)*

These examples demonstrate that racism cannot be separated from young BME women's individual experiences of sexual violence and contributes to young BME women feeling vulnerable or at risk of harassment escalating into racist, or racialised, violence and abuse.

Whilst racism and sexism intersect to frame individual experiences of sexual violence, they also occur and intersect on a structural level to produce a wider context that shapes experiences and perceptions of sexual violence. For example, studies suggest that the racialised objectification, exoticisation and commodification of BME women in mainstream media and pornography is routine and pervasive. This representation affects attitudes towards 'race', gender and BME women's bodies specifically (Dines, 2010; Larasi, I, 2013; Coy, 2014).

Seeking support

We know that disclosure of, and seeking support for, sexual violence is difficult for many young people (Allnock and Millar, 2013), but that BME young people are likely to face additional barriers (Warrington *et al.*, 2017). These barriers include racism, inaccessible services and lack of knowledge among services and staff about the specific experiences of BME young people (Imkaan and University of Warwick, 2015).

Within the wider context of structural racism and patriarchy detailed above, young BME women who have experienced sexual harassment voiced a sense of feeling like they are less entitled to space or support than their white peers. This tells us something about how racism operates in ways that mean some children and young people may be less likely to seek support following sexual violence and abuse. This was evident in a recent study into young people's experiences of help-seeking and support following an experience of familial sexual abuse (Warrington *et al.*, 2017). In the study, young people from 'minority ethnic' communities identified that protection of their community would be a contributing factor to their decision about whether to disclose or not. Young people from 'minority ethnic' backgrounds cited the racism their communities already face and the risk of exacerbating prejudice and discrimination as factors that would act as barriers to disclosure[7] (Warrington *et al.*, 2017).

Barriers to disclosure also include professionals' responses to certain young people, with research demonstrating that some young people receive different treatment to others (Beckett *et al.*, 2016). Young people have spoken about the ways in which aspects of their identity, such as ethnicity, socio-economic status and perceived class, have a bearing on the professional response they receive (Beckett *et al.*, 2016). In a piece of research that looked at young people's perceptions of the police when they are responding to safeguarding concerns, a number of young people identified experiencing or perceiving differential treatment due to aspects of their, or other's, identity. For example, this young woman notes that:

Me and my mate got arrested, and my mate was like black and even like she saw like they were treating me different because like, like they handcuffed me, but they hand-cuffed me at the front with my handcuffs all loose and with her they just pushed her onto the floor and handcuffed her from the back.

(13-year-old female cited in Beckett et al., 2016, p. 53)

Identification by professionals

Sometimes, however, this differential treatment is not as obvious and is instead structural, meaning these forms of oppression may be more likely to go unchallenged and/or unex-amined. For example, research shows us that services including statutory agencies such as police and local authority children's services are less likely to identify BME young people in need of support (Berelowitz *et al.*, 2012; Gohir, 2013; Fox, 2016). BME children and young people with learning disabilities are further under-represented in services (Franklin, Raws and Smeaton, 2015). BME children and young people are disproportionately placed in the youth justice system (Berelowitz *et al.*, 2012; Youth Justice Board, 2016) and black boys from low income families are faced with exclusion from school far more often than their peers (Berelowitz *et al.*, 2013). Whilst these facts do not necessarily provide evidence that BME young people are less likely to be identified as in need of support post sexual violence specifically, it does require us to ask questions about why BME young people are dispropor-tionately given punitive responses and what impact a range of intersecting inequalities can have on young people?

This is occurring within a context of social discourse that problematises minoritised groups, whilst neglecting the social structures that create and reinforce inequality. Some of these social discourses were evident in the campaigns leading up to the 2016 referendum on United Kingdom (UK) membership to the European Union (EU); the United Nations Committee on the Elimination of Racial Discrimination has since reported deep concerns about the anti-immigrant and xenophobic rhetoric surrounding the campaigns and suggested that both politicians and the media helped to fuel the rise in violence and intimidation towards BME communities over this period (Committee on the Elimination of Racial Discrimination, 2016). Furthermore, there is ongoing construction of CSE as a racialised crime (Cockbain, 2013) that produces a specific 'type' of perpetrator and victim which not only further stigma-tises minoritised communities, but also hides certain young people from being recognised as victims (Gohir, 2013; Larasi, M., 2013). It is important to build constructive dialogue on 'race' and CSE that acknowledges the complexities related to this issue and the broader context of structural inequalities (Larasi, M., 2013).

Accessing services

These examples demonstrate why, when looking at individual cases of sexual violence, it is important to consider external societal attitudes and oppressions that may influence and constrain young people's views of their abuse and how accessible or safe any form of support feels. In response, Imkaan recognises the critical need for safe spaces as forms of resistance, support and justice that are defined and provided 'by and for' BME women and girls them-selves (Larasi with Jones, 2017). Similarly, for some young people, an accessible service is one that can adequately and appropriately respond to their individual and specific needs, relating to different/all aspects/intersections of their identity. Minoritised children and young people who experience violence, including CSE, have the right to resist and heal in a 'by and for' context that centres around them and understands and responds to the totality of their identities and experiences to ensure all children and young people have a voice.

The availability of specialist services, however, is limited in the current economic context of severe cuts to public services which disproportionately affect those already more deprived communities (Hastings *et al.*, 2015; Imkaan, 2015). This holds significant implications for those young people who require access to services following an experience of sexual violence. To illustrate, Childline's annual report for 2016 highlighted an 87 per cent increase in the number of counselling sessions where young people talked about struggling to access appropriate professional support locally, especially for mental health problems, some of which were linked to experiences of abuse (Childline, 2016). Findings from a mapping study of the availability of therapeutic services for children and young people affected by sexual abuse completed in 2015 show that there is a current overall gap of 12 per cent in service provision, and this is predicted to rise to 17 per cent (Allnock and Sneddon with Ackerley, 2015). The study also highlighted the precarious and short-term funding arrangements for specialist, in demand services. Furthermore, it highlighted the long and often complicated commissioning processes which divert services from their primary aim of delivering quality services to young people (Allnock and Sneddon with Ackerley, 2015).

Often more severely affected by the current economic context, given the already disproportionately low number of specialist services, are those services that offer a specialist service for children and young people related to specific aspects of their identity, such as their ethnicity or whether they have a disability (Franklin, Raws and Smeaton, 2015; Warrington *et al.*, 2017). Although demographic data varied considerably across services, the 2015 mapping study found that it is white British girls without disabilities who comprise the largest group receiving services (Allnock and Sneddon with Ackerley, 2015). Therefore, a context of multiple inequalities, lack of access to appropriate support and significant gaps in research around the specificities of young people's experiences means that some young people's needs are not being adequately met.

Adopting an intersectional lens

Understanding intersecting oppressions, which are 'simultaneously subjective, structural, about social positioning and everyday practices' (Brah and Phoenix, 2004, p. 80) gives us a truer picture of the realities of young people's lives, including their whole experiences of harm and treatment in services, policy and wider society.

Taking an intersectional lens to research and practice allows us to develop nuanced understandings about vulnerability to sexual violence and exploitation, intersections with other forms of harm and inequality, and why some young people may be less visible to researchers and practitioners. It also allows us to consider the intersections in and between the contexts where young people experience harm, for example at home, at school, in their local areas and within peer networks, and how these contexts are influenced by a wider societal context of inequalities.

Implementing intersectionality

Acknowledgment of power imbalances and the need for an intersectional approach is important. However, putting this into practice requires ongoing effort. While there is no one way of delivering intersectional practice, and we do not aim to provide any blueprint for doing so, there are steps individuals and organisations can take to begin to embed intersectionality into their work.

Imkaan (2017) highlights the importance of considering the impact of structural inequality on young people's journeys and experiences, staff attitudes and practice, and organisational governance and staffing. In particular, recognising entrenched power imbalances and having the reflexivity to deal with and change relationships of power and oppressive practice to ensure that all children and young people are seen, valued and supported.

Involving children and young people in decision-making about their care and creating opportunities for young people to have a say in matters that affect their lives is one way of challenging unequal power structures (Warrington, 2017). Young people who have been affected by sexual violence often describe feelings of powerlessness and a loss of control (Beckett and Warrington, 2015; Beckett et al., 2016; Warrington et al., 2017). Opportunities to participate are therefore crucial to attempt to redress this balance and often serve a therapeutic purpose (Brodie et al., 2016a; Warrington, 2017).

Within CSE policy, young people's participation is seen as increasingly important and many services are adapting and evolving to make space for young people's voices, which is an important step forward (Brodie et al., 2016a). There is still, however, a significant gap in the literature relating to the specific experiences of certain groups of young people, including BME young people, and therefore more work needs to be done to make sure that services are accessible and inclusive of all young people's needs (Brodie et al., 2016a). An intersectional approach requires us to actively identify which young people do not 'show up' in our services or research and carve out spaces for their voices to be heard and their needs supported in ways that work for them.

Whilst these are in no way meant to be prescriptive, questions that might be useful to consider in practice and research could include:

- Do I embed reflective practice into my work, and if not, how can I go about doing this?
- How am I influenced by my own identity and experience of the world and what impact does this have on how I interact with people?
- Which young people use my service/are included in my research and which young people are not included? Does this need to change? How can I go about doing this?
- Are the young people who are using my service or who are involved in my research representative of the young people in this area?
- Is my service truly accessible to all young people? If not, what do I need to do to change this?
- What methods am I using to engage young people in my service/research? Are these appropriate and accessible?
- If there are barriers to young people accessing my service/taking part in my research how will I address these?

- Have I asked any young people about what they think or what they want from services/research?
- Is there anything we do as an organisation/I do as an individual that reinforces structural inequalities?

(Adapted and developed from Brodie et al., 2016b;
Warrington, 2016; and Imkaan, 2017)

Acknowledging the value and specificity of work and partnerships with specialist services is also important (Imkaan, 2017). Recognising, for example, the importance of supportive partnerships with organisations that hold specialisms in particular areas, such as 'by and for' organisations for BME women and girls, in order to provide the best response to all young people who experience sexual violence. This might be about knowledge or skill exchange, but may also be about the 'type' of space or access that another organisation provides (Imkaan, 2017).

Conclusion

Taking an intersectional approach to address sexual violence is an ongoing process that requires continuous reflection and action. Further research into how different groups of young people experience services and how intersectionality theory can be applied to strengthen service responses to young people affected by sexual violence is needed to continue learning in this area. Structural inequalities must also be acknowledged and addressed in order to meet the needs of all young people.

Truly intersectional approaches would enable researchers and practitioners to better safeguard young people and better consider their needs at every stage of support, from service design through to evaluation. It would also provide the opportunities for all young people, including minoritised young people, to participate in service development and practice, as key partners to prevention (Warrington, 2010, 2013).

Only by recognising who we do not see in research and practice, and taking meaningful steps to begin to work with these young people, can we hope to disrupt structures of power and better support all young people affected by sexual violence. In the current political context of austerity, rising racism and xenophobia following the referendum on UK membership to the EU, and local commissioning processes that do not value specialist services, understanding the specificities of young people's experiences of oppression and violence is as important as ever.

Notes

1 Given the current debate on the distinctions and overlaps of different forms of sexual harm (see Chapter 1), this chapter will use the more generic term sexual violence defined as any behaviour that is 'perceived to be of a sexual nature, which is unwanted or takes place without consent or understanding' (DHSSPSNI, 2008).
2 We have put 'race' in inverted commas to acknowledge that it is a social construct with real consequences. Although we critique the impact of inequality based on gender, we are not critiquing gender as a construct in the same way.
3 Whilst we recognise that the term 'minority ethnic' is widely used in research, policy and practice, we use quotation marks here in line with Imkaan's stance to acknowledge that minoritisation is itself a process that can be problematic in that it can erase the specificity of individual identities (Larasi with Jones, 2017).

4 For a powerful critique of the importance of intersectionality theory in understanding and responding to violence against South Asian women see Thiara and Gill, 2010.
5 In line with the author's preference, bell hooks is not capitalised.
6 Within the media discourse (and research) exploitation of boys and young men, disabled young people and LGBTQ young people is also not given due consideration (see McNaughton Nicholls *et al.*, 2014; Albert Kennedy Trust, 2015; and Franklin, Raws and Smeaton, 2015). Whilst this chapter is focused specifically on 'race' and gender, we recognise and acknowledge the myriad ways in which young people are discriminated against.
7 In this study, all focus group participants were of British South Asian heritage due to geographical location and focus of the organisations and communities who agreed to take part. Therefore, whilst care must be taken not to generalise across these experiences and to consider these findings in this context, it is clear that BME young people from many different backgrounds may face additional, complex and intersecting barriers to disclosure and help-seeking and support that require further exploration and research (Warrington *et al.*, 2017, p. 59).

References

Albert Kennedy Trust (2015) *LGBT youth homelessness: A UK national scoping of cause, prevalence, response, and outcome.* London: Albert Kennedy Trust. Available at: www.akt.org.uk/webtop/modules/_repository/documents/AlbertKennedy_researchreport_FINALinteractive.pdf (Accessed: 6 January 2017).

Allnock, D. and Millar, P. (2013) *No one noticed, no one heard: A study of disclosures of childhood abuse.* London: NSPCC. Available at: www.nspcc.org.uk/globalassets/documents/research-reports/no-one-noticed-no-one-heard-report.pdf (Accessed: 30 July 2017).

Allnock, D. and Sneddon, H. with Ackerley, E. (2015) *Mapping therapeutic services for sexual abuse in the UK in 2015.* Luton: University of Bedfordshire. Available at: www.beds.ac.uk/__data/assets/pdf_file/0004/504283/mapping-therapeutic-services-sexual-abuse-uk-2015.pdf (Accessed: 7 July 2017).

Barter, C., McCarry, M., Berridge, D. and Evans, K. (2009) *Partner exploitation and violence in teenage intimate relationships.* London: NSPCC. Available at: www.nspcc.org.uk/globalassets/documents/research-reports/partner-exploitation-violence-teenage-intimate-relationships-report.pdf (Accessed: 8 February 2017).

Beckett, H. (2011) *Not a world away: The sexual exploitation of children and young people in Northern Ireland.* Belfast: Barnardo's.

Beckett, H., Brodie, I., Factor, F., Melrose, M., Pearce, J., Pitts, J., Shuker, L. and Warrington, C. (2013) *'It's wrong but you get used to it.' A qualitative study of gang-associated sexual violence and exploitation.* Luton: University of Bedfordshire.

Beckett, H. and Warrington, C. (2015) *Making justice work: Experiences of criminal justice for children and young people affected by sexual exploitation as victims and witnesses.* Luton: University of Bedfordshire.

Beckett, H., Warrington, C., Ackerley, E. and Allnock. D. (2016) *Children's voices research report: Children and young people's perspectives on the police's role in safeguarding: A report for Her Majesty's Inspectorate of Constabularies.* Luton: University of Bedfordshire. Available at: www.beds.ac.uk/__data/assets/pdf_file/0011/496136/HMIC-UoB-Report-FINAL.pdf (Accessed: 10 March 2017).

Berelowitz, S., Firmin, C., Edwards, G. and Gulyurtlu, S. (2012) *'I thought I was the only one, the only one in the world': The Office of the Children's Commissioner's inquiry into child sexual exploitation in gangs and groups interim report.* London: Office of the Children's Commissioner for England.

Berelowitz, S., Clifton, J., Firmin, C., Gulyurtlu, S. and Edwards, G. (2013) *If only someone had listened: Office of the Children's Commissioner's inquiry into child sexual exploitation in gangs and groups.* London: Office of the Children's Commissioner for England.

Brah, A. and Phoenix, A. (2004) 'Ain't I a woman? Revisiting intersectionality'. *Journal of International Women's Studies,* 5(3), pp. 75–86.

Brayley, H., Cockbain, E. and Gibson, K. (2014) *Rapid evidence assessment: The sexual exploitation of boys and young men*. London: UCL, Barnardo's and NatCen.

Brodie, I. with D'Arcy, K., Harris, J., Roker, D., Shuker, L. and Pearce, J. (2016a) *The participation of young people in child sexual exploitation services: A scoping review of the literature*. Available at: www. alexiproject.org.uk/assets/documents/Alexi-Project-Participation-Scoping-Review.pdf (Accessed: 29 July 2017).

Brodie, I. with D'Arcy, K., Harris, J., Roker, D., Shuker, L. and Pearce, J. (2016b) *The participation of young people in child sexual exploitation services: A scoping review of the literature. Summary for practice*. Available at: www.alexiproject.org.uk/assets/documents/Alexi-Project-Participation-Scoping-Review-Practice-Summary.pdf (Accessed: 29 July 2017).

Childline (2016) *'It turned out someone did care': Childline annual review 2015/16*. London: NSPCC.

Cockbain, E. (2013) 'Grooming and the "Asian sex gang predator": The construction of a racial crime threat'. *Race and Class*, 54(4), pp. 22–32.

Collins, P. H. (2000) *Black feminist thought: Knowledge, consciousness, and the politics of empowerment*. New York and London: Routledge.

Committee on the Elimination of Racial Discrimination (2016) *Concluding observations on the twenty-first to twenty-third periodic reports of United Kingdom of Great Britain and Northern Ireland*. London: CERD. Available at: http://tbinternet.ohchr.org/Treaties/CERD/Shared%20Documents/GBR/CERD_C_GBR_CO_21-23_24985_E.pdf (Accessed: 6 January 2017).

Cossar, J., Brandon, M., Bailey, S., Belderson, P., Biggart, L. and Sharpe, D. (2013) *'It takes a lot to build trust': Recognition and telling: Developing earlier routes to help for children and young people*. London: Office of the Children's Commissioner for England.

Coy, M. (2014) *'Pornographic performances': A review of research on sexualisation and racism in music videos*. London: EVAW, Imkaan and Object. Available at: www.endviolenceagainstwomen.org.uk/data/files/Pornographic_Performances_FINAL_Aug_2014.pdf (Accessed: 7 January 2017).

Crenshaw, K. (1989) 'Demarginalizing the intersection of race and sex: A black feminist critique of antidiscrimination doctrine, feminist theory and antiracist politics'. *University of Chicago Legal Forum*, 1(8), pp. 139–167.

Crenshaw, K. (1991) 'Mapping the margins: Intersectionality, identity politics, and violence against women of color'. *Stanford Law Review*, 43(6), pp. 1241–1299.

Department for Health, Social Services and Public Safety (DHSSPSNI) (2008) *Tackling sexual violence and abuse: A regional strategy 2008–2013*. Belfast: DHSSPSNI.

Dines, G. (2010) *Pornland: How porn has hijacked our sexuality*. Boston: Beacon Press.

Firmin, C. (2015) *Peer on peer abuse: Safeguarding implications of contextualising abuse between young people within social fields*. Professional Doctorate Thesis. Luton: University of Bedfordshire.

Firmin, C. with Curtis, G., Fritz, D., Olaitan, P., Latchford, L., Lloyd, J. and Larasi, I. (2016) *Towards a contextual response to peer-on-peer abuse: Research and resources from MsUnderstood local site work 2013–2016*. Available at: www.beds.ac.uk/__data/assets/pdf_file/0006/517704/Towards-a-Contextual-Response-to-Peer-on-Peer-Abuse.pdf (Accessed: 12 January 2017).

Fox, C. (2016) *'It's not on the radar': The hidden diversity of children and young people at risk of sexual exploitation in England*. Ilford: Barnardo's.

Franklin, A., Raws, P. and Smeaton, E. (2015) *Unprotected, overprotected: Meeting the needs of young people with learning disabilities who experience, or are at risk of, sexual exploitation*. Barkingside: Barnardo's.

Gohir, S. (2013) *Unheard voices: The sexual exploitation of Asian girls and young women*. Birmingham: Muslim Women's Network UK.

Hastings, A., Bailey, N., Bramley, G., Gannon, M. and Watkins, D. (2015) *The cost of the cuts: The impact on local government and poorer communities*. London: Joseph Rowntree Foundation. Available at: www.jrf.org.uk/sites/default/files/jrf/migrated/files/CostofCuts-Full.pdf (Accessed: 7 January 2017).

hooks, b. (1994) *Teaching to transgress: Education as the practice of freedom*. New York: Routledge.

Imkaan (2015) *State of the Sector: Contextualising the current experiences of BME ending violence against women and girls organisations*. London: Imkaan.

Imkaan (2017) *Safe pathways? Exploring an intersectional approach to addressing violence against women and girls – Good practice briefing.* Available at: https://thelondonvawgconsortium.org.uk/wp-content/uploads/2017/03/CORRECT-Good-Practice-Briefing-Imkaan-Intersectionality.pdf (Accessed 20 June 2017).

Imkaan and University of Warwick (SWELL) (2015) *Between the lines research briefing: Service responses to black and minority ethnic women and girls experiencing sexual violence.* London: Imkaan and University of Warwick.

Imkaan and EVAW (2016) *'I'd just like to be free' – young women speak out about sexual harassment.* Available at: www.youtube.com/watch?v=lJ-qpvibpdU (Accessed: 7 April 2017).

Jago, S., Arocha, L., Brodie, I., Melrose, M., Pearce, J. and Warrington, C. (2011) *What's going on to safeguard children and young people from sexual exploitation? How local partnerships respond to child sexual exploitation.* Luton: University of Bedfordshire.

Larasi, I. (2013) 'Sexed-up music videos are everyone's problem', *The Guardian*, 13 December. Available at: www.theguardian.com/commentisfree/2013/dec/13/sexed-up-music-videos-problem-beyonce (Accessed: 13 June 2017).

Larasi, M. with Jones, D. (2017) *Tallawah: A briefing paper on black and 'minority ethnic' women and girls organising to end violence against us.* Available at: https://drive.google.com/file/d/0B_MKSoEcCvQwcGo0NHRWbGVjdFk/view (Accessed: 13 June 2017).

Larasi, M. (2013) *[Re]Constructing the sexual terrorist: The racialisation of contemporary media debates on child sexual exploitation.* Master's Thesis. Birkbeck.

Lewis, G. (1985) 'From deepest Kilburn' in L. Heron (ed.) *Truth, dare or promise: Girls growing-up in the fifties.* London: Virago.

Lewis, G. (2000) *Race, gender, social welfare.* Cambridge: Polity.

Lewis, G. (2013) 'Unsafe travel: Experiencing intersectionality and feminist displacements'. *Signs: A journal of women in culture and society*, 38(4), pp. 869–892.

McNaughton Nicholls, C., Cockbain, E., Brayley, H., Harvey, S., Fox, C., Paskell, C., Ashby, M., Gibson, K. and Jago, N. (2014) *Research on the sexual exploitation of boys and young me: A UK scoping study. Summary of findings.* London: Barnardos, NatCen and UCL.

Melrose, M. and Pearce, J. (2013) 'Introduction: Critical perspectives on child sexual exploitation and related trafficking' in Melrose, M. and Pearce, J. (eds) *Critical Perspectives in Child Sexual Exploitation and Related Trafficking.* Basingstoke: Palgrave Macmillan.

Pearce, J. (2009) *Young people and sexual exploitation: 'It's not hidden, you just aren't looking'.* London: Routledge.

Thiara, R. K. and Gill, A. K. (2010) 'Understanding violence against South Asian women: What it means for practice' in Thiara, R. K. and Gill, A. K. (eds) *Violence against women in South Asian communities: Issues for policy and practice.* London: Jessica Kingsley Publishers.

UNCRC (1989) *United Nations convention on the rights of the child.* Available at: https://downloads.unicef.org.uk/wp-content/uploads/2010/05/UNCRC_united_nations_convention_on_the_rights_of_the_child.pdf?_ga=2.220355928.1153835827.1501409561-1507349448.1499682569 (Accessed: 30 July 2017).

Ward, J. and Patel, N. (2006) 'Broadening the discussion on "sexual exploitation": Ethnicity, sexual exploitation and young people'. *Child Abuse Review*, 15(5), pp. 341–350.

Warrington, C. (2010) 'From less harm to more good: The role of children and young people's participation in relation to sexual exploitation'. *Youth and Policy*, 104, pp. 62–79.

Warrington, C. (2013) 'Partners in care? Sexually exploited young people's inclusion and exclusion from decision making about safeguarding' in Melrose, M. and Pearce, J. (eds) *Critical perspectives in child sexual exploitation and related trafficking* (pp. 110–124). Basingstoke: Palgrave Macmillan.

Warrington, C. (2016) *International Centre's working paper on children and young people's participation in research and evaluation.* Luton: University of Bedfordshire.

Warrington, C. (2017) *Young person-centred approaches in CSE – promoting participation and building self-efficacy: Frontline briefing.* Dartington: Research in Practice.

Warrington, C. with Beckett, H., Ackerley, E., Walker, M. and Allnock, D. (2017) *Making noise: Children's voices for positive change after sexual abuse in the family environment*. Luton: University of Bedfordshire.

Youth Justice Board (2016) *Youth justice statistics 2014/15*. London: Youth Justice Board/Ministry of Justice. Available at: www.gov.uk/government/uploads/system/uploads/attachment_data/file/495708/youth-justice-statistics-2014-to-2015.pdf (Accessed: 7 January 2017).

PART II

Contemporary perspectives on prevention and response

5

LET'S TALK ABOUT SEXUAL VIOLENCE

Involving young people in preventative peer education

Silvie Bovarnick with Kate D'Arcy

Introduction

This chapter explores the role of youth participation in sexual violence prevention. It builds on Cody's (2015a/b) work by introducing hitherto unpublished data from 'Our Voices', a pan-European initiative promoting youth participation in sexual violence prevention across Europe (for more information, see www.our-voices.org.uk). This is presented with reference to the existing evidence base around sexual violence prevention and participation.

Having briefly highlighted issues of terminology, the chapter commences with an exploration of the need for educative work around sexual violence. Having considered this, it then explores the potential contribution that peer education can make in this regard, alongside some of the ethical and practical challenges associated with pursuing such efforts.

Recognising the relatively limited degree to which young people with experience of sexual violence have been given the opportunity to engage in participatory initiatives (preventative or otherwise), the chapter also considers the benefits that such an opportunity can offer young people, particularly those with experiences of sexual violence themselves. We argue that youth participation should be an integral part of sexual violence prevention and draw on illustrative examples from four youth-led initiatives developed as part of 'Our Voices' to highlight the benefits of peer education that is supported by trained facilitators.

Terminology

In this chapter, the term 'child'[1] refers to any person under the age of 18 years. We use the term 'young people' and 'youth' to include any person between the ages of 18 and 30. This is to reflect the full age range (15 to 30) of participants involved in 'Our Voices' and to differentiate between those aged under and over 18.[2]

The term 'sexual violence against children' refers to:

> Engaging in sexual activities with a child where use is made of coercion, force or threats; or abuse is made of a recognised position of trust, authority or influence over the child, including within the family; or abuse is made of a particularly vulnerable situation of the child, notably because of a mental or physical disability or a situation of dependence.
>
> *(Council of Europe, 2007, Articles 18–23)*

We use the term 'children with experience of sexual violence' to refer to those who are both known victims and/or known perpetrators of such incidents of sexual violence. The broader category of 'children affected by sexual violence' includes those indirectly affected by such violence, such as those who have witnessed sexual violence, those who know someone who has experienced it and/or those who live in environments with a high incidence of sexual violence.

> We define peer education as a process in which 'young people undertake informal or organized educational activities with their peers (those similar to themselves in age, background, or interests) . . . aimed at developing young people's knowledge, attitudes, beliefs, and skills.'
>
> *(adapted from Youth Peer Education Network, 2005, p. 13)*

Sexual violence against children

Sexual violence against children is a serious and pervasive problem (Radford *et al.*, 2011; Finkelhor *et al.*, 2014; WHO, 2017). Although estimates vary, prevalence data suggests that approximately one in five children in Europe experiences some form of sexual violence (May-Chahal and Herczog, 2003; Lalor and McElvaney, 2010).

Over the past decade, concerted efforts have been launched at the highest European policy level to prevent, report and raise awareness of sexual violence against children. Policy developments in the region have included the global learning initiative 'Know Violence in Childhood', UNICEF's 'Ending Violence against Children: Six Strategies for Action' report and Child Rights International Network's 'Stop violence against children' campaign. We have also seen the introduction of the Council of Europe (CoE) Convention on Protection of Children against Sexual Exploitation and Sexual Abuse (also known as the 'Lanzarote Convention') in 2007 and the CoE's (2012) 'one in five' campaign supporting its implementation.

Sexual violence can affect many areas of life; it can negatively impact relationships, physical health, mental health, educational achievement and employment (Saied-Tessier, 2004; Currie and Spatz-Widom, 2010; NAESV, 2011). While the specific impact of sexual violence on individual children may vary, a range of effects on children's psychosocial development have been evidenced through research (Finkelhor and Browne, 1985). There is evidence to suggest that about half of all children affected by child sexual abuse (CSA) suffer from mental health problems including depression, Post Traumatic Stress Disorder (PTSD), disturbed behaviour, attachment disorders, or a combination of these (Monck and New, 1996; Cawson *et al.*, 2000; OCC, 2012a/b). Children who are sexually abused or exploited can experience 'sexualised trauma'[3] (Finkelhor and Browne, 1985) and the importance of 'trauma-informed' practice responses is increasingly recognised (Hickle and Hallett, 2016; La Valle and Graham with Hart, 2016; Sweeney *et al.*, 2016; Bovarnick, Scott and Pearce, 2017).

Given these impacts, it is important that we not only focus efforts on responses to abuse, but also invest in efforts to prevent it occurring in the first place. Whilst we recognise that prevention is a multi-faceted endeavour (Beckett, Holmes and Walker, 2017; Dfe, 2017), for the purposes of this chapter we focus specifically on that relating to awareness raising amongst children and young people. Drawing on data from our 'Our Voices' – a European project looking at peer education around sexual violence – we particularly consider the role that young people themselves can play within awareness raising efforts.

'Our Voices': involving young people in peer education on sexual violence

In line with human rights principles, children's rights under the United Nations Convention on the Rights of the Child are indivisible and interdependent (OHCHR, 1989). This means that all rights are equally important and interrelated; they cannot be enjoyed without one another. However, in the context of sexual violence against children, child protection concerns tend to frequently override children's right to participation (Brown, 2006; Warrington, 2016). Concerns over retraumatisation and a lack of knowledge, training and confidence around how to navigate the risks associated with engaging vulnerable groups in participation can often mean that such groups are excluded from participation projects and unable to harness the potential benefits such initiatives have to offer (Horwarth *et al.*, 2012; Warrington, 2013; Houghton, 2015).

However, as Warrington (2016, p. 19) argues, participation and empowerment are necessary conditions of a protective response and can add therapeutic value to recovery from sexual abuse: 'put simply, it is not "protection or participation"; participation is a fundamental part of protecting young people.'

This is recognised at the heart of the 'Our Voices' programme of work. In 2016, 'Our Voices' supported the development of four youth-led 'mini-projects' in Europe, during which 39 youth advocates[4] (aged between 15–30) in England, Albania and Bulgaria developed ideas about how to address the gap in awareness around sexual violence they had identified in their communities (Cody, 2015a). The four mini-projects facilitated a series of youth-led awareness raising activities that reached over 500 peers. The 39 youth advocates used a range of creative methods to produce information materials around sexual violence prevention, including film (Albania and England), photography (Bulgaria), designing a poster (Albania), writing a blog (Albania), and developing a brochure (Bulgaria). These resources were used in 'information sessions' that were delivered by the youth advocates to young people in a range of educational and community settings.

The data discussed here draws on the evaluations of these youth-led initiatives. These evaluations compiled detailed feedback from both the youth advocates and the project staff who supported them on a range of issues relating to their experiences and involvement in the mini-projects. We explore the findings in relation to two key elements of the evaluation: (a) perspectives on existing challenges around sexual violence prevention and (b) how these could be addressed through peer education initiatives. We present these with reference to the existing evidence base around these issues.

Challenges around sexual violence prevention

Cultures of silence

The youth consultations conducted by the youth advocates as part of 'Our Voices' identified 'cultures of silence' to be a pervasive problem in their communities, reporting that sex as well as sexual violence were taboo topics that were rarely discussed in their immediate environments (Cody, 2015a). As a blog developed by the youth advocates in Albania observes, 'even today it is considered shameful and a taboo to talk about sexual issues in Albania, though things are slowly changing' (Our Voices blog, 2016). This is an observation mirrored within much of the research evidence on sexual violence against children, with issues around unacceptability of, and embarrassment in relation to, discussions about sexual violence – or even sex – highlighted as contributing to our failure to protect children and young people from such harm (Beckett, 2014; Warrington *et al.*, 2017).

Lack of information and understanding

Youth advocates also pointed to a dearth of information and resources on sexual violence prevention and victim support in schools, families and communities. Without safe spaces to openly discuss sex and sexuality, young people have limited opportunities to develop an understanding of what constitutes sexually harmful behaviour and to develop risk-awareness around sexual violence. Many young people who took part in the awareness raising activities knew relatively little about different types of sexual violence or its prevalence. A similar lack of knowledge was observed around risk factors, grooming and issues of 'agency' and 'consent'.

Similar issues have been identified within the existing body of research. A lack of adequate sex and relationships education, and information on sexual violence specifically targeted at children and young people, has repeatedly been identified in research with young people (Coy *et al.*, 2013; Beckett, 2014; Cody, 2015a; Girlguiding, 2015; Firmin, 2016; Bovarnick and Scott, 2016). Studies have shown consequent gaps in knowledge amongst young people around 'consent'[5] and other issues associated with sexual violence (Beckett, 2011; Coy *et al.*, 2013; Beckett, 2014).

In the UK, a recent parliamentary inquiry into sexual harassment and sexual violence in schools warned that, without adequate guidance young people are left to find out for themselves what is 'normal' and receive unhelpful messages from media or popular culture (House of Commons Women and Equalities Committee, 2016). This affirms the need for age-appropriate information that engages young people and challenges beliefs, perceptions and attitudes that sustain sexual harmful behaviours (Pearce, 2009a/b; Beckett *et al.*, 2013; Firmin, 2016). Whilst recognition of the importance of healthy relationship education has led to the inclusion of relationships and sexual education (RSE) as an obligatory component of mainstream education in the England,[6] evaluations on the effectiveness of such programmes are still scarce (Department for Children, Schools and Families, 2009; Hale, Coleman and Layard, 2011; Bovarnick and Scott, 2016).

'Victim-blaming' attitudes

The 'Our Voices' findings demonstrate that a limited understanding of issues surrounding sexual violence was compounded by the 'victim-blaming' mentality reported to exist in places. Data from a mini-project in Bulgaria, for example, showed that victim–blaming attitudes could permeate authorities, such as police and legal and health care providers, and inform practitioners' attitudes towards victims. Youth advocates and facilitators spoke of an 'institutionalisation of prejudice', whereby victims were frequently disbelieved, blamed and discouraged from speaking out. As one youth advocate explained, 'if I address the police, it is most likely that they make me guilty. . . . There was much discussion about the usefulness of institutions in cases of sexual violence.' Similar messages have been captured in both UK research and serious case reviews (Coffey, 2014; Jay, 2014; Bedford, 2015; Beckett, Holmes and Walker, 2017).

Youth advocates also highlighted the 'stigma' that was attached to sexual violence in their local contexts. Stigma and shame are known to be common features in experiences of sexual violence. They can fuel children's feelings of self-blame (Finkelhor and Browne, 1985; Warrington *et al.*, 2017); undermining children's ability to disclose abuse and access support (Pearce, Hynes and Bovarnick, 2013). As Warrington and colleagues observe in their 2017 study:

> In keeping with previous research about experiences of sexual abuse (Finkelhor and Browne, 1988; McElvaney, 2008; Children's Commissioner, 2015; Smith *et al.*, 2015; Sneddon et al., 2016), a common and pervasive theme in interviewees' narratives was feelings of shame and embarrassment, and fears about the stigma associated with abuse . . . recurring themes from [survey] respondents' answers about why a character would not tell someone (or may be unlikely to do so) highlighted the significance of being believed; fear for physical safety; concerns about stigma, blame and shame.
>
> *(Warrington* et al.*, 2017, p. 51 and 56)*

The contribution of peer education to sexual violence prevention

The use of peer education

The rationale for 'peer education' arguably stems from an increasing recognition of the significance of peer relationships (Allnock, 2015; Hellevik *et al.*, 2015). There is evidence to suggest that, in some cases, peers can be more influential than family members in providing support and information to young people (Allnock, 2015; Barter *et al.*, 2015). Young people may feel more comfortable to discuss sensitive matters with peers, rather than adults, because they may share similar experiences and 'speak the same language', which can facilitate rapport (Hellevik *et al.*, 2015; Bovarnick and Scott, 2016).

At the same time, peer education should not be presumed to necessarily be 'participatory', risk-free or appropriate in all contexts. Barter *et al.* (2015) note that not all children will trust their peers or feel confident in sharing personal issues with them. It is therefore crucial that peer educators are trained and adequately supported to avoid further trauma, either for themselves or other young people (Cody, 2017).

Peer education in the field of sexual violence

The use of peer education in addressing sexual violence is relatively new and, to date, there is relatively little research to establish whether or not, or under which conditions, peer education is an effective tool for sexual violence prevention. Existing evidence, however, suggests that involving young people in preventative education can add authenticity, credibility and acceptability, which are key factors for impact (Bovarnick and Scott, 2016). Personal narratives or testimonials can further add authenticity to campaigns by 'making it real' (Rigotti and Wakefield, 2012; Cody, 2017).

In the UK, an evaluation of the 'Tender whole school approach'[7] – aimed at addressing gender-based violence and promoting healthy relationships – found that developing peer influence was one of three key ingredients shown to facilitate change (McNeish and Scott, 2012).[8] Engaging young people as peer educators is believed to be particularly effective when peer educators and the groups they engage with are well matched (Hotaling *et al.*, 2004; Rawsthorne, Hoffman and Kilpatrick, 2010).

The 'Our Voices' evaluation also identified clear potential benefits to peer education on sexual violence prevention when appropriately designed and supported. Despite the caveats relating to the small sample size and methodological limitations[9] of the study, the lessons from the mini-projects suggest that participatory peer education can be a powerful tool for raising awareness around sexual violence prevention and an empowering experience for participants, as explored below.

Breaking the 'taboo' that surrounds sexual violence

In responding to the aforementioned challenges about stigma and social taboos, the 'Our Voices' youth advocates stressed the need to 'talk about sexual violence more openly to make it less taboo'. To this end, youth advocates designed and developed a number of awareness raising activities aimed at peer education. These included youth-led photography and film-based work, a blog on sexual violence prevention, and a series of workshops and information sessions on sexual violence prevention that they developed and delivered to peers (aged 16–30) in a range of education and community settings. Information materials were designed and developed 'by young people for young people' with support of local project staff. By facilitating opportunities to discuss these issues, the youth advocates and those supporting them made inroads into addressing the taboo nature of such conversations.

Spreading the message about sexual violence prevention

Peer education activities, based on participatory methods of engagement, were found to be an effective tool for introducing the topic of sexual violence to young people. The information sessions met an educational need identified by the youth advocates in their communities and provided a safe platform for young people to discuss sexual violence. Reflecting on their experiences of delivering such workshops to peers, youth advocates in Albania noted that 'young people in Albania are very interested in this topic and asked many questions about the causes and ways to prevent sexual violence' (Our Voices blog, 2016). A snowballing effect was noted in the aftermath of the workshops as the information sessions sparked further conversations amongst peers. This multiplying effect helped to spread the message about sexual violence prevention and was perceived to facilitate change through a 'bottom-up approach'.

Encouraged by the impact that information sessions had on peers, youth advisors in Albania highlighted the need to scale-up prevention efforts from local to regional/national level:

The good thing is that we found young people to be open to new information and willing to learn. We wish this project could reach out to other areas of Albania where people lack information about sexual violence and refuse to talk about it. It would be good to also involve adults and other institutions, not just young people.

(Our Voices blog, 2016)

Empowering young people

'Youth participation' generally describes forms of social engagement and relates to children's right to be involved in decisions that affect their lives (Lansdown, 2010; see Chapter 9). According to Lansdown (2002, p. 273), it can be defined as 'children taking part in and influencing processes, decisions, and activities that affect them, in order to achieve greater respect for their rights'. A deeply political concept and activity, participation challenges existing power structures. Decisions as to whether or not youth participation is promoted are rooted in relationships of power that exist in theory and practice and relate to wider questions around young people's agency, their role and say in society (Brodie *et al.*, 2016).

Debates about youth participation in relation to sexual violence are often further complicated by the fact that adults may perceive the topic to be too sensitive and/or young people to be too vulnerable to engage in such efforts. Yet, where granted or negotiated, the opportunity to be involved in participatory initiatives that begin to tackle wider societal issues around sexual violence can be an empowering experience. This can be particularly true for someone who has personal experience of such issues, as explored below.

The project evaluation showed that both facilitators and youth advocates noted an increase in confidence, reflection, communication and group work skills amongst the young people who participated in the mini-projects. Youth advocates felt proud of what they had achieved, of speaking out on behalf of victims, and many felt as if they were making a real difference in raising awareness and educating themselves and others about sexual violence. They felt passionate about becoming active 'agents for change' who challenge sexual violence in their local contexts. This resonates with existing evidence on the positive effects of young people's involvement in campaigns (Oliver *et al.*, 2006; Batsleer, 2011; Hagell, 2013; Houghton, 2015).

Validating children's voices

Children's voices continue to be silenced though violence and abuse whilst they are also too often overlooked in policy and practice responses (Warrington, 2013). Recognising and promoting children's own voices and capacity to inform debate arises out of a rights–based ethical imperative, both as a means of personal empowerment and a means of challenging 'cultures of silence', in which abuse and impunity thrive (Ibid.). Involving children affected by sexual violence in prevention campaigns can be particularly meaningful in this context – it can offer children an opportunity to speak out against injustice.

Abusive and exploitative relationships are typically characterised by experiences of isolation and powerlessness (Finkelhor and Browne, 1985). These dynamics can sometimes be replicated in practice. Research shows that children affected by violence and abuse are often ignored or disbelieved, and their disclosures are frequently not heard or understood (Allnock and Miller, 2013). Evidence from public inquiries and court cases on young people's experiences of CSE in the UK suggests that child victims are often blamed or their accounts remain ignored by professionals (Warrington, 2013; Brodie *et al.*, 2016). Creating opportunities for these children and young people to exert control and express their opinions is therefore significant (Beckett, Holmes and Walker, 2017).

There is evidence to suggest that strength-based strategies, which harness and promote children's resilience and innate capabilities, are instrumental in overcoming trauma and abuse (Pearce, 2007). Youth participation that is based on sharing power and fostering young people's control can promote young people's self-esteem and self-efficacy (Houghton, 2015). By providing young people with opportunities to develop skills and access to a new protective network, participation can enhance a young person's sense of belonging and connectedness (Oliver *et al.*, 2006; Cody, 2015b). This can counter the feelings of isolation, loss of control and powerlessness that are common features of abuse (Finkelhor and Browne, 1985) and promote protective factors.

Recognising the value of children and young people's contributions can have a positive impact on participants' mental health and well-being (Brown, 2006; Oliver *et al.*, 2006). Evidence shows that activities aimed at improving the situation for others can be very meaningful and empowering for young people affected by sexual violence; it can increase their sense of self-worth (Batsleer, 2011; Levy, 2012; Hagell, 2013; Houghton, 2015). This suggests that ethical and meaningful participation in sexual violence prevention campaigns can be part of a strength-based and capacity-building response to sexual violence against children.

Extending engagement opportunities

Opportunities for participation have generally been limited to those children and young people who are deemed 'reliable' and 'capable' (Hill, 2006; Horwath, Kalyva and Spyru, 2012; Brodie *et al.*, 2016). Conversely, children who are considered 'vulnerable' or 'marginalised' have often been excluded (Horwath, Kalyva and Spyru, 2012). Undoubtedly, engaging children and young people who have experienced sexual violence in participation initiatives around the issue presents a number of risks. Warrington (2016), however, stresses the importance of 'working with and managing risk, as opposed to adopting more risk averse approaches'. Involving children in decision-making entails moving away from seeing children's agency as a problem towards reframing it as a resource (Warrington, 2016).

Whilst a participatory approach may not be appropriate in all contexts, it is important to widen access to participation and to create opportunities and choice. Sexual violence prevention initiatives offer a clear opportunity in this regard, and young people have clear views on how and when they would like to get involved in such initiatives (Cody, 2015a). The 'Our Voices' consultations showed that young people want to be asked whether or not they wish to participate in sexual violence prevention. They also want to be involved in conversations around what level of engagement is ethical and appropriate, to be part of risk assessments and set boundaries in terms of their involvement in a project (Houghton, 2015; Cody, 2017).[10]

The challenges of peer education on sexual violence

Engaging with risk, rather than avoiding it, inevitably entails a number of difficulties and challenges. Here we briefly consider some of the ethical issues that arose in relation to the

'Our Voices' project's efforts to facilitate peer involvement in sexual violence prevention and the ways in which they were resolved. We also highlight the wider debate around the validity of participatory findings, which holds significance not only for our work but for the work of others who seek to elicit learning via participatory means.

Ethical challenges

Despite risk assessments and ethical protocols being in place, there were some challenges along the way. Youth advocates were sometimes met with rudeness, scepticism, hostility and mockery during dissemination events; they were challenged by peers who refuted that sexual violence against children existed; and they had to engage with peers who were reluctant to speak about sexual violence because they were embarrassed. Youth advocates were also at times confronted with 'victim-blaming' views from peers during dissemination events. In these instances, the local project facilitators stepped in to support the youth advocates in handling the situation. Whilst reiterating the need for awareness raising across peer groups, these incidents illustrate that meaningful and ethical youth participation must be adequately supported through skilled and experienced facilitators. Youth participants, as well as facilitators of participation, benefit from ongoing opportunities to share learning, build confidence and to develop tools and strategies to manage these risks appropriately.[11]

Epistemological and methodological considerations

Tendencies to dismiss children's experiences or views as 'anecdotal' on one hand and a 'tokenistic' utilisation of children's voices on the other hand, represent a common ethical and methodological dilemma in participatory work. Issues around the validity of data emerging from participatory-based engagements raise wider epistemological questions in research. They challenge traditional notions relating to what constitutes 'evidence' and what degree of rigour is required in its elicitation.

Data resulting from participatory projects contain an inherent tension. A commitment to youth participation requires researchers to relinquish some control over the design, methodology and implementation of youth-led activities. At the same time, researchers are required to produce methodologically sound data and ensure that findings are 'credible'. The less prescriptive nature of participatory studies provides both a challenge and an opportunity. Whilst the findings may feel less 'robust', it is precisely the flexible and informal nature of participative methodologies that facilitates engagement and creates an environment in which children and young people feel more inclined to share their views. In this context, child participation not only serves as a methodological but also as a political tool, giving children a voice and constituting their experiences as 'evidence' (Warrington *et al.*, 2017).

Conclusion

Illustrative examples from 'Our Voices' suggest that peer education, informed by participatory practice, can play an important role in sexual violence prevention. However, to mitigate against some of the ethical and practical challenges associated with this work, it must be carefully planned and appropriately supported by trained and experienced facilitators.

If adequate attention is given to such matters, there are a number of significant benefits that can ensue from involving young people in sexual violence prevention. These relate not only to those delivering the preventative work, but also those at whom the work is targeted and the service seeking to deliver the preventative work. Though not without its challenges, youth engagement in preventative initiatives can offer a degree of credibility and relevance that may not otherwise be achieved, thereby potentially enhancing receptivity of the audience and the effectiveness of the messaging.

In terms of benefits for the young people given the opportunity to engage in preventative efforts, particularly those who have experienced abuse, involvement in participatory peer education offers the opportunity to reframe their experiences and reclaim their voices as powerful and active agents for change. This is important both as a means of personal empowerment and as a way of challenging the wider cultures of silence in which abuse flourishes with impunity. It not only serves as a methodological tool, creating spaces in which children may feel more comfortable to share their views and experiences, but also as a political tool that constitutes children's voices and experiences as important evidence.

Notes

1 We use the term to conceptually distinguish between 'children' and 'adults' whilst acknowledging a continuum of children's diverse and evolving capacities in their journeys towards adulthood. Our intention is to constitute children as political agents, recognising existing power structures and dynamics that can curtail children's ability to influence decisions that affect their lives.

2 Whilst the project involved young people between the ages of 15 and 30, the majority of youth participants were between 15 and 18 years old. Involvement of 'older young people' (in their mid or late twenties) enabled the project to draw from specific experiences (e.g. service users living in assisted care or protected homes). Peers attending dissemination events were between the ages of 13 and 19, with the majority being 16 and 17 years old.

3 'Sexualised trauma' is defined in Finkelhor and Browne's (1985) traumagenic model to include: traumatic sexualisation, stigmatisation, betrayal and powerlessness.

4 The majority of the young people involved in the mini-projects were described as 'marginalised' and were known to the partner organisations. Most of the local partner organisations had expertise in working with young people affected by sexual violence and had experience of, or interest in, working in participatory ways. Whilst the gender ratio amongst the groups of youth advocates was female-dominated, the mini-projects reached a wider gender diversity of young people through their dissemination events.

5 A study commissioned by the Office of the Children's Commission for England (OCC) suggests that, whilst young people were familiar with the meaning of 'consent' in theory, their understanding was less clear in real life scenarios (Coy et al., 2013). The findings show that young people's understanding of 'consent' was gendered and informed by double-standards relating to particular constructions of 'masculinity' that viewed young men as 'collecting man points' and gaining respect from peers by having sex (Ibid., p. 10).

6 Announced by government on 1 March 2017.

7 In the UK, Tender's 'whole school' approach to challenging gender-based violence and promoting healthy relationships across eight London secondary schools was evaluated as effective. Some schools created peer mentoring schemes, or peer led campaigns and advisory groups, whilst others developed drama presentations or DVDs which students delivered in assemblies and to young people in other schools (McNeish and Scott, 2012).

8 The other key ingredients included the commitment of participating schools and the quality of Tender's work (McNeish and Scott, 2012).

9 The authors were not directly involved in the delivery of the mini-projects, instead local partner organisations reported back on the findings that emerged from the youth-led activities. As data were collected through partner agencies the information was, with the exception of the project in

England, translated into English by the local partners. This harbours the possibility that some aspects may have been 'lost in translation' or were not relayed exactly as intended by the young people because of our incomplete understanding of the local contexts.

10 Young people can be very cognisant of the risks; youth advisors in 'Our Voices', for example, stressed the importance of making sure that young people were 'ready' and highlighted risks to involving young people with 'recent, fresh, raw' experiences of sexual violence, as these young people may just want to forget and not want to relive their abusive experiences (Cody, 2017, p. 10).

11 A current initiative that addresses this need is the 'LEAP' ('Life skills, leadership, limitless potential: Supporting children and young people affected by sexual violence in Europe by strengthening and facilitating participatory practice') project. More information can be found on the 'Our Voices' programme website (www.our-voices.org.uk/about/projects/leap-against-sexual-violence-2015-2017).

References

Allnock, D. (2015) Child maltreatment: How can friends contribute to safety? *Safer Communities*, 14(1), pp. 27–36.

Allnock, D. and Miller, P. (2013) 'No one noticed – no one heard': a study of disclosures of childhood abuse. London: NSPCC.

Barter, C., Stanley, N., Wood, M., Aghtaie, N., Larkins, C., Øverlien, C., Lesta, S. and Deluca, N. (2015) *Safeguarding teenage intimate relationships. (STIR): Connecting online and offline*. Available at: http://stiritup.eu/wp-content/uploads/2015/06/STIR-Exec-Summary-English.pdf (Accessed 28 May 2017).

Batsleer, J. (2011) 'Voices from an edge. Unsettling the practices of youth voice and participation: arts-based practice in The Blue Room, Manchester'. *Pedagogy, Culture and Society*, 19(3), pp. 419–434.

Beckett, H. (2011) *Not a world away: The sexual exploitation of children and young people in Northern Ireland*. Belfast: Barnardo's. Available at: www.barnardos.org.uk/13932_not_a_world_away_full_report.pdf (Accessed 28 May 2017).

Beckett, H. with Brodie, I., Factor, F., Melrose, M., Pearce, J., Pitts, J., Shuker, L. and Warrington C. (2013) 'It's wrong . . . but you get used to it': A qualitative study of gang-associated sexual violence towards, and exploitation of, young people in England. London: Office of the Children's Commissioner.

Beckett, H. (2014) 'Sexual violence and exploitation in adolescence' in Schubotz, D. and Devine, P. (eds) *Not so different. Teenage attitudes across a decade of change in Northern Ireland*. Belfast: Russell House Publishing.

Beckett, H. and Warrington, C. (2015) *Making justice work: Experiences of criminal justice for children and young people affected by sexual exploitation as victims and witnesses*. Luton: University of Bedfordshire. Available at: www.beds.ac.uk/__data/assets/pdf_file/0011/461639/MakingJusticeWorkFull Report.pdf (Accessed 28 May 2017).

Beckett, H., Holmes, D. and Walker, J. (2017) *Child sexual exploitation. Definition and guide for professionals: Extended text*. Available at: www.beds.ac.uk/__data/assets/pdf_file/0009/536175/UOB-RIP-CSE-GuidanceFeb2017.pdf (Accessed 28 May 2017).

Bedford, A. (2015) *Serious case review into child sexual exploitation in Oxfordshire: From the experiences of Children A, B, C, D, E, and F*. Oxford: Oxford Safeguarding Children Board. Available at: www.oscb.org.uk/wp-content/uploads/SCR-into-CSE-in-Oxfordshire-FINAL-FOR-WEBSITE.pdf (Accessed 2 August 2017).

Bovarnick, S. and Scott, S. (2016) *Child sexual education prevention: A rapid evidence assessment*. Available at: www.beds.ac.uk/__data/assets/pdf_file/0004/540490/FINAL-REA-1.pdf (Accessed 28 May 2017).

Bovarnick, S., Scott, S. and Pearce, J. (2017) *Direct work with sexually exploited or at risk children: A rapid evidence assessment*. Available at: www.beds.ac.uk/__data/assets/pdf_file/0006/540492/FINAL-REA-3.pdf (Accessed 28 May 2017).

Brodie, I. with D'Arcy, K., Harris, J., Roker, D., Shuker, L. and Pearce, J. (2016) The participation of young people in child sexual exploitation services: A scoping review of the literature. Available at: www.alexiproject.org.uk/assets/documents/Alexi-Project-Participation-Scoping-Review.pdf (Accessed 28 May 2017).

Brown, K. (2006) 'Participation and young people involved in prostitution'. *Child Abuse Review*, 15(5), pp. 294–312.

Cawson, P., Wattam, C., Brooker, S. and Kelly, G. (2000) *Child maltreatment in the United Kingdom*. London: NSPCC.

Cody, C. (2015a) 'They don't talk about it enough': Report on the 2014 consultations with Youth Advisors for 'Our Voices'. Luton: Guildford Street Press. Available at: http://childhub.org/sh/system/files/dont_talk_report_new.pdf (Accessed 28 May 2017).

Cody, C. (2015b) *Child and youth participation for prevention and protection: The 'Our Voices' Project*. Presented at the High Level, Cross Regional Meeting on Protection of Children from Sexual Violence, Council of Europe and the Special Representative of the UN Secretary General on Violence Against Children, Strasbourg, 19 June, 2015.

Cody, C. (2017) '"We have personal experience to share, it makes it real"': Young people's views on their role in sexual violence prevention efforts'. *Children and Youth Services Review*, 79, pp. 221–227.

Coffey, A. (2014) Real voices: Child sexual exploitation in greater Manchester – An independent report by Ann Coffey, MP. Manchester.

Coy, M., Kelly, L., Elvines, F., Garner, M. and Kanyeredzi, A. (2013) '*Sex without consent, I suppose that is rape': How young people in England understand sexual consent*. London: Office of the Children's Commissioner. Available at: www.childrenscommissioner.gov.uk/sites/default/files/publications/Sex_without_consent_I_suppose_that_is_rape_newprint.pdf (Accessed 28 May 2017).

Council of Europe (CoE) (2007) *Lanzarote Convention*. Strasbourg: Council of Europe. Available at: www.coe.int/en/web/young personren/lanzarote-convention (Accessed 28 May 2017).

Council of Europe (CoE) (2012) *Is it really one in five?* Strasbourg: Council of Europe. Available at: www.coe.int/t/dg3/young personren/1in5/Source/I%20in%205%20fact%20argumentation%20_en.pdf (Accessed 28 May 2017).

Currie, J. and Spatz Widom, C. (2010) 'Long-term consequences of child abuse and neglect on adult economic well-being'. *Child Maltreatment*, 15(2), pp. 111–120.

Department for Children, Schools and Families (2009) *Personal, social, health and economic (PSHE) education: Research evidence note*. London: Analysis and Research Division, Schools Research Team.

Department for Education (DfE) (2017) Child sexual exploitation. Definition and a guide for practitioners, local leaders and decision makers working to protect children from child sexual exploitation. Available at: www.gov.uk/government/uploads/system/uploads/attachment_data/file/591903/CSE_Guidance_Core_Document_13.02.2017.pdf (Accessed 28 May 2017).

Finkelhor, D., Shattuck, A., Turner, H. and Hamby, S. (2014) 'The lifetime prevalence of child sexual abuse and sexual assault assessed in late adolescence'. *Journal of Adolescent Health*, 55, pp. 329–333.

Finkelhor, D. and Browne, A. (1985) 'The traumatic impact of child sexual abuse: A conceptualization'. *American Journal of Orthopsychiatry*, 55(4), pp. 530–541.

Firmin, C. (2016) *Evidence submission to parliamentary inquiry: Sexual harassment and sexual violence in schools*. Luton: University of Bedfordshire.

Girlguiding (2015) *Girls attitudes survey 2015*. Available at: http://new.girlguiding.org.uk/latest-updates/making-a-difference/girls-attitudes-survey-2015 (Accessed 28 May 2017).

Hagell, A. (2013) *AYPH Be Healthy project evaluation*. London: Association for Young People's Health.

Hale, D., Coleman, J. and Layard, R. (2011) *A model for the delivery of evidence-based PSHE (personal wellbeing) in secondary schools: Discussion paper*. London: Centre for Economic Performance, London School of Economics. Available at: http://cep.lse.ac.uk/pubs/download/dp1071.pdf (Accessed 28 May 2017).

Hellevik, P., Överlien, C., Barter, C. *et al.* (2015) 'Traversing the generational gap: Young people's views on intervention and prevention of teenage intimate partner violence'. in Humphreys, C. and Stanley, N. (eds) *Domestic violence and protecting children: New thinking and approaches*. London: Jessica Kingsley.

Hickle, K. and Hallett, S. (2016) 'Mitigating harm: Considering harm reduction principles in work with sexually exploited young people'. *Children and Society*, 30(4), pp. 302–313.

Hill, M. (2006) 'Children's voices on ways of having a voice. Children's and young people's perspectives on methods used in research and consultation'. *Childhood*, 13(1), pp. 69–89.

Hotaling, N., Burris, A., Johnson, J., Bird, Y. and Melbye, K. (2004) 'Been there done that: SAGE, a peer leadership model among prostitution survivors'. *Journal of Trauma Practice*, 2(3–4), pp. 255–265.

Horwath, J., Kalyva, E. and Spyru, S. (2012) '"I want my experiences to make a difference": Promoting participation in policy-making and service development by young people who have experienced violence'. *Children and Youth Services Review*, 34, pp. 155–162.

Houghton, C. (2015) 'Young people's perspectives on participatory ethics: Agency, power and impact in domestic abuse research and policy-making'. *Child Abuse Review*, 24, pp. 235–248.

House of Commons Women and Equalities Committee (2016) *Sexual harassment and sexual violence in schools: Third report of session 2016–17*. Available at: https://publications.parliament.uk/pa/cm201617/cmselect/cmwomeq/91/91.pdf (Accessed 28 May 2017).

Jay, A. (2014) *Independent inquiry into child sexual exploitation in Rotherham 1997–2013*. Available at: http://www.rotherham.gov.uk/downloads/file/1407/independent_inquiry_cse_in_rotherham (Accessed 28 May 2017).

Lansdown, G. (2002) *Taking part: Young person's participation in decision-making*. London: Institute for Public Policy Research.

Lansdown, G. (2010) 'The realization of children's participation rights: Critical reflections' in Percy-Smith, B. and Thomas, N. (eds) *A handbook of children and young people's participation: Perspectives from theory and practice*. London: Routledge.

Lalor, K. and McElvaney, R. (2010) *Overview of the nature and extent of young person sexual abuse in Europe*. Dublin: Dublin Institute of Technology.

La Valle, I. and Graham, B. with Hart, D. (2016) *Child sexual exploitation: Support in children's residential homes research report*. London: Department for Education. Available at: www.gov.uk/government/uploads/system/uploads/attachment_data/file/582354/Child-sexual-exploitation-support-in-childrens-homes.pdf (Accessed 28 May 2017).

Levy, L. (2012) 'Hidden nobodies: Female youth in care participate in an arts-based trauma informed empowerment intervention program'. *Relational Child and Youth Care Practice*, 25(1), pp. 5–19.

May-Chahal, C. and Herczog, M. (2003) *Child sexual abuse in Europe*. Strasbourg: Council of Europe Publishing.

McNeish, D. and Scott, S. (2012) *Tender's healthy relationship education in schools: Final evaluation summary report*. DMSS Research & Consultancy.

Monck, E. and New, M. (1996) *Report of a study of sexually abused children and adolescents and of young perpetrators of sexual abuse who were treated in voluntary agency community facilities*. London: HMSO.

National Alliance to End Sexual Violence (NAESV) (2011) *The costs and consequences of sexual violence and cost-effective solutions*. Available at: www.nsvrc.org/sites/default/files/CostsConsequencesSV.pdf (Accessed 28 May 2017).

Office of the High Commissioner for Human Rights (OHCHR) (1989) *Convention on the rights of the child*. www.ohchr.org/EN/ProfessionalInterest/Pages/CRC.aspx (Accessed 28 May 2017).

Office of the Children's Commissioner for England (OCC) (2012a) *The inquiry into the child sexual exploitation in gangs and groups*. London: OCC. Available at: www.childrenscommissioner.gov.uk/inquiry-child-sexual-exploitation-gangs-and-groups (Accessed 28 May 2017).

Office of the Children's Commissioner for England (OCC) (2012b) *Briefing for the Rt Hon Michael Gove MP, Secretary of State for Education, on the emerging findings of the Office of the Children's Commissioner's inquiry into child sexual exploitation in gangs and groups, with a special focus on children in care*. Available at: www.childrenscommissioner.gov.uk/sites/default/files/publications/Accelerated_Report_for_the_Secretary_of_State_for_Education.pdf (Accessed 28 May 2017).

Oliver, K. G., Collins, P., Burns, J. and Nicholas, J. (2006) 'Building resilience in young people through meaningful participation'. *Australian e-Journal for the Advancement of Mental Health (AeJAMH)*, 5(1), pp. 1–7.

Our Voices blog (2016) *Youth advisors in Albania produce a film and poster to raise awareness about the need to speak out about sexual violence.* Available at: www.beds.ac.uk/research-ref/iasr/centres/ourvoices/news/2016/youth-advisors-in-albania-produce-film-and-poster (Accessed 28 May 2017).

Our Voices Mini-project Evaluation (2016) *Evaluation of mini-projects in England, Albania and Bulgaria.* (Analysis of OV data; internal document – not published).

Pearce, J. (2007) 'Risk and resilience: a focus on sexually exploited young people' in Thom, B., Sales, R. and Pearce, J. (eds) *Growing up with risk.* Bristol: The Policy Press.

Pearce, J. (2009a) *Young people and sexual exploitation: It's not hidden, you just aren't looking.* London: Routledge.

Pearce, J. (2009b). *Young people and sexual exploitation.* London: Routledge.

Pearce, J., Hynes, T. and Bovarnick, S. (2009) *Breaking the wall of silence: Practitioners' responses to trafficked children and young people.* London: NSPCC.

Pearce, J., Hynes, T. and Bovarnick, S. (2013) *Trafficked young people: Breaking the wall of silence.* London: Routledge.

Radford, L., Corral, S., Bradley, C., Fisher, H., Bassett, C., Howat, N. and Collishaw, S. (2011) *Child abuse and neglect in the UK today.* London: NSPCC.

Rawsthorne, M., Hoffman, S. and Kilpatrick, E. (2010) 'Women educating each other . . . women in safe and equal relationships'. *Women in Welfare Education*, 9, pp. 13–27.

Rigotti, N. A. and Wakefield, M. (2012) 'Real people, real stories: A new mass media campaign that could help smokers quit'. *Annals of Internal Medicine*, 157(12), pp. 907–909.

Saied-Tessier, A. (2004) *Estimating the cost of child sexual abuse in the UK.* London: NSPCC.

Sweeney, A., Clement, S., Filson, B. and Kennedy, A. (2016) 'Trauma-informed mental healthcare in the UK: What is it and how can we further its development?' *Mental Health Review Journal*, 21(3), pp. 174–192.

UNICEF (2014) *Ending violence against children: Six strategies for action.* Available at: www.unicef.org/publications/files/Ending_Violence_Against_Children_Six_strategies_for_action_EN_9_Oct_2014.pdf (Accessed 28 May 2017).

Warrington, C. (2013) 'Partners in care? Sexually exploited young people's inclusion and exclusion from decision making' in Melrose, M. and Pearce, J. (eds) *Critical Perspectives on Child Sexual Exploitation and Related Trafficking.* Basingstoke: Palgrave Macmillan.

Warrington, C. (2016) *Young person-centred approaches in child sexual exploitation (CSE) – promoting participation and building self-efficacy.* Dartington: Research in Practice.

Warrington, C. with Beckett, H., Ackerley, E., Walker, M. and Allnock, D. (2017) *Making noise: Children's voices for positive change after sexual abuse.* Luton: University of Bedfordshire.

World Health Organisation (WHO) (2017) *Child maltreatment.* Available at: www.who.int/violence_injury_prevention/violence/child/Child_maltreatment_infographic_EN.pdf?ua=1&ua=1 (Accessed 28 May 2017).

Youth Peer Education Network (2005) *Youth peer education toolkit. Training of trainers manual.* New York: United Nations Population Fund.

6

THE ROLE OF DETACHED YOUTH WORK IN PREVENTING AND IDENTIFYING SEXUAL HARM

Jenny Lloyd and Danielle Fritz

Introduction

Research into child sexual exploitation (CSE) and other forms of harm has highlighted the need for prevention, education and opportunities for disclosure (Berelowitz, 2013; Allnock and Miller, 2013; Department for Education, 2017). In some places, greater awareness of these issues has resulted in investment into preventative work for those (at risk of) experiencing and/or perpetrating harm. Whilst this work is crucial to how we respond to the harm young people experience, it is often one-off or ad-hoc in nature – a theatre performance within schools, a three-week course or targeted one-to-one work. However, what research into CSE and broader work on disclosures has highlighted is that relationships developed over time are key (Beckett and Warrington, 2015; Warrington *et al.*, 2017). If we want to develop holistic responses to tackling CSE and other forms of harm we must move beyond these discrete educative initiatives and ensure that the wider environment in which young people live their day-to-day lives works to minimise harm and is conducive to disclosure of any harm that may occur.

It is well documented that young people experience sexual harm not only in the home (as has traditionally been the focus), but in the wide range of places in which they spend time – this includes parks, shopping centres, schools and estates to name a few (Messerschmidt, 2012; Beckett *et al.*, 2013; Firmin, 2013). Responding to abuse in these environments calls for a more contextual approach to safeguarding that moves beyond a focus on risk and protection within the home and seeks to create safety within extra-familial spaces (Firmin *et al.*, 2016b).[1] This requires the involvement of a wider range of partners with knowledge of, and familiarity with, these spaces.

In this chapter, we draw upon existing literature and new empirical research to highlight the key role that detached youth workers can play in supporting prevention of harm and creating environments conducive to disclosure within these spaces. Whilst we do not, in any way, suggest that detached youth workers are the only people who can fulfil these roles, we do purport that being physically present within young people's contexts and communities provides them with a unique opportunity to prevent, identify and tackle harm. In what follows we highlight how the physical presence of detached youth workers in young people's spaces is instrumental to building relationships that offer scope for prevention and identification of abuse. We begin by summarising pertinent themes from the existing body of literature on detached youth work provision and the study's methodology. We then turn to the empirical findings, exploring four themes: understanding young people's spaces, engaging young people and prevention through informal education and identification. We conclude by exploring the implications of current cuts to youth work provision.

Detached youth work in the United Kingdom

Although varying according to local context, detached youth work broadly involves working with young people in locations and on issues of the young person's choosing. As workers spend time within an area and form relationships with young people, they come to understand the contexts in which they live and are able to better empathise with young people's realities (Lavie-Ajayi and Krumer-Nevo, 2013). By establishing voluntary relationships with young people – one that is not a statutory requirement but relies on young people choosing to spend time with workers – detached workers can recognise what issues are important and integrate education within the young people's own contexts without relying on them going to a centre or office (Crimmens *et al.*, 2004; Jeffs and Smith, 2008).

The origins of detached youth work lie in nineteenth century efforts of philanthropic organisations to draw young people into particular activities or services, with the aim of improving the health and development of (then called) lower class children. The modern iteration of detached youth work took form in the 1960s after the Ministry of Education released the Albermale report (HMSO, 1960), which argued that the state must provide 'social education' to young people outside of the school setting so that young people would become active and responsible citizens (Crimmens *et al.*, 2004). However, in recent years detached youth work has increasingly become aimed at controlling 'at risk' populations of young people, particularly those who are not in employment, education or training (Cullen, 2013; Bradford and Cullen, 2014). Shifts in government policy over the past few decades have led to the application of market approaches and ideologies to youth work, including detached youth work (Jeffs and Smith, 2008). As Bradford and Cullen (2014) observe, this has often led to the 'commissioning out' of youth work services to third-sector organisations.

Despite austerity measures that have cut youth services, some detached youth work provision still exists. However, the provision that remains is often part of a targeted approach to youth work where detached workers are expected to work towards achieving prescribed outcomes, such as getting young people into education or employment or stopping a particular behaviour like alcohol abuse (Jeffs and Smith, 2008; Bradford and Cullen, 2014). Literature on detached youth work has begun to capture the changing landscape of detached youth and the effects of national policy (Davies, 2013). It has also explored some of the ways that it can tackle different forms of harm such as alcohol abuse (Fletcher and Bonell, 2008). However, not a lot has been written on the role of detached youth work in relation to safeguarding children from abuse, including CSE and other forms of sexual harm. This is in spite of the repeated mandate within government guidance on CSE that clearly states that 'safeguarding children is everyone's responsibility' (Department for Education, 2017).

Many authors have emphasised the need for a breadth of partnership working to prevent and respond to CSE and other forms of sexual harm (Pearce, 2006; Beckett, 2011). In relation to prevention, Beckett *et al.* (2017) highlight the importance of involving a wide range of partners in appropriate educative initiatives, together with the importance of resilience building work with young people and their families and identification of (potential) harm. In relation to post-harm responses, Pearce (2006) argues that support must be holistic, recognising the often-intersecting needs that many young people have. She argues that, as such, statutory social services must work with community-based services to improve young people's social inclusion and quality of life. This chapter builds upon the work of these and other authors to argue that detached youth work provides a critical opportunity to implement a contextual approach to safeguarding young people that can form part of wider efforts to prevent and identify harm.

Method

In addition to reviewing existing literature, this chapter draws on qualitative data collected on the role of detached youth work in creating safety for young people in public spaces (Fritz, Firmin, and Olaitan, 2016). Over a six-month period, three researchers observed eight detached youth work sessions and conducted separate focus groups with detached youth workers, young people and other professionals, such as police, social workers, health practitioners and the youth offending team, in two London boroughs. The chapter also draws upon data collected from contextual safeguarding audits carried out in three London boroughs (Firmin *et al.*, 2016a).[2] As the experiences of young people and detached youth workers are shaped by their locality, the studies do not claim to be representative of issues facing young people or detached youth work provision on a larger scale. What they do, however, is provide rich qualitative data on young people's experiences of detached youth work provision within the areas studied and others' perceptions of this.

Findings

A clear benefit of detached youth work is that workers are able to understand and engage with young people in the contexts that they live in, which helps them to better empathise with young people's realities (Lavie-Ajayi and Krumer-Nevo, 2013). Our research highlighted four distinct advantages of this that supported prevention, education and disclosure with young people affected by sexual exploitation and other forms of harm. Firstly, working in young people's spaces allows them to observe and understand their experiences in non-adult environments. Secondly, this allows workers to build relationships and trust with young people. Thirdly, it offers them the opportunity to engage in preventative informal education. And fourthly, it means they are well placed to identify potential harm. We explore each of these elements in turn below.

Understanding young people's spaces

In order to understand young people's experiences of harm we need to appreciate the contexts within which they experience this harm. The serious case review into CSE in

Oxford noted how a lack of such understanding, and the associated judgements made about individuals' behaviours and actions, were significant barriers to identifying them as victims of CSE (Bedford, 2015). Inadequate knowledge about the environments young people live in, can result in focus shifting solely onto the individual young people themselves. For example, using labels such as 'streetwise' – which we heard many times during formal multi-agency meetings on sexual exploitation and serious youth violence – highlights how safeguarding discussions can often focus on individual behaviour with limited recognition of how young people develop strategies and skills to feel safe on the street (Cahill, 2000). Instead, by having a developed knowledge of local neighbourhoods, professionals can explore and understand how spaces can be unsafe and the necessity of understanding the context of harm or perpetration of abuse (Bedford, 2015).

The very nature of detached youth work, means that workers are present within young people's spaces. Lavie-Ajayi and Krumer-Nevo (2013, p. 1700) suggest several benefits of this:

> The lengthy duration of actual physical presence on the streets, working evening and nights, means that the youth workers are learning the 'rules of the game' on the streets, understanding the context in which the youth live, and seeing them as active agents in any process of change. This enables the youth workers to learn 'the grammar of exploitation' to see and interpret reality from the point of view of the youth.

Detached youth workers in our own research echoed this sentiment. By engaging young people in the public spaces where they spend their time, youth workers felt they were able to *understand* contexts and embed themselves within these, rather than just observe them:

> We are out there, we are in the community. We become a part of where they live. We are not scared of being there. When you see someone there every week, coming back the next month, year, two years – we take our time to come out of our comfort zone to go to their comfort zone. We are not asking them to come to an office. We are just there trying to understand the issues they're going through and be there for them.
> *(Sarah, detached youth worker)*[3]

By being out on the street, detached youth workers are able to see the challenges young people face day to day. Being physically present within these spaces they are able to understand the social norms of young people, the language they use and the histories and experiences of young people and the community. For example, several noted how working with older siblings and generations of families meant that they could use their knowledge of where they are coming from to talk through issues affecting young people now.

It is clear that the ability to understand contexts is a key step towards understanding the harm young people may experience and the environment within which this can occur, but it is also crucial to how that harm is responded to by professionals. As Firmin *et al.* (2016b) demonstrate, if abusive behaviours are not viewed within the contexts in which they occur, then professionals may inadvertently condone abuse or focus entirely on individuals rather than the locations that facilitated it. Greater understanding of contextual dynamics can help agencies to develop CSE interventions that both recognise and engage with the realities that young people are living in. For example, in an observation made during a CSE multi-agency meeting, the presence of a youth worker meant that discussions and actions were informed through knowledge of particular locations and peer dynamics. This meant that agencies, with advice from youth workers, could develop work with greater chances of success because they recognised what was happening on the ground for young people experiencing CSE, what would be effective and what issues were of concern at that time.

Engaging young people

Research has noted the challenges practitioners face in identifying when something is wrong (Jago et al., 2011; Shephard and Lewis, 2017). This work demonstrates how time, flexibility, accessibility and trust are crucial elements of ensuring that practitioners are able to identify abuse and support young people to feel able to speak out. As Beckett, et al. (2017, p. 27) state:

> It is those who know and have a relationship with the child or young person who are generally best placed to identify potential concerns about, and assess associated risk around, child sexual exploitation. They will have the contextual understanding to identify changes that represent something more than adolescent behaviours and make sense of the range of vulnerabilities that the child or young person may be facing.

However, what has become clear in recent years is that larger workloads, cuts to services and ever-increasing targets have reduced the time that many of those tasked with safeguarding, such as social workers, have available for meaningful engagement with service users (Munro, 2010; Featherstone et al., 2011; Broadhurst and Mason, 2012). This is not to say that social workers are not capable and able to engage young people, but that these systemic barriers pose significant challenges to practitioners' abilities to have meaningful face-to-face interactions, which are recognised as vital to forming relationships (Broadhurst and Mason, 2012).

For young people (at risk of) experiencing harm the ability to develop close trusting relationships with professionals is crucial, both in order for professionals to recognise if something is wrong and to support young people if and when they decide to speak to someone (Hallett et al., 2003; Warrington et al., 2017). Whilst youth work is also experiencing cuts to services, the location of workers in the communities they serve offers opportunities to overcome many of the challenges that statutory services experience. The ability for youth workers to build trust and engage with people was clearly important in enabling young people to speak with them, as highlighted by one young man:

> Like if you came – I'm not going to lie or be rude yea. Like if you came up to me today and said – started asking me about my mum and all that, I would tell you – I would be like, 'Who are you? I don't even know you?' I wouldn't tell you fuck all. But you see Diana [detached youth worker] and that, I would tell them about my mum and tell them about my family or whatever is going on, to a certain point, obviously.
>
> *(Tom, young man)*

The professionals in our research observed how a community based approach made them physically available to young people and took the onus off young people 'coming to them' should they wish to engage. This accessibility appeared to support young people to use services and increased awareness of what help is available. The importance of youth workers going to young people is inferred in the following conversation with a young man talking about a detached youth worker:

David: She's been helping me out – telling me what she thinks I'm good at, what she thinks I could be good at – like helping me go about getting my building card and my CSCS [construction skills certificate card] card. That's the only reason that I turned up today [to the focus group], because she's helped me so much.

Researcher: That's really amazing, that's a really powerful message actually. So, aren't there other people that can do that?

David: Not that, no one – I'm not even going to lie, they approached me. I didn't even go to them. They approached me about it and they helped me out, so. I'm not going to lie – I probably would've just carried on doing what I was doing.

Youth workers interviewed felt that working in the community was important not only in terms of physical accessibility but also in terms of the message it sent in relation to typical provider/service user power dynamics:

> You're taking the work to them in their territory, whether it's on their estate under some stairways, the park. When you do that, there is – not always, but on the whole – that mutual respect in the sense that you're going to them.
>
> *(Becky, detached youth worker)*

Within offices and buildings, other professionals may be viewed as in positions of authority, whereas detached youth workers must negotiate their relationships on young people's terms within the young person's territory. One youth worker explained that when young people go to a 'centre' or place of business for an appointment with a professional, they are removed from some of the influences that negatively impact their behaviour. When meeting with detached youth workers, however, young people are in a less controlled environment. This is not meant to suggest that youth workers cede all decision-making power to young people or that the relationships between a detached youth worker and a young person are not affected by the race, gender, age or professional status of both parties. Rather, we argue that situating relationships in spaces chosen by young people reduces some of the hierarchies that may hinder relationship building between professionals and young people.

Another aspect that supported the ability to successfully work with young people is that they *choose* to engage with detached workers; it is not imposed on them by a statutory service or court.

> That's where the work develops – in their communities, in their space where they feel comfortable. . . It's very much about the work going to the young people, not them coming to us.
>
> *(Gemma, team manager)*

The physical availability and accessibility of detached youth workers – and their ability to develop sustained relationships in situ with young people – make them well placed to undertake informal educative work around CSE and other forms of harm. It also offers a unique opportunity to observe harm, or escalation towards this, and to be a conduit for disclosure should a young person want to seek support. These are explored in turn below.

Prevention: informal education

Research shows that normalisation of abuse and exploitation in different contexts may prevent young people from seeing their actions or experiences as harmful to them and/or others (Barter, 2009; Beckett *et al.*, 2013; Coy *et al.*, 2013). Research has also noted that by developing trusting relationships detached youth workers can create temporary spaces of safety and prevent harm by challenging this normalisation through informal education (Batsleer, 2013). By doing so young people can explore and interrogate their own opinions and behaviours and those of others around them. In our own research detached youth workers observed that whilst young people assess their physical safety in some situations, they possess much less awareness around sexual health, the nature of consent and what constitutes healthy relationships. One worker recalled a group work session with young women who did not understand the concept of grooming. Another detached youth worker clarified that young people's awareness of these issues varies greatly, but even where young people understand a term like 'grooming', they do not see it as a problem. This replicates Beckett *et al.*'s (2013) findings where some young people, repeatedly exposed to harmful sexual behaviours and beliefs, came to accept such violence as normal or inevitable.

Young people require high-quality, age appropriate sex and relationship education and information to prevent sexual harm. Detached workers were observed engaging young people in a range of such discussions around issues of personal safety, behaviours and attitudes. According to one worker:

> We create safe spaces for young people…We try to provide a safe space where young people feel comfortable to talk about anything – it could be race, gender, sexuality, faith. Just giving them that space where they feel safe and can talk.
>
> *(Esther, detached youth worker)*

The impact of this was discussed by three young people:

Researcher: And you think having youth workers around makes a difference?
Alyshia: Yeah.
Camilla: Yeah.
Researcher: What kind of difference does it make?
Alyshia: I don't know.
Camilla: Well like, Gemma she kinda like helps us, like, be safe. She tells us what to do in case anything happens. She gives us an idea of what to do in that situation.
Selena: She gives good advice.
Alyshia: Yea, advice.

Being physically present within the spaces young people might occupy, ones where workers rarely inhabit, provides the opportunity for detached workers to not only *form* relationships with young people, but then *use* those relationships to educate and, where necessary, challenge young people's behaviour and opinions.

It was clear in several discussions that the trust that detached youth workers had built up with young people over time enabled them to work with young people in ways that other professionals may not be able to because they are able to speak on a more relational level:

Tom: Cause what – because I got arrested because I got probation, you [social workers] think you can just ask me everything because you see me in the system – you don't know me, man, and I don't know you.

Researcher: So, what happens then when you get this from social workers, teachers, or whatever – what happens, what do you do?

Akeem: You don't say shit to them.

Tom: I don't say nothing. It's annoying, innit. It builds up anger. That's when you hear people doing this to a teacher, this to a police officer or a social or, you get me. It's just anger building up. That's all it is. Like, why are you asking me all these questions for?

Researcher: Do you ever hear the youth workers say to you that you shouldn't have done that?

Group: Yea, yea. Of course.

Tom: Yea, but they'll speak to you in a reasonable way. [. . .]. Like 'I expect better from you. I have worked with you, so I know – it's me speaking to you personally. You opened up to me – I know you're not stupid, so for you to do that is…I'm disappointed in you.'

A particular strength of the role of detached youth work is that it can provide young people with opportunities to critically interrogate their actions and opinions in an environment with which they are familiar and where the worker has earned their trust and respect. Detached youth workers can use their skills as informal (trained) educators to address some of the underlying gender and sexual norms that create a risk of exploitation and abuse. In describing preventative work around CSE one worker stated:

> I've got a girl's group which we set up quite a while back and we go through themes. No one in that girls group has been involved in CSE at this stage. I would like to think that is because of the group work that we have done, because it is preventative in its nature. These girls are in a high-risk environment, where a lot of their peers who do not attend the girls group are very well known and they're getting involved in all sorts of stuff. So, I would like to think that – if we can and when we can go in early enough to do preventative work, and that is only achieved via detached, then we are hitting it right on the head and we're able to empower them and give them the skills.
>
> *(Tara, detached youth worker)*

During one observation, researchers noted how a detached youth worker subtly yet adeptly challenged one young man's use of degrading language towards the young women present. When asked why he used the term, the young man responded he was joking. The detached youth worker pressed on and asked the young man to explain the joke. After a short exchange, the young man appeared to understand that the term was not funny. Whilst all professionals are able to challenge young people's language in various settings, detached youth workers are in the unique position (literally) to challenge language and behaviours as they arise in young people's preferred social spaces. Furthermore, such challenges are more likely to be successful when they come from someone who gained the trust of the young people they are with.

The nature of detached youth work as a flexible practice means that workers can recognise what are the pressing issues that need addressing and develop approaches that adapt to how young people engage and learn. Furthermore, by being connected to multi-agency meetings and work within local authorities, workers suggested that they are able to tailor the work they do in response to local needs and issues. Being situated in young people's social spaces allows workers to observe and intervene with these peer group dynamics in ways that may be hard to replicate in one-on-one service provision within professional environments.

Identification and support: being present and available

Research on disclosure has highlighted the significance of having someone notice that something isn't right, to be able to ask young people if there are concerns and then be available and trusted to hear if they do disclose (Allnock and Miller, 2013; Warrington *et al.*, 2017). Detached youth workers are well-positioned to identify young people who may be experiencing, or are at heightened risk of experiencing, harm as they are able to build trust over time and notice changes in a young person's behaviour. Their proven commitment and the trust they have developed makes them an important conduit for help-seeking. As one young male observed:

> It's because we've got a certain level of trust that I can have the confidence to tell them things. But if they came up to me and kept asking questions and nagging me… But again, that comes through the years. It don't just come straightaway. Like they've been there since we were little.
>
> *(Brandon, young man)*

Research on abuse has noted how inconsistency of professional relationships and an inability to establish and maintain rapport can conspire against potential disclosures and undermine any potential supportive relationships (Hickle and Hallett, 2016; Warrington *et al.*, 2017). Yet, establishing rapport and relationships with young people can take months, if not years.

Many young people who participated in our focus groups perceived detached workers as more understanding, less judgmental and better equipped to help them with a problem than other professionals. The consistent and long-term presence of detached youth workers in an area gives young people the time and opportunity to develop relationships and trust with them, and ultimately talk to them about issues they may not talk to other professionals about. Building trust and being available to speak is essential for the identification and disclosure of abuse. This was discussed by a young man in our focus group:

> There are certain persons – you don't have the confidence to tell them or something. In other terms, don't get me wrong – when I have problems where, I would tell her [detached youth worker], cause she's there and she says she wants to help.
>
> *(Akeem, young man)*

Whilst arguably, there are a range of professionals that work with and are able to engage with young people, young people suggested they were more likely to go to a detached youth worker than other professionals they engage with:

> I know that people would expect you to go to a teacher, but you can't really go to a teacher. You can, but not with everything, whereas with the youth worker you can tell them, like, most things and they will actually help.
>
> *(Ryan, young man)*

One of the unique features of most detached youth workers is that they do not have a set agenda or work programme, and as such discussions are generally determined by the young people themselves.

Young people interviewed suggested that they were more willing to speak with detached youth workers because relationships had been established over years, and that workers were able to understand where they were coming from, both figuratively and literally. The ability to understand young people's contexts, build trust and speak in a relational manner are benefits of their position within communities. In the following conclusion we highlight the importance of these principles and some of the barriers to successful youth work.

Conclusion

In this chapter we have argued that detached youth workers are well placed to build relationships with young people in a contextual way. By being based in the environments where young people spend time, detached youth workers can understand young people's spaces and the contexts in which they may experience harm. They can also educate to prevent harm through relationship based dialogue, their physical and relational availability mean they are well placed to identify potentially harmful behaviours and be a conduit for help and support. It is clear from research into abuse and our own work that the principles of what young people want from professionals – time and availability, the ability to build trust and for them to understand the young person – is what detached youth work does well. It is not our intention to suggest that youth workers are the only people capable of this but that their ability to be welcomed into places others often struggle to work in, places them in a unique position. We argue that other professionals could learn from detached youth work principles that would support the engagement of young people.

However, workers noted to us their frustration that increasingly the youth work context is changing – to be more target driven with predetermined work – and that this constrains the practice and impacts workers' ability to be responsive to issues identified by young people. In the study, more experienced detached youth workers and team managers lamented the loss of the sense of community that detached youth workers were able to inculcate in the past. They perceived a shift – that detached youth work is no longer a community-based service, despite the work itself taking place within public spaces. According to one participant:

> We haven't got enough time to invest in the old style – going into the area and meeting with the neighbourhood and the parents. I often find myself these days more – almost like – like avoiding certain roads because I know that we'll walk there and the parents will be hanging out on their balcony... I know that sounds awful.
>
> *(Carly, detached youth worker)*

At its core, detached youth work delivers informal education and social support to young people on their own terms and in spaces of their choosing. Rather than prescribing a focus on CSE – or indeed any other issue – detached youth workers need flexibility and time to establish relationships with young people and their communities and respond to issues as they emerge. If detached youth work becomes too enmeshed with other service agendas and workers do not have the necessary time and flexibility, we risk losing what makes it a unique service for young people.

Notes

1 'Contextual safeguarding' is an approach to safeguarding young people that recognises and engages with the contexts young people spend time and supports practitioners to identify, assess and intervene in extra-familial spaces and tackle harmful environments. Visit www.contextualsafeguarding.org.uk for more information.
2 The research involved observations of detached youth workers as they travelled through their local 'patch' and within multi-agency meetings.
3 All names have been changed.

References

Allnock, D. and Miller, P. (2013) *No one noticed, no one heard: A study of disclosures of childhood abuse.* London: NSPCC.

Barter, C. (2009) 'In the name of love: Partner abuse and violence in teenage relationships'. *British Journal of Social Work*, 39(2), pp. 211–233.

Batsleer, J. R. (2013) 'Informal learning in youth work', in Curran, S., Harrison, R. and MacKinnon, D. (eds.) *Working with Young People.* London: SAGE.

Beckett, H. (2011) *Not a world away: The sexual exploitation of children and young people in Northern Ireland.* Belfast: Barnado's Northern Ireland.

Beckett, H. and Warrington, C. (2015) *Making justice work: Experiences of criminal justice for children and young people affected by sexual exploitation as victims and witnesses.* Luton: University of Bedfordshire:.

Beckett, H., Holmes, D. and Walker, J. (2017) *Child sexual exploitation. Definition and guide for professionals: Extended text.* Luton: University of Bedfordshire.

Beckett, H., Brodie, I., Factor, F., Melrose, M., Pearce, J. J., Pitts, J., Shuker, L. and Warrington, C. (2013) *'It's wrong, but you get used to it': A qualitative study of gang-associated sexual violence towards, and exploitation of, young people in England.* Luton: University of Bedfordshire.

Bedford, A. (2015) *Serious case review into child sexual exploitation in Oxfordshire: From the experiences of Children A, B, C, D, E, and F.* Oxford: Oxfordshire Safeguarding Children Board.

Berelowitz, S. (2013) *If only someone had listened: Office of the Children's Commissioner's inquiry into child sexual exploitation in gangs and groups: Final report.* London: Office of the Children's Commissioner.

Bradford, S. and Cullen, F. (2014) 'Positive for youth work? Contested terrains of professional youth work in austerity England'. *International Journal of Adolescence and Youth*, 19(sup. 1), pp. 93–106.

Broadhurst, K. and Mason, C. (2012) 'Social work beyond the VDU: Foregrounding co-presence in situated practice – Why face-to-face practice matters'. *British Journal of Social Work*, 44(3), pp. 578–595.

Cahill, C. (2000) 'Street literacy: Urban teenagers' strategies for negotiating their neighbourhood'. *Journal of Youth Studies*, 3(3), pp. 251–277.

Coy, M., Kelly, L., Elvines, F., Garner, M. and Kanyeredzi, A. (2013) *'Sex without consent, I suppose that is rape': How young people in England understand sexual consent.* London: Office of the Children's Commissioner.

Crimmens, D., Factor, F., Jeffs, T., Pitts, J., Pugh, C., Spence, J. and Turner, P. (2004) *Reaching socially excluded young people: A national study of street-based youth work.* Discussion Paper. Leicester: National Youth Agency.

Cullen, F. (2013) 'From DIY to teen pregnancy: New pathologies, melancholia and feminist practice in contemporary English youth work 1'. *Pedagogy, Culture and Society*, 21(1), pp. 23–42.

Davies, B. (2013) 'Youth work in a changing policy landscape: The view from England'. *Youth and Policy*, 110(6), pp. 6–33.

Department for Education. (2017) *Child sexual exploitation: Definition and a guide for practitioners, local leaders and decision makers working to protect children from child sexual exploitation*. London: Department for Education.

Featherstone, B., Broadhurst, K. and Holt, K. (2011) 'Thinking systemically – thinking politically: Building strong partnerships with children and families in the context of rising inequality'. *British Journal of Social Work*, 42(4), pp. 618–633.

Firmin, C. (2013) 'Something old or something new: Do pre-existing conceptualisations of abuse enable a sufficient response to abuse in young people's relationships and peer-groups?', in Melrose, M. and Pearce, J. (eds.) *Critical Perspectives on Child Sexual Exploitation and Related Trafficking*. Basingstoke: Palgrave Macmillan.

Firmin, C., Curtis, G., Fritz, D., Olatain, P., Latchford, L., Lloyd, J. and Larasi, I. (2016a) *Towards a contextual response to peer-on-peer abuse*. Luton: University of Bedfordshire.

Firmin, C., Warrington, C. and Pearce, J. (2016b) 'Sexual exploitation and its impact on developing sexualities and sexual relationships: The need for contextual social work interventions'. *British Journal of Social Work*, 46(8), pp. 2318–2337.

Fletcher, A. and Bonell, C. (2008) 'Detaching youth work to reduce drug and alcohol-related harm'. *Juncture*, 15(4), pp. 217–223.

Fritz, D., Firmin, C. and Olaitan, P. (2016) *Practitioner briefing #5: The role of detached youth work in creating safety for young people in public spaces*. London: MsUnderstood Partnership.

Hallett, C., Murray, C. and Punch, S. (2003) 'Young people and welfare: Negotiating pathway', in Hallett, C. and Prout, A. (eds.) *Hearing the voices of children: Social policy for a new century*. Falmer: Routledge.

Hickle, K. and Hallett, S. (2016) 'Mitigating harm: Considering harm reduction principles in work with sexually exploited young people'. *Children and Society*, 30(4), pp. 302–313.

HMSO (1960) *The Youth Service in England and Wales (The Albemarle Report)*. London: HMSO.

Jago, S., Arocha, L., Brodie, I., Melrose, M., Pearce, J. J. and Warrington, C. (2011) *What's going on to safeguard children and young people from sexual exploitation? How local partnerships respond to child sexual exploitation*. Luton: University of Bedfordshire.

Jeffs, T. and Smith, M. (2008) 'Valuing youth work'. *Youth and Policy*, 100, pp. 277–302.

Lavie-Ajayi, M. and Krumer-Nevo, M. (2013) 'In a different mindset: Critical youth work with marginalized youth'. *Children and Youth Services Review*, 35(10), pp. 1698–1704.

Messerschmidt, J. W. (2012) *Gender, heterosexuality, and youth violence: The struggle for recognition*. Rowman and Littlefield.

Munro, E. (2010) *The Munro review of child protection interim report: The child's journey*. Available at: www.gov.uk/government/publications/munro-review-of-child-protection-final-report-a-child-centred-system (Accessed 21 July 2017).

Pearce, J. (2006) 'Who needs to be involved in safeguarding sexually exploited young people?' *Child Abuse Review*, 15(5), pp. 326–340.

Shephard, W. and Lewis, B. (2017) *Working with children who are victims or at risk of sexual exploitation: Barnardo's model of practice*. London: Barnardo's.

Warrington, C. with Beckett, H., Ackerley, E., Walker, M. and Allnock, D. (2017) *Making noise: Children's voices for positive change after sexual abuse*. Luton: University of Bedfordshire.

7

CSE IS EVERYONE'S BUSINESS?

The role of the night-time economy

Roma Thomas

Introduction

'CSE is everyone's business' is a resonant campaign slogan for child sexual exploitation (CSE) awareness raising which underlines the need for all in the community to take responsibility for safeguarding children. Like the African proverb 'it takes a village to raise a child' the phrase may appeal to our better selves and, arguably, it gives a welcome emphasis to the wider role of society in child protection. However, whilst the message that protecting children extends beyond those with legal responsibilities for safeguarding may be widely known, there remain significant challenges and debates about how to make this a reality. The question of how people and organisations that are outside of welfare and safeguarding systems can be empowered to protect children and young people is a central concern for this chapter. In other words, how do we ask a hotel manager or the corporate director of a multi-million pound fast food chain to ensure that children are safe in their outlets?

In answering this question the chapter aims to address gaps in the evidence base concerning CSE prevention and community awareness raising (Dhaliwal *et al.*, 2015; Radford *et al.*, 2015). Whilst the importance of the role of the community in safeguarding is recognised (Berelowitz *et al.*, 2013; Jay, 2014), evidence of what works in developing effective strategies for prevention in the community remains lacking, with few published evaluations.

The arguments in this chapter are positioned as a contribution to debates about CSE awareness raising in the community in the specific context of the night–time economy, a term which describes hospitality and entertainment services provided at night (Hobbs, 2005; Shaw, 2015). The chapter focuses primarily on risks of CSE in the night–time economy for young people; teenagers rather than children below the age of 12. This is in recognition of teenagers' growing independence during this phase in their lives (Coleman, 2010) the increased time in spaces without adult supervision and the implications of this for safeguarding (Pearce, 2013). 'Community' is conceptualised within the chapter as a wide range of publics who are outside of statutory child protection responsibilities.

The chapter begins by defining what is meant by the 'night–time economy' and asks firstly why the night–time and the night–time economy are significant in the context of CSE? It is acknowledged that CSE risks and abuse take place at different times (day and night) and in a variety of spaces. However, I contend that the night-time economy is a distinct space which merits attention for the prevention of CSE in the community. I argue that CSE risks and vulnerabilities may at times be heightened and/or overlooked, precisely because they occur at night and because the characteristics of the night-time economy may amplify these effects.

Secondly, the chapter explores the ways in which young people in public space at night are frequently 'produced' as problems and/or made invisible. Drawing on theoretical constructs from Melrose (2013) and Puwar (2004) I argue that such positioning has the effect of placing children and young people beyond protection, and that this may be reinforced by the characteristics of the night-time economy. In the final part of the chapter I present evidence from an evaluation of a pilot project in England which aimed to increase awareness and action against CSE among workers employed in the night-time economy. This research is used to explore potential learning for community awareness and CSE prevention in the night-time economy.

When darkness falls – the social space of the night-time economy

In many Western cultures night-time is seen as a time of pleasure seeking and risk. It is associated in the popular imagination with 'the marginal' (a space that is edgy, beyond day-to-day routine) and as an adults-only space, 'a time for doing things that your children are too young to understand' (Lovatt, 1994, p. 5). Melbin's (1978) conceptualisation of the night as a 'frontier' provides a useful metaphor. The 'night frontier' is used extensively in the social sciences (Hobbs, 2005; Shaw, 2015) to mark the night as a significant time and space that is 'both dangerous and alluring' (Shaw, 2015, p. 2). The distinctiveness of night from day is an essential part of the context for understanding the development of the night-time economy and its implications for safeguarding young people.

The 1990s saw the emergence of the night-time economy, a term coined by Hobbs (2005) and other commentators to describe the rapid expansion of night-time bars and leisure outlets with extended licensing hours which began in the post-industrial 1990s era. The night-time economy was used as a way of earning revenue to replace lost industries and expand city economies (Roberts, 2006; Smith, 2014). In contemporary public discourse 'night-time economy' provides shorthand to describe a vibrant, out-of-hours urban culture. This marketisation of the night has created the night-time economy as a distinct social space which has transformed urban centres:

> The commercial and civic remnants of past economic eras having morphed into 'themed' pubs and 'designer' bars and clubs. . . These licensed premises are often clustered into easily identifiable zones, notable for their youth-orientation and focus upon alcohol consumption as key social activity, economic driver, and cultural motif.
>
> *(Hadfield et al., 2009, p. 466)*

There is a hard business edge to the creation of this 24/7 party culture. Figures from the Home Office in 2000 cited in Smith (2014) estimate the United Kingdom (UK) night-time economy to be worth £1 billion a year with the turnover of the club and pub industry worth three percent of gross domestic product. The sector employs around 650,000 people in production and retail of alcohol and a further 1.1 million in the wider economy. Whilst the literature is dominated by the UK (Chatterton and Hollands, 2003; Hobbs, 2005; Hadfield, 2006) this is not solely a UK phenomenon. Europe, the United States (US) and Australia are a particular focus for night-time economy studies (Waitt *et al.*, 2011; Brands *et al.*, 2013) and Shaw (2015, p. 643) refers to 'a spread of nocturnal capitalism globally'.

However, the focus on promoting the night-time economy in urban centres as a 'happening' space has not yet led to significant attention to attendant risks and safeguarding concerns for young people. Policy and academic studies still largely focus on traditional problems of alcohol, disorder and policing (Association of Town Centre Management, 2012; Wickham, 2012) rather than risks of sexual harm and safeguarding. Teenagers below the age of 18 are not fully visible in night-time economy policy and studies. Young people feature mainly as older, 18 or 21 plus, actors whose presence in public space at night is linked with alcohol and problems of anti-social behaviour (Hadfield, 2006; Smith, 2014). This leads to a paradox of night-time economies which make use of youth culture (Smith, 2014) to attract young people but which do not address their need for protection. I suggest below two ways in which we can usefully draw on theory to understand this gap.

Bracketed children and space invaders – strangers and dangers in the night

In this section I briefly draw on two theoretical concepts to reflect on the social positioning of young people. In considering the relationship between ideas about young people, victimhood and agency within dominant CSE discourses, Melrose (2013, p. 17) discusses society's need to 'bracket' young people off from the category of 'child' or 'victim':

> They (these young people) also need to be bracketed off from the category of 'victim' since if they are acting autonomously they clearly cannot be considered 'victims' of abusive or predatory adults.

Melrose (2013) develops the point further by highlighting a discourse where young people cannot be understood as innocent victims and must instead be understood as individuals who have something wrong with them either as 'children' or as 'victims'. According to Melrose, this fails to take account of the relationship between young people's agency and the impact of structural issues arising from the commercialisation of sex. The underplaying of the seriousness of abuse and the apparent contempt and blaming of victims among some professionals highlighted in the Rotherham Inquiry (Jay, 2014) and elsewhere in research (Beckett and Warrington, 2015) provides further evidence of the impact of this positioning of young people affected by sexual exploitation. Melrose's concept is helpful in developing our understanding in ways that may help to challenge more simplistic assumptions about young people as 'transgressors' who have 'something wrong with them', and who can, as a result, be included in a 'bracketed off' category of young people.

The second theoretical construct drawn upon here is Puwar's (2004) concept of 'space invaders'. Rather than applying the concept directly, I argue that it provides a useful parallel by focusing attention on processes of 'othering' diverse peoples in social spaces. Drawing on intersectional analyses of power and the positioning of women and racial minorities within what are traditionally deemed white, male spaces in political and cultural institutions, Puwar (2004, p. 11) highlights the sense of 'terror and threat' when 'dissonant bodies' take up space in positions that have not been 'reserved' for them: 'known through a limited set of framings, these bodies jar and destabilise an exclusive sense of place'.

She describes ways in which negative constructions of black people in senior positions serve to render black people as both 'highly visible' space invaders and 'invisible' as bodies who are out of place (Puwar, 2004, p. 60). We can draw a comparison here with young people who may be 'seen' as a negative presence, as well as overlooked, in risky situations within the purported 'adults only' zone of the night-time economy. In this way young people become 'space invaders' (that is people who are not supposed to be there) and they are also rendered invisible in our social world. I suggest that the night-time economy is a key exemplar of this effect. This is significant because thinking about the social space of the urban night and ways in which young people are blamed or pathologised directs our attention towards spaces and places outside of office hours. These are areas which might otherwise appear to be 'fenced' off from child safeguarding considerations by the barrier of night-time. Established and developing knowledge about CSE tells us that we need to examine spaces in social life in order to raise awareness and prevent CSE (Pearce, 2009; Firmin, 2017). With this in mind I now turn to empirical evidence of approaches employed in the social space of the night-time economy.

Seeing in the dark – the Nightwatch project

'Nightwatch: CSE in Plain Sight' was a year-long UK Department for Education (DfE) funded pilot project run by Barnardo's, a leading UK children's charity. The project was developed partly as a response to findings on CSE and community awareness raising in an earlier evaluation of the Barnardo's Families and Communities Against Sexual Exploitation project (D'Arcy et al., 2015). Nightwatch was designed specifically to target risks and vulnerabilities for children and young people at night as part of efforts to extend the reach of CSE prevention work in the community. The project aims were:

> To safeguard children and young people from child sexual exploitation (CSE) by increasing awareness of CSE among businesses and services working in the night-time economy, and by developing strategies, in co-production with these businesses and others, to identify and protect children at risk at night, and intervene early by providing advice, support, training and guidance.
>
> *(DfE cited in D'Arcy and Thomas, 2016, p. 4)*

Nightwatch was implemented across 12 sites in England using a range of training, outreach and guidance methods to 'increase ability, confidence and awareness in identifying and reporting (CSE risks) among night-time economy workers' (D'Arcy and Thomas, 2016, p. 5). Nightwatch targeted a range of night-time economy businesses and services in the private sector including hospitality, leisure, food and services industries. This included workers in fast food outlets, hotels, bars and security roles. Within the public and voluntary sector, accident and emergency services and community outreach services which operated at night were also targeted.

Initial targets devised centrally by Barnardo's were refined at an early stage of the pilot by the Barnardo's practitioners. Changes to the targets were based on gathering local intelligence around CSE risks and 'hotspots' and a pragmatic approach to what was possible for one to two workers to deliver locally in the pilot. The programme was delivered by 14 Barnardo's practitioners recruited specifically to deliver the pilot. Notably, a significant proportion of the staff had previously worked for Barnardo's in other roles. Practitioner experience of CSE prevention and response work ranged from 0–20 years' experience. In addition, four of the practitioners had previously undertaken outreach work in the night-time economy sector.

Nightwatch was delivered by Barnardo's practitioners using a range of methods including direct training of night-time economy staff and distribution of guidance materials which comprised written information such as leaflets, posters and videos. Other strategies used were awareness raising through community events, typically through running an information stall or workshop at public events and 'meaningful engagement' (D'Arcy and Thomas, 2016, p. 11). The latter term was used to describe brief conversations about key CSE awareness messages with individuals or small groups of night-time economy workers at their place of work as well as at specified locations outside the workplace. It included localised elements and written guidance material as well as answering questions from night-time economy worker(s). Barnardo's monitoring figures for Nightwatch programme outputs showed that a large proportion of the 'take-up' by private sector night-time economy workers comprised receipt of shorter 'guidance' documents and fell within the 'meaningful engagement' category of activity described above. This is commented upon in the context of time constraints later in the chapter.

The outcomes of the project showed that during the year of operation a total of 16,944 night-time economy workers participated in Nightwatch receiving one or more of the programme interventions (see Table 7.1).

TABLE 7.1 Night-time economy sector breakdown of Nightwatch participants

Night-time economy sector	Number of recipients of advice, support, training, guidance and engagement
Hotels/Bed and Breakfast	788
Community groups	2,166
Convenience stores/petrol stations	41
Fast food eateries	142
Gambling premises	8
Leisure centre/area	107
Licensed premises	686
Private sector – mixed audience	831
Public and voluntary sector audience	4,935
Public transport	188
Security	358
Shisha bars	4
Higher education sector	3,032
Taxi establishments	3,401
Other	257
Grand total Nightwatch participants	16,944

(D'Arcy and Thomas, 2016, p. 34)

The evaluation

The evaluation of Nightwatch aimed to understand the approaches employed in the project and its effectiveness in increasing the ability of workers in the night-time economy to protect children at risk of CSE. Notably the Nightwatch study is the first known evaluation that has engaged private sector businesses in an assessment of CSE prevention. Both qualitative and quantitative data was gathered to examine the project's effectiveness: Quantitative data was drawn from Barnardo's own evaluations of training events. Qualitative data was gathered using a range of methods, as noted below:

- Interviews with Barnardo's Nightwatch practitioners (n = 9);
- Three focus group discussions with Barnardo's Nightwatch practitioners and night-time economy workers;
- Questionnaires completed by night-time economy workers who attended Nightwatch training (n = 9). The questionnaires were used to assess night-time economy workers' understanding of the aims of Nightwatch and to monitor changes in levels of ability, knowledge and confidence in reporting suspicions relating to CSE;
- Researcher observation of a training and awareness event (n = 1);
- Case studies produced from the data to illustrate different localised approaches to achieving the aims of the project (n = 4).

The evaluation received ethical approval from the University of Bedfordshire and Barnardo's ethics committees. All the evaluation participants received information about the project and gave written consent to participating in the study. Data was deemed to be confidential unless there were disclosures of information which indicated that a young person or child was at significant risk of harm. In reporting on the evaluation all quotes have been anonymised in line with ethical procedures.

Data were coded manually and analysed thematically. Data were then compared to a previous evaluation of community awareness raising within the Barnardo's Families and Communities Against Sexual Exploitation project (D'Arcy et al., 2015). The analysis was informed by a realist evaluation framework focusing on what works for whom and in what circumstances (Pawson and Tilley, 1997).

The evaluation has three main limitations which are worth briefly highlighting here. Firstly, although an exploration of the views of young people (as part of considering the impact of this project) would have been a valuable extension to the study remit, this was not possible within the funding and time constraints of the evaluation. Secondly, the project and evaluation was funded for one year; shortness of time therefore meant that it was not possible to consider long-term impacts. Finally, the evaluation also faced methodological challenges similar to those encountered in the Nightwatch project delivery itself; namely it was difficult to locate workers in the night-time economy who were able and/or willing to give time to participate in the evaluation.

Study findings

In a review of the international evidence base for responses to and prevention of CSE and child abuse, Radford et al. (2015, p. 57) found that approaches to prevention fell into three categories:

1) those aimed at mobilization to change social norms, attitudes and behaviour (most common);
2) situational prevention (altering the environmental and situational context that provide opportunities for abuse); and
3) prevention by reducing risks and vulnerabilities of children to victimisation via programmes for social and economic empowerment.

The Nightwatch project can be placed in the second category, focusing on the night-time economy as environmental and situational contexts for exploitation. The project was an attempt to move beyond problematic notions of young people in public space and engage in a practical way with the social realities of some young people's worlds. Whilst this engagement speaks to theoretical points described earlier, the evaluation found there was limited scope for engaging night-time economy workers in more complex ideas about agency and victimhood in young people. Time constraints and other reasons for this lack of scope will become clear in the findings presented below. For the remainder of the chapter I focus on key findings from the study and seek to draw out learning which can be applied to extending safeguarding responsibilities more widely in the community.

Localised approaches and flexible working

The Nightwatch study found that the '*complex web of businesses*' and '*transitory*' nature of employment (Smith, 2014, p. 48) in the night-time economy demanded localised and flexible responses for raising awareness and preventing CSE. Use of local approaches enabled the Nightwatch project to respond effectively to diverse business types and varied patterns of working hours. This also allowed it to adapt to the shortness of time available for night-time economy workers to absorb key messages about CSE prevention.

Barnardo's practitioners gathered local intelligence in a variety of ways. This included walking the streets, observing neighbourhood activity, approaching local businesses in person or by telephone and making strategic partnerships with local safeguarding hubs. This localised approach, coupled with degrees of autonomy exercised by the practitioners, gave rise to different emphases for each of the project sites. Approaches ranged from outreach to a reliance on the creation and operation of strategic partnerships. In cases where the strategic approach was observed to be highly effective, it was characterised by joint efforts with existing services.

However, 'joined up' strategic approaches between the Nightwatch project and local, mainly statutory services, did not work well across all sites. In one site the Nightwatch worker felt that their autonomy and ability to respond more flexibly was limited by the fact that they were tied into an existing partnership with statutory child protection services which had pre-defined strategies for working. This left limited space for the aims of the Nightwatch project. In another site, the worker spoke of a contrast between a close working relationship with Children's Services in one local authority and distant relations with Children's Services in a neighbouring borough. The Barnardo's worker expressed the view that this was in part due to a concern from the neighbouring borough about the potential for duplication of existing CSE specialist services funded in the local area. This was against a backdrop of competition for scarce resources.

The evaluation found adopting a local approach to be both necessary and a particular strength of the Nightwatch project. It enabled Barnardo's practitioners to reach out to numerous diverse local businesses such as hotels, bars and taxi firms. Constructive relationships between statutory child protection agencies and Barnardo's staff in the voluntary sector contributed greatly to this. The challenges encountered in forging local partnerships between statutory child protection services and voluntary sector CSE specialist services, such as Barnardo's, also highlights the need for detailed thinking and negotiation of project remits if the aim of extending safeguarding services into the community is to be achieved. This example has implications for a wider rollout of the Nightwatch project, underlining the need to consider local 'politics' and other heterogeneous factors.

While the international evidence base broadly supports the case for localised approaches in CSE prevention (Radford *et al.*, 2015), difficulties in demonstrating impact mean that this evidence is partial. The transitory nature of employment in the night-time economy where workers frequently move on from casual and short-term work provides further challenges to sustaining the impact of awareness raising in the sector. The Nightwatch evaluation contributes to the evidence base for localism, but it still remains a qualified claim. Longer term research is needed to fully demonstrate impact.

Having considered the study findings that a localised approach is more effective as a means of genuine engagement of night-time economy staff, I turn now to discuss 'flexibility'. Flexibility in Nightwatch took a variety of forms including adapting the timing and style of delivery of the programme. This meant adapting to a wide range of working hours among night-time economy workers, an approach which proved to be a critical component in engaging workers. A key finding for the study was the short amount of time night-time economy workers had available to receive training and guidance. This time constraint limited the depth of information and education that could be offered in Nightwatch. It required skilled interpretation of the Nightwatch project guidelines by Barnardo's staff. Nightwatch direct training was fairly closely defined in Barnardo's staff guidance as a classroom based session lasting two to three hours using PowerPoint and videos (D'Arcy and Thomas, 2016). However, in practice Nightwatch workers adapted this approach to deliver the programme:

> I cannot go in takeaways and taxi ranks with a PowerPoint, so flexibility is really important. Yesterday we went into a bowling alley and we spoke to the staff and talking to them about the basic signs, giving them all the information. . . My colleague spotted two of her high-risk clients.
>
> *(Nightwatch Worker 1)*

The level of adaptation undertaken by Barnardo's practitioners to fit the circumstances of night-time economy workers required a combination of knowledge, skill and agility and a degree of autonomy in programme delivery. These are notable characteristics for the design and effectiveness of future programmes which aim to raise awareness in the night-time economy. The limited existing evidence base also supports the study finding about the importance of flexibility for community approaches to CSE prevention (D'Arcy *et al.*, 2015).

Gaining access and engagement

> You have got to keep going and keep going. Some organisations remain negative about child protection, don't want to get involved, just keep chipping away.
>
> *(Nightwatch Worker 1)*

Nightwatch workers experienced a critical challenge in gaining access to staff and in conveying the 'CSE is everyone's business' message to night-time economy outlets. Nightwatch workers deployed a range of approaches to good effect in a significant number of cases. Access was gained through use of both strategic and grassroots networks. However, all the Nightwatch workers interviewed reported mixed levels of uptake and interest from the organisations they approached. This included slow (or no) responses to emails and phone calls. In some cases there was confusion over the role of the Barnardo's charity and people assumed they were collecting donations:

> The vast majority of people we spoke to heard 'Barnardo's' and told us they already gave to charities, they were busy and could we call back or plain hang up.
>
> *(Nightwatch Worker 3)*

Some organisations did not see the relevance of the training offered and were unwilling to release staff to attend. Gaining 'buy-in' was therefore a crucial task which required persistence and a significant amount of time on the part of Barnardo's workers. This included, for example, chasing responses and establishing contact with the right person(s) in local businesses or in corporate headquarters.

Many of the Nightwatch sites undertook initial outreach work to raise awareness with brief key messages followed up by more detailed advice, guidance and training. The ability to adopt the right tone, build rapport and demonstrate a friendly, non-judgemental approach were observed to be key skills for programme delivery. This was particularly the case in some locations due to the stigma attached to receiving CSE prevention messages. At the outset of the project some audiences felt they were being unfairly 'targeted'. For example, at one site taxi drivers spoke of being 'unhappy' that the issue was being seen by wider society as an 'Asian taxi driver' issue and, as a consequence, they were hesitant about being involved in CSE prevention work. Nightwatch workers dealt with this by adopting a practical approach, building up relationships with the aim of empowering night-time economy workers. The core message here was that the training would help taxi drivers gain essential knowledge about safeguarding and that this would add to their skillset. This approach proved effective in a number of cases.

More generally, a strengths-based approach provided a useful way to overcome barriers created by a fear of stigma among local businesses. However, it may be that fear of stigma and reluctance to engage in CSE awareness was a larger barrier to dealing with businesses at a corporate level. Only one Barnardo's worker in the project managed to establish significant links at a corporate level. This was fruitful as it led to embedding CSE prevention training in the annual training cycle of a large entertainment organisation. Although a significant number of the businesses engaged by Nightwatch were part of larger chains and franchises, engagement was usually at an individualised level rather than addressing the corporate management personnel of these services. The large-scale significance of corporate ownership in the night-time economy sector (Chatterton and Hollands, 2003) suggests that this is an important area for future initiatives. The main strengths of Nightwatch are in local neighbourhood approaches. The project was not so well equipped in gaining entry and influence at the corporate level. The evaluation cannot tell us all the reasons businesses did not, or were reluctant to, engage with Nightwatch. However, the importance of soft skills such as rapport building, avoiding stigma combined with the tenacity required from Barnardo's practitioners to 'sell' CSE prevention indicates that barriers to engagement were high. I reflected during the study that this may suggest that CSE prevention messages can be perceived as irrelevant or out of place in business contexts.

Responding to distress and disclosures

In a number of cases Nightwatch workers found that despite prior communication stressing the importance of explaining the sensitive nature of the training in advance, attendees were not always informed about and/or prepared for this. In one example a bus worker became visibly upset following introduction of the training. She had no prior knowledge of the content of the programme. The painfulness of her distress was vividly recalled by the Nightwatch worker during a focus group discussion. The Nightwatch worker was particularly concerned that it was difficult to provide follow up support for the woman concerned.

It also became evident that, in the process of Nightwatch reaching out to night-time economy workers, disclosures of past abuse were occurring among some night-time economy workers who were themselves past victims. In some cases these disclosures came about through staff attending the Nightwatch training programme. For example, in a focus group discussion one of the Barnardo's practitioners recalled that a bar manager had disclosed, as part of introducing his team to the training, that he had been a past victim of abuse. According to the Barnardo's worker the bar manager made the disclosure to help emphasise the importance of the training. The unexpected nature of the disclosure was described by the Barnardo's worker as creating a 'difficult and uncomfortable' atmosphere for the subsequent delivery of the training. This occurred despite Nightwatch staff having been trained in managing disclosures, and despite all Nightwatch staff explaining ethics and disclosure protocols in advance of delivering training.

The difficulties encountered suggest a need to prepare staff more effectively to deliver this type of training in community environments. Greater levels of awareness of the possibility that Nightwatch participants might have experienced abuse, or might have otherwise been affected by CSE, would have been beneficial in the project. During the pilot, additional training and support in dealing with disclosures was required for Nightwatch practitioners who had less experience of CSE work. This is consistent with knowledge about the need for emotional support for those who work to assist adult survivors of abuse (Allnock and Wager, 2016) and the need for specialist skills and knowledge for workers undertaking awareness raising (D'Arcy et al., 2015).

Established evidence also highlights the importance of access to support for victims (Sneddon et al., 2016), but at the same time shows that there is a dearth of services available for victims of non-recent abuse (Allnock and Wager, 2016). The evaluation showed that in some cases Nightwatch practitioners were able to talk through issues with people who had made disclosures and refer them to victim support services. However, patchiness in the availability of support and therapeutic services for adults meant that this was a considerable challenge for a number of sites. Further rollout of initiatives such as Nightwatch requires resources beyond support for awareness training and guidance that tells people how to report their suspicions, important though this is. There is a clear need for access to therapeutic help and support for adult victims and young people affected by CSE.

Conclusion

I began this chapter with the slogan 'CSE is everyone's business' and I have explored how this might become a reality in the night-time economy, where young people may face particular risks and vulnerabilities. I have argued that young people at risk of CSE are frequently overlooked and invisible and that there may even be hostility to the presence of young people in public space at night-time. Community awareness raising seeks to empower individuals, businesses and others to be alert to safeguarding issues and to take appropriate action. In most cases this means people understanding when and how to report causes of concern to statutory authorities. The empirical evidence outlined here has shown that taking safeguarding out to workers in the night-time economy (even at a relatively basic level) presents significant challenges.

The Nightwatch evaluation demonstrates that awareness raising requires skilled, determined and flexible practitioners and working patterns as well as the ability to act on local intelligence. Nightwatch provides a contribution to the evidence base for community awareness raising. However, there remain larger questions to answer. For example, how can we change a society where it is possible to ignore the sight of a young person in the company of an older adult checking into a local hotel in suspicious circumstances, for instance where the young person appears upset or afraid to speak? This question needs to be addressed in corporate board rooms as well as targeting local night-time economy workers with CSE prevention messages. It also needs to be addressed in policy protocols for nurturing night-time economies in our cities. Finally, there is a need for a fundamental shift in the way we think about young people's presence in the social space of the night. The task of making CSE everyone's business is truly a labour for both day and night.

References

Allnock, D. and Wager, N. (2016) *Victim support's adult survivors of child sexual abuse project: An evaluation of a co-created service delivery model.* Luton: University of Bedfordshire.

Association of Town Centre Management (2012) *Purple flag's night-time economy best practice guide.* London: Association of Town Centre Management.

Beckett, H. and Warrington, C. (2015) *Making justice work – Full report.* Luton: University of Bedfordshire.

Berelowitz, S., Clifton, J., Firmin, C., Gulyurtu, S. and Edwards, G. (2013) *If only someone had listened: The Office of the Children's Commissioner's inquiry into child sexual exploitation in gangs and groups – Final report.* London: Office of the Children's Commisioner.

Brands, J., Schwanen, T. and van Aalst, I. (2013) 'Fear of crime and affective ambiguities in the night-time economy'. *Urban Studies*, 52(3), pp. 439–455.

Chatterton, P. and Hollands, R. (2003) *Urban nightscapes: Youth cultures, pleasure spaces and corporate power.* London: Routledge.

Coleman, J. C. (2010) *The Nature of Adolescence.* Fourth Edition, London: Routledge.

D'Arcy, K. and Thomas, R. (2016) *Nightwatch: CSE in plain sight – Final evaluation report.* Luton: University of Bedfordshire.

D'Arcy, K., Dhaliwal, S., Thomas, R., Brodie, I. and Pearce, J. (2015) *Families and communities against child sexual exploitation (FCASE) – Final evaluation report.* Luton: University of Bedfordshire.

Dhaliwal, S., D'Arcy, K. and Thomas, R. (2015) 'Community awareness raising on child sexual exploitation: possibilities and problems'. *Safer Communities*, 14(1), pp. 4–15.

Firmin, C. (2017) 'Contextualizing case reviews: A methodology for developing systemic safeguarding practices'. *Child and Family Social Work*. Advance Access 27 June 2017.

Hadfield, P. (2006) *Bar wars: Contesting the night in contemporary British cities*. Oxford: Oxford University Press.

Hadfield, P., Lister, S. and Traynor, P. (2009) '"This town's a different town today": Policing and regulating the night-time economy'. *Criminology and Criminal Justice*, 9(4), pp. 465–485.

Hobbs, D. (2005) *Bouncers: Violence and governance in the night-time economy*. Oxford: Oxford University Press.

Jay, A. (2014) *Independent inquiry into child sexual exploitation in Rotherham 1997–2013*. Rotherham: Rotherham Council.

Lovatt, A. E. (1994) *The 24-hour city: National conference on the night-time economy: Selected papers and edited transcripts*. Manchester: Manchester Institute for Popular Culture.

Melbin, M. (1978) 'Night as frontier'. *American Sociological Review*, 43(1), pp. 3–22.

Melrose, M. (2013) 'CSE: A critical discourse analysis', in Melrose, M. and Pearce, J. (eds.) *Critical perspectives on child sexual exploitation and related trafficking*. Basingstoke, Hampshire: Palgrave Macmillan, pp. 9–22.

Pawson, R. and Tilley, N. (1997) *Realistic evaluation*. SAGE Publications.

Pearce, J. (2009) *Young people and sexual exploitation: 'It's not hidden, you're just aren't looking'*. London: Taylor and Francis.

Pearce, J. (2013) 'A social model of "abused consent"', in Melrose, M. and Pearce, J. (eds.) *Critical perspectives on child sexual exploitation and related trafficking*. Basingstoke, Hampshire: Palgrave Macmillan, pp. 52–68.

Puwar, N. (2004) *Space invaders: Race, gender and bodies out of place*. London. New York: Berg.

Radford, L., Allnock, D. and Hynes, P. (2015) *Preventing and responding to child sexual abuse and exploitation: Evidence review*. Unpublished, authors' permission to cite.

Roberts, M. (2006) 'From "creative city" to "no-go areas" – The expansion of the night-time economy in British town and city centres'. *Cities*, 23(5), pp. 331–338.

Shaw, R. (2015) 'Night as fragmenting frontier: Understanding the night that remains in an era of 24/7'. *Geography Compass*, 9(12), pp. 637–647.

Smith, O. (2014) *Contemporary Adulthood and the Night-Time Economy*. Basingstoke, Hampshire: Palgrave Macmillan.

Sneddon, H., Wager, N. and Allnock, D. (2016) *Responding sensitively to survivors of child abuse: An evidence review*. Luton: University of Bedfordshire.

Waitt, G., Jessop, L. and Gorman-Murray, A. (2011) '"The guys in there just expect to be laid": Embodied and gendered socio-spatial practices of a "night out" in Wollongong, Australia'. *Gender, Place and Culture*, 18(2), pp. 255–275.

Wickham, M. (2012) *Alcohol consumption in the night-time economy: Policy interventions*. London: Greater London Assembly.

8

PROFILING CSE

Building a contextual picture of a local problem

Carlene Firmin and David Hancock

Introduction

Over recent years research has increasingly evidenced the social, public and networked nature of child sexual exploitation (CSE) and related forms of abuse (Barter *et al.*, 2009; Beckett *et al.*, 2013; Melrose, 2013; Pearce, 2013; Cockbain, Brayley and Sullivan, 2014; Firmin *et al.*, 2016; Sidebotham *et al.*, 2016). CSE often occurs within social spaces, whether online or offline, with its nature informed by the social rules of those spaces (Beckett *et al.*, 2013; Firmin, Warrington and Pearce, 2016). Increased identification of group-based perpetration by both adults and children has further evidenced the social dynamic of this phenomenon (CEOP, 2011; Cockbain, Brayley and Sullivan, 2014; Pitts, 2013; Firmin, 2017), as has the identification of 'CSE locations' or 'hotspots'. Public spaces such as transport hubs, take away shops, high streets, parks and stairwells have provided environments in which contact with children and young people can be made and exploitative relationships can be formed (Cockbain, 2013; D'Arcy *et al.*, 2015; Curtis, 2016; Firmin, 2017).

Capturing these social and environmental elements of CSE cases means moving beyond interventions focusing on individual case management and more towards the identification and disruption of the trends that those cases share in common. One way of realising this ambition in the United Kingdom (UK) has been through the process of 'problem profiling'; the activity of analysing trends across cases to build a picture of the CSE profile within a given local area.

This chapter explores the contribution that problem profiling has made to CSE practice within the UK and considers the implications of this work for local, national and international policy and practice. Using empirical data from a seminar series on peer-on-peer abuse for local analysts, and supplementing this material with local examples of profiling activity, this chapter will:

- Provide a brief introduction to the concept of problem profiling;
- Outline the methodology of the seminar series, and the theoretical framework that informed both it and the approaches taken to research and practice by the authors;

- Consider three thematic issues that emerged from the series that have implications for how profiling activity is used as part of a response to CSE;
- Discuss the learning from this process to make recommendations for policy and practice development.

The chapter explores the interdependent relationships between the objectives of problem profiling, approaches to information sharing and the dissemination/presentation of CSE profiles. Each of these elements informs the other, and all need to build upon a contextual understanding of CSE in order to address the dynamics within which it occurs. Whilst profiling has the potential to illuminate the contextual nature of CSE and drive interventions which change the social conditions of abuse, it will only do so if built on a contextual understanding of the issue. In the absence of this, despite its potential, profiling activity locally, nationally and internationally will continue to inform, and be informed by, an individualised account of a social issue.

Understanding problem profiling

A problem profile draws together all known intelligence from the range of agencies working within a specific locality. In this sense, it is a multi-agency activity drawing on relevant data pertaining to a particular issue that professionals want to address. The issues that can be addressed through problem profiling vary considerably, including, for example, hate crimes or educational underachievement. Irrespective of the issue being addressed, relevant data held across different agencies will be drawn together and analysed to inform strategic decision-making and the development of local practice (College of Policing, 2015).

In the main, a local area will have a lead data analyst who will be responsible for profiling. This analyst has to work with partners to identify what data is available for inclusion and ensure that all data used is 'clean', i.e. does not double count individuals or incidents which is a common risk when synthesising various, distinct data sources. Once all the data has been collected the process of analysis can begin. In the case of CSE, this will involve identifying trends/patterns relating to the known victims, offenders and locations associated to CSE within a demarcated geographical area.

Upon completion, key findings from profiling activity are disseminated to relevant partners. In the main this is social care and policing, although health, education and youth justice may also be included. Partners will then, ideally, agree on a plan for addressing the identified issues.

Regular reviews of both the profile and the outcomes of interventions that have been designed to respond to identified issues should be undertaken to ensure that the profile can be updated as the risk reduces, increases or changes. This is particularly critical in relation to CSE which is often dynamic in nature, with locations, affected individuals and risk levels changing over time. This means problem profiles are often outdated fairly soon after completion and therefore require monitoring and amendments in order to helpfully direct intervention. The degree to which this occurs is, however, questionable, with a review of London local authorities in 2014 capturing problems in relation to, and a frequent absence of, such updating (Beckett and Firmin, 2014).

Increasingly, inspectorates and policymakers have argued that problem profiling is a crucial element of a local area response to safeguarding, crime and/or community safety issues (Office of Children's Commissioner, 2013; Ofsted, 2016). In the absence of a problem profile, local areas are unable to identify and/or target trends related to the prevalence or nature of an issue and instead are restricted to individual case management and responsive (rather than preventative or proactive) intervention. Profiling not only allows local services to identify trends within an area, providing them with data of their own as well as, often, neighbouring areas, but it also informs discussions/design of measures put in place to respond to the issue and provides a baseline for measuring how effective such responses have been (Office of Children's Commissioner, 2013; College of Policing, 2015; Ofsted, 2016).

Methodology

From 2015 to 2016, academics at the University of Bedfordshire ran a seminar series for CSE and gangs analysts across six (bordering) urban local authorities to develop their profiling of peer abuse. The objectives of the seminar series were to:

- Share the research evidence base on peer-on-peer CSE, and other forms of peer abuse, to support a shared conceptualisation of the issue across the six local authorities;
- Develop a shared recognition of the contextual dynamics of peer-on-peer CSE and other forms of peer abuse in order to facilitate contextual profiling;
- Identify datasets that would be of use in enhancing existing profiling work beyond that which is held by children's social care and policing.

Theoretical basis

The seminar series was designed as part of a wider programme of work that applied the theory of contextual safeguarding to develop local responses to peer-on-peer abuse (Firmin et al., 2016; Firmin, Warrington and Pearce, 2016). Contextual safeguarding is built upon the social theory of Pierre Bourdieu (1990). Bourdieu viewed the social world as one in which individuals navigate social fields, each of which have a set of social rules. According to Bourdieu, individuals embody these social rules through their 'habitus' and engage in a reflexive process in which they are constructed by, and construct, the social fields of which they are a part. Individuals bring social, economic, cultural and symbolic capital into any given social field and draw upon these in pursuit of status within that field. If one views the social world through this Bourdieusian lens then human behaviour is best explored with reference to the social rules at play within the contexts in which it occurs.

Applying this to CSE, contextual safeguarding argues that in order to change behaviours, professionals need to address the social contexts in which the abuse occurs. For peer-on-peer CSE, and other forms of peer abuse, these behaviours are therefore best understood when the contexts in which young people exploit their peers are explored alongside the behaviours of the individuals involved. This approach provided the scaffold upon which to base the structure of the seminar series. Each seminar focused on data which would illuminate the contexts of peer abuse, the social rules at play there and the characteristics of the individuals who engaged with those rules.

Planning the seminar series

To establish the seminar series, an initial planning workshop was held with eight local CSE and/or serious youth violence analysts and seven regional data holders from the six bordering local authorities (herein referred to as 'sites'). The regional data holders were those who held or managed large datasets that research had identified as potentially useful for local profiling of peer-on-peer abuse, such as transport and public health data (i.e. Office of the Children's Commissioner, 2013).

During the planning workshop a researcher provided a presentation on research into peer abuse and the extent to which the phenomenon was contextual. It was demonstrated that should profiling want to sufficiently capture context, it would need to identify the families, peer networks, schools and public/neighbourhood spaces associated with peer abuse in a local area, in addition to the number of individuals affected and their characteristics (see Figure 8.1).

Following this, workshop attendees engaged in small group discussion to identify priority datasets and challenges to be addressed by the seminar series. Through this process of co-creation a three-part series was designed to capture data that could cumulatively provide information about potential warning signs for, and contexts of, abuse:

- Seminar 1: Capturing education data (exclusions, absences and children missing from education) to identify schools in which young people are being abused by peers and to identify children displaying the potential warning signs of exploitation (missing/disengaged from school).
- Seminar 2: Capturing health data (sexual health, mental health and A&E) to identify peer groups affected by peer abuse (who may attend/access sexual health services or hospitals together) or locations in which victims of abuse are found by health practitioners (mental health outreach services and paramedics).
- Seminar 3: Capturing community safety and transport data to identify transport routes/hubs, public spaces and housing stock in which young people are being abused by their peers.

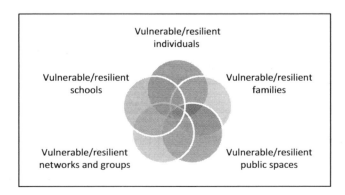

FIGURE 8.1 Aspirational categories for contextual profiling

Ethical approval to run the seminar series was granted by the University of Bedfordshire as part of a wider programme of action research delivered in 11 local authorities across England from 2013 to 2016. Consent to participate (and for findings to be used for publications, so long as sites were not identified) was obtained in advance, and participants also provided approval of the written record that was circulated to them following each seminar. At the close of the seminar series all members of the core group were invited to co-create written materials with the researchers. Written materials included a practice briefing (Firmin *et al.*, 2016) and this chapter. The data collected during the seminars are held by, and co-owned by, all core group members and researchers.

The seminar series

A core group of analysts, whose role was to profile the nature of CSE and/or gang violence within a local authority area, were booked to attend each seminar. They came from community safety, policing and social care contexts, but all used policing and social care data to profile the nature of peer abuse. This core group of analysts were joined by data holders relevant to each seminar topic. For example, those working within local authorities who held data on education attended the first seminar; clinical commissioning groups, public health analysts and designated safeguarding nurses attended the second; and transport and community safety analysts participated in the third.

Each seminar followed the same structure. Researchers provided a contextual account of peer abuse at the start of each seminar with a specific focus on the datasets due for discussion. Following reflections on the introductory presentation, members from the analyst core group presented papers on the ways in which they had used the datasets under consideration and any challenges that they had in accessing them. Following a discussion on those papers, the invited data-owners presented their perspectives on the potential usage of the datasets they managed and the ways that these could be accessed and used to better profile CSE and other forms of peer abuse in the future. Seminar attendees then broke into smaller groups to discuss these issues of potential usage and associated challenges.

In keeping with the ethical agreements for the project, each seminar discussion was recorded and transcribed. The conclusions from smaller group discussions were written onto flip chart paper and shared verbally with the wider group. A written record of each seminar was circulated to attendees along with the slides produced for each paper presentation. These were agreed by the core group and used to develop a briefing for analysts on aspirational profiling of peer abuse.

Data analysis

For the purposes of this chapter, the minutes of each seminar and the paper presentations have been subjected to qualitative analysis to identify thematic lessons around the profiling of peer-on-peer CSE, which in turn could be of relevance to profiling CSE more broadly. In the text that follows, this seminar series data is supplemented with examples from a local analyst to illustrate their practical application or implication. As such, the chapter, along with the data collected for it, has been co-created between researchers and a local authority analyst.

Limitations

While this process has surfaced findings associated with profiling methodologies, it has a number of limitations. Firstly, as noted, it was representatives from six local authorities who participated in the seminar series. The approaches they take, the data they hold and the challenges that they face may not reflect experiences in other local areas. Secondly, confining the series to three seminars practically limited the number of datasets that could be considered. For example, data from youth service provision which could yield further knowledge about contextual profiling practice were not included in the process. Thirdly, the seminar series was focused on profiling peer abuse more generally and therefore considered the identification of abusive behaviours that went beyond CSE and likewise were not directly concerned with profiling CSE perpetrated by adults. As a result, the authors have had to consider the implications of the learning from the series for wider work on CSE beyond that which is peer perpetrated.

Findings: developing contextual CSE profiles

By knowing how CSE, or other forms of harm and abuse, manifests within their geographical area of responsibility, local partnerships are better placed to understand the risks posed to young people and identify the most appropriate ways to respond (CEOP, 2011; Beckett and Firmin, 2014). While the important place of profiling within the local response to CSE is accepted in policy and research (Firmin et al., 2016; Ofsted, 2016; Beckett, Holmes and Walker, 2017), it remains a relatively young component of local practice. Analysis of data generated during the seminar series has identified three key areas which would benefit from further development:

- The objectives of problem profiling;
- Approaches to data collection including information sharing;
- Methods for presenting/sharing profiles and using these to inform practice.

This section of the chapter explores the opportunities and challenges in relation to these, with the aim that they will inform the development of more consistent and purposeful profiling as part of local responses to CSE both nationally and internationally.

The objectives of profiling CSE

Many of the local partnerships represented in the seminar series were yet to establish a shared objective for problem profiling. While in one sense participants were clear on the purpose and benefits of profiling work, analysts recognised that their contribution to the profiling of CSE wasn't always understood and saw this as directly related to differing objectives within the partnership. Critical questions that were raised during seminar discussions included:

- Do we profile to gather intelligence for criminal justice investigations or to safeguard young people?
- When profiles identify young people associated to one another, and to CSE, to what extent do all of those who feature require a response?

- Are we profiling to count the number of those affected or to document the nature of the local issue; for example, models of abuse or the demographics of those involved?
- Should we generate profiles to better understand what is known or to gather information to identify what is not known?
- Should profiling enable proactive identification of risk or be used to guide reactive interventions?

Of course, there is no 'one size fits all' answer to these questions, and the purpose of a problem profile will likely vary according to local context and need at any given point in time. One way of resolving these challenges, however, is to ensure that a discussion takes places amongst a multi-agency partnership before an area is selected for profiling.

To illustrate, in one site, emerging themes/patterns that indicate the need for a profile are brought to the multi-agency CSE meeting to decide which area/elements will be profiled in more depth. Through this discussion the local partnership agrees what data sources will be used. Once developed, the profile is presented to the partnership who can agree how best to circulate and use it amongst the wider workforce.

Within this model, one analyst created a peer exploitation profile for the local authority. The objective of the profiling work was to understand contextual trends across cases of peer abuse identified by social care and the police. By analysing the individual cases with reference to the type of abuse and school attended by the victim, the analyst identified associations between schools and particular models of abuse across individually managed cases (see Table 8.1).

This process proved particularly useful in capturing and addressing issues emerging within particular settings that had not yet been identified through individual case management processes (for example, online bullying in School A and gang-associated CSE in Schools C and E). It has also strengthened the relationships between multi-agency safeguarding partnerships and education providers, resulting in a considerable increase in the rates of intelligence being shared by schools associated to suspected cases of CSE more broadly.

Shared objectives are critical not only for ensuring the effective use of problem profiling, but for determining the nature of profiling activity. During the seminar attended by

TABLE 8.1 Numbers of peer exploitation cases, by school and exploitation type

School	Model type				
	Online (including coercion to send sexual images and online bullying)	Sexual bullying at school	Gang associated abuse and exploitation	Other Sexual assault	Teenage relationship abuse
A	7	0	0	1	2
B	0	1	0	0	1
C	0	0	3	0	1
D	0	0	0	1	0
E	4	0	4	3	4
F	1	0	1	0	0
G	1	0	1	1	0
H	0	0	2	1	0

practitioners focusing on child health care, for example, significant questions were raised about why health data is required for CSE profiles – what does it add? Such questions stemmed from a lack of an agreed and shared objective for profiles in the first place. Likewise a number of partner agencies who attended seminars, including those from public transport providers (not private companies), health and education, commented that they were unaware of the local profiles that had been generated and therefore were not using them to inform practice or commissioning decisions. If profiling is only undertaken to inform an analyst or a small local partnership, its objectives are quite different from profiling that aims to inform, or gather information from, wider activities across local services.

Sources of information

All analysts participating in the seminars stated that they largely drew upon police and children's social care data to develop profiles at present, outlining the benefits that such analysis could add to our understanding of these datasets. Drawing together information from across CSE referrals, for example, can produce new insights about cases already known to services and is an approach in keeping with advice on the management of multi-agency CSE meetings (Curtis, 2016; Metropolitan Police Service, 2015). To illustrate, an analyst drawing on such data may find that 6 out of 30 young people being individually managed as CSE cases all went missing on the same evening. This can surface questions about whether they were missing together – a discussion that would not be possible without identifying trends across these individual cases.

Discussions during seminars indicated that this approach to profiling could be extended and analysts believed that their work would benefit from access to a wider dataset. This ambition was particularly informed by their objective to use profiling for the purposes of identifying those issues/concerns not already known by the multi-agency CSE partnership.

To illustrate, we can consider the example of mapping connections between young people. Data explored during seminars provided some opportunities to identify hitherto unknown young people or hitherto unknown patterns of behaviour amongst a known friendship group. For example, accessing details of young people's journeys on the local public bus network could identify young people consistently travelling together in the same group. It might then be possible to identify other (as yet unknown) individuals associated with a group around which there are concerns. Similarly it may be possible to identify that a known group is attending a previously unknown address in the evenings. There was consensus amongst seminar participants that schools were also likely to hold information on connections between young people who may be at risk of CSE, not all of whom would already be known to statutory services.

Applying these lessons, one analyst who attended the seminar series has now started to use data provided by those working with a specific brief on community safety within their profiling work. They have overlaid this information with that of known CSE hotspots and intelligence from missing reports for young people. Incorporating this new data into problem profiles has led to the identification of new hotspots of concern. It has also enabled the analyst to link episodes of young people going missing with some reported incidents of anti-social behaviour. In this latter case, children who were seen as anti-social and involved in problematic behaviours can now be viewed as those who were likely to be vulnerable and missing from home or care at the time the behaviour took place.

Additionally, accessing datasets connected to different issues impacting the safety of young people can advance local understandings of CSE. For example, in one site, cross-referencing datasets helpfully revealed that:

- 60.7% of missing/concerning absence episodes in 2015/2016 were by young people identified at risk of CSE;
- 25% of young people who had a CSE Risk Assessment completed were identified as having links to a gang.

In the absence of information from a wider set of partners, profiling will largely be confined to the practice of communicating themes across known cases. Whilst this practice is beneficial for enabling strategic discussion of known cases, it does not necessarily facilitate the identification of young people who are at risk of CSE but unknown to services. Instead, thematic profiling of known cases could be used as a foundation for identifying contexts upon which wider partnership discussions could be launched. For example, if analysis of a number of known cases of CSE identified young people within the same peer group who attended the same educational establishment, this information could be used to:

- Contact the school to identify if there were other peers associated to that group who may be vulnerable to CSE but who had not been identified by statutory services;
- Draw local detached youth workers into the response if they have pre-existing relationships with some members of that group;
- Contact transport providers to identify where this group of young people travel to when they go missing in the evening, and whether there are others in the group who travel with them but are not known to services.

Working in this way may also help the partnership identify the public spaces where these young people spend their time and, by proxy, the localities in which they are being exploited.

Information sharing

While different services such as schools and transport companies may hold information to inform problem profiles, seminar discussions indicated that they were not aware of what to share, how to share it, when to share it and with whom to share it. Social care and policing organisations often felt challenged in requesting/accessing this data from data holders in other services. The importance of knowing what information to share, and when and how, was consistently referenced across seminars and was particularly important to the profiling of contexts.

Core analysts and other participants commented that in terms of individual case management, information sharing arrangements were largely effective. This was demonstrated by them explaining that if policing or social care professionals had a named person of concern they were able to contact their school, health services and even a transport provider and request specific information to build a profile about an individual child. Health professionals, for example, commented on the clarity that they had in regards to conducting searches on named children and the clarity they experienced knowing when and how to bring information to multi-agency planning meetings or strategy discussions with regards to those children.

However, matters appeared far more complex with regards to sharing broader, or contextual, data for the purposes of identifying young people who were yet to be the subject of a referral. In these instances, communicating the purpose of the profiling activity and developing personal relationships between agencies seemed to be critical to enabling agencies to proactively contact and share information with analysts. Practice questions remain, however, regarding the ability of analysts to access some datasets, particularly those held by private organisations, with regards to both the number of organisations and businesses this may involve and the legal frameworks required to leverage this type of information sharing.

The benefits of accessing broader datasets and working with other partners are aptly demonstrated by one site which, following engagement in the seminar series, has begun to meet with schools that have the highest number of young people identified as being at risk of CSE in attendance. These meetings have given the analysts a foundation for mapping peer networks within one school. This in turn has identified that young people from multiple local authorities are part of one peer group in one school. This identification has resulted in cross-borough strategy meetings to link information held on the different members of that peer network within that school. In the absence of partnership working between education practitioners and analysts, it would not have been possible to proactively identify social connections between individuals known to different local authorities in this way.

In the same site the CSE analyst has begun working with schools to capture data on children who are missing from school during the day. This missing behaviour has been identified as a potential indicator of both CSE (with children drawn from schools by those who have groomed them) and peer abuse within schools (with children not attending school or certain classes to avoid students who pose a risk to their safety). It is thought that some of these children are only missing during the school day and not overnight, and are therefore unlikely to have been reported missing to the police by their parents/carers. In the absence of formal missing reports, it is unlikely that these types of missing episodes will be reported and shared with a local partnership. The analyst in the site has worked with one school to design a template for recording occasions where young people go missing during the school day; this template is being reviewed before it is disseminated amongst other schools in the local authority. Once completed templates are received by the analyst, the site will be able to review the data generated against information on children reported missing from home/care. Once duplicates are removed, they will have a more complete picture of missing episodes for young people in the area.

While seminars offered a number of recommendations for improving information sharing, the one that appeared of central importance above all others was the access that the wider partnership had to profiles that were produced. Seminar participants stated that if they knew how the information they provided was used, and could access the resultant profile to inform their practice, then it was more likely that data could/would be shared. Approaches to disseminating/presenting profiles, and the ethics and legalities of information sharing, then become integral to building contextual responses to CSE.

Disseminating profiles

All analysts participating in the seminar series had presented problem profiles to small multi-agency groups established to drive the local response to CSE. These groups mainly consisted of social care, policing, specialist CSE services and – less commonly – youth justice, health and education representatives. In these environments problem profiles enabled a group of professionals to focus on and discuss trends across cases, thereby going beyond case discussions to strategically plan interventions.

In one site, for example, the analyst presented a contextual problem profile to the CSE meeting regarding cases of online exploitation within the local authority. The profile provided information on the gender and age of the individuals affected, the social media site on which the exploitation had occurred and the point of contact between the young person and the alleged perpetrator. In collating this data it became clear that while all examples involved some form of online CSE, in 90% of cases the young person didn't actually meet the alleged perpetrator online. In close to half of the cases, contact happened either in school (the vast majority of these being peer-on-peer online CSE cases) or in the community. Contact also varied by the type of social media site of concern. Bringing this level of contextual information to the profile was critical to informing the type of interventions that were developed. For example, producing this profile has led to both the identification of specific education settings where online exploitation amongst peers is particularly prevalent and guided the direction of group work for those young people who have been affected. The local authority has also produced a social media guide for parents highlighting the most prevalent social media apps being used by young people and any potential concerns about them. Local partners have engaged with particular social media companies to highlight identified issues that analysts have found on their sites. This targeted approach has proved effective in that an increased number of young people are raising concerns directly about online exploitation with professionals within the partnership, who are then able to notify relevant social media companies regarding inappropriate content.

Beyond presenting profiles to inform the work of specialist CSE meetings, seminar discussions identified the importance of profile presentation to other local and regional strategic groups with a responsibility or strategic priority for safeguarding young people. Rather than presenting the numbers of CSE referrals made within a local area, strategic partnerships could benefit from knowledge of the local contextual profile. This would include how many families (particularly sibling associations), peer groups, educational establishments and public spaces are associated to, or affected by, CSE. Presenting a local CSE profile in this manner could direct the commissioning of services to intervene with public and social contexts, such as detached youth workers for peer groups or supportive provision for schools.

Beyond strategic partnerships, discussions during seminars prompted analysts to proactively share redacted/sanitised versions of their profiles with partner agencies as a means of yielding improved information sharing. For example, the CSE problem profile in one site is now shared with professionals in key health organisations and has been made available on their intranet system. While a health representative is often on a multi-agency CSE group, health itself is a broad sector covering sexual health services, GPs, Accident and Emergency provision in hospitals, midwifery and mental health provision. One health representative is rarely able to engage all of these services within a local area. One CSE analyst has therefore proactively presented the profile to frontline Accident and Emergency staff, sexual health clinics and school nurses directly, and there is an agreement that this will continue on a quarterly basis as new trends/patterns are identified.

New information can be generated by the sharing of redacted profiles with partners who are unable to access the details discussed at CSE-specific meetings. If services know what they are looking for, or know that what they are seeing is in keeping with the local area profile, they will be arguably better placed to proactively share information with analysts.

Interdependent activities for contextual profiling

The data presented above has provided a foundation for exploring the role/s of problem profiling in advancing both how CSE is responded to and understood. Beyond identifying the need to consider (a) agreed objectives for profiling activity, (b) information sharing arrangements and (c) the best approach to disseminating profiles, the findings indicate a mutually dependent relationship between these three components and profiling activity (Figure 8.2).

To expand, the objective of profiling activity needs to be agreed in order to best facilitate information sharing and proactive data collection. The ability to proactively collect data related to CSE is informed by the use that the wider multi-agency partnership is able to make of the profile. If a range of agencies understand the purpose of the profile and how they may use it, it appears that they will be able to understand what information is required and why, and will therefore be willing to provide access to it. The ability to make partner organisations aware of a local profile will be determined by the objectives of the analyst role. If their objective is to inform the work of meetings that are limited to a small number of individuals directly involved in the management of known CSE cases, for example, then the extent to which profiles can be shared with and used by others is limited.

Conclusion

Achieving the aspirational profiling detailed in this chapter requires strategic investment in research, policy and practice locally, nationally and internationally. Analysts are a critical element of a local authority research team, and investment in analytical support creates an evidential capacity within safeguarding which has often been missing. Our work in sites over the past three years has seen an increased investment in CSE analytical support amongst some local authorities (Firmin et al., 2016), ensuring that children's social care have access to data

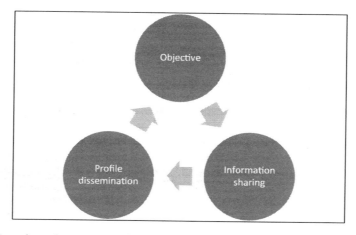

FIGURE 8.2 Interdependent activities for contextual profiling

which will inform their assessments and intervention plans, rather than just monitor their performance for the purposes of local authority reporting.

Some ethical and practical challenges also require further attention. Firstly, contextual profiling risks labelling those individuals, groups and environments that are more visible to professionals as problematic. For example, it would be problematic to conclude that every student in the school class of a young person identified as having been sexually exploited is also at increased risk of CSE and requires intervention. Similarly it would be problematic to suggest that all young people who are identified as spending time with a young person known to social care as having displayed harmful sexual behaviour are also involved in crime or exploitation simply by association. In order to address this tension it is important to articulate, and keep under review, the intention of profiling activity and the evidence base upon which conclusions are drawn. It is critical that contextual profiling is conducted using a wide source of data, beyond those individuals and places already known to social care and policing, to ensure that a different discourse around risk, safety and vulnerability is developed. It is also important to acknowledge that contextual profiling does not only have to adopt a deficit-based model. Analysts could, for example, profile protective peer networks, school environments or public places of safety which provide contexts in which young people can safely socialise and develop.

These are debates worth investing in, as a contextual approach to problem profiling offers significant benefits in our efforts to combat CSE and other related forms of harm. If the objective of profiling is to inform policing and social care, and is generated from case management and investigations of individual cases, then these are the services that will dominate a largely reactive and individualised response. Broadening profiling activity in the ways suggested in this chapter enables the realisation of contextual practice, commissioning and strategic planning. It alerts professionals to the social conditions which are facilitating, enabling, or failing to protect children from CSE, and provides a mechanism for exploring interventions to address them. Understanding how an individual case fits within the patterns at play in a local area has the potential to drive attention towards changing the broader social conditions which are informing individual behaviours. Involving a wider partnership in profiling ensures that the contexts with which those agencies are engaged become part of the discussion, and so too do their services.

The seminar series upon which this chapter has been built also indicates the potential for contextual theories and research evidence to advance the methodological approaches adopted by analysts. By working in partnership with analysts, we identified roles for researchers, academic institutions and government departments to disseminate and enable theory-informed profiling work. In the sites where we worked our relationships with analysts ensured that safeguarding practices and policies are built upon both theoretical and empirical data.

Finally, at an international level the global profiling of CSE and the monitoring of sexual violence prevalence rates more broadly could learn much from the local profiling activity in the UK. International counts of CSE are often focused on the individual characteristics of those affected by it, and, like national and local profiling work, are yet to consistently report the social contexts in which this abuse manifests. This is particularly important given the various global contexts in which CSE occurs; each one having social conditions that, although distinct from each other, all facilitate the abuse of young people. If international efforts are to intervene with, and change, the contexts of abuse, rather than only provide assistance to those affected, then contextual profiling needs to be an aspiration amongst global as well as local leaders. The efficacy of interventions would therefore be measured in relation to monitored change in the nature of exploitative environments as well as the outcomes for young people who have experienced CSE.

References

Barter, C., McCarry, M., Berridge, D. and Evans, K. (2009) *Partner Exploitation and Violence in Teenage Intimate Relationships*. London: NSPCC.

Beckett, H. with Brodie, I., Factor, F., Melrose, M., Pearce, J., Pitts, J., Shuker, L. and Warrington, C. (2013) *'It's wrong but you get used to it': A qualitative study of gang-associated sexual violence towards, and sexual exploitation of, young people in England*. London: Office of the Children's Commissioner.

Beckett, H. and Firmin, C. (2014) *Tackling child sexual exploitation: A study of current practice in London*. Summary Report. London: London Councils.

Beckett, H., Holmes, D. and Walker, J. (2017) *Child sexual exploitation: Definition and guide for professionals*. Luton: University of Bedfordshire.

Bourdieu, P. (1990) *The logic of practice*. California: Stanford University Press.

CEOP (2011) *Out of mind, out of sight: Breaking down the barriers to understanding child sexual exploitation*. London: Child Exploitation and Online Protection Centre.

Cockbain, E. (2013) 'Grooming and the "Asian sex gang predator": The construction of a racial crime threat'. *Race and Class*, 54(4), pp. 22–32.

Cockbain, E., Brayley, H. and Sullivan, J. (2014) 'Towards a common framework for assessing the activity and associations of groups who sexually abuse children'. *Journal of Sexual Aggression*, 20(2), pp. 156–171.

College of Policing (2015) *Authorised professional practice: Intelligence management*. Available at: www.app.college.police.uk/app-content/intelligence-management/intelligence-products/ (Accessed: 9 January 2017).

Curtis, G. (2016) *Practitioner briefing #4: Developing the multi-agency sexual exploitation (MASE) meetings to respond to peer-on-peer CSE*. London: MsUnderstood.

D'Arcy, K., Dhaliwal, S., Thomas, R. with Brodie, I. and Pearce, J. (2015) *Families and communities against child sexual exploitation (FCASE) Final evaluation report*. Luton: University of Bedfordshire.

Firmin, C. (2017) *Abuse between young people: A contextual account*. London: Routledge.

Firmin, C. with Curtis, G., Fritz, D., Olaitan, P., Latchford, L., Lloyd, J. and Larasi, I. (2016) *Practitioner briefing #6: Developing a contextual peer-on-peer abuse profile – Messages for Analysts*. London: MsUnderstood.

Firmin, C., Warrington, C. and Pearce, J. (2016) 'Sexual exploitation and its impact on developing sexualities and sexual relationships: The need for contextual social work interventions'. *British Journal of Social Work*, early view.

Melrose, M. (2013) 'Young people and sexual exploitation: A critical discourse analysis', in Melrose, M. and Pearce, J. (eds) *Critical perspectives on child sexual exploitation and related trafficking*, pp. 9–22. Hampshire: Palgrave Macmillan.

Metropolitan Police Service (2015) *The London child sexual exploitation operating protocol*. London: MPS.

Office of the Children's Commissioner (2013) *'If only someone had listened': Inquiry into child sexual exploitation in gangs and groups*. London: Office of the Children's Commissioner.

Ofsted (2016) *Ofsted social care annual report 2016*. London: Ofsted.

Pearce, J. (2013) 'A social model of "abused consent"', in Melrose, M. and Pearce, J. (eds) *Critical perspectives on child sexual exploitation and related trafficking*, pp. 52–68. Basingstoke: Palgrave Macmillan.

Pitts, J. (2013) 'Drifting into trouble: Sexual exploitation and gang affiliation', in Melrose, M. and Pearce, J. (eds) *Critical perspectives on child sexual exploitation and related trafficking*, pp. 23–37. Basingstoke: Palgrave Macmillan.

Sidebotham, P., Brandon, M., Bailey, S., Belderson, P., Dodsworth, J., Garstang, J., Harrison, E., Retzer, A. and Sorensen, P. (2016) *Pathways to harm, pathways to protection: A triennial analysis of serious case reviews 2011–2014*. London: Department for Education.

9

DEVELOPING PARTICIPATORY PRACTICE AND CULTURE IN CSE SERVICES

Camille Warrington and Isabelle Brodie

Introduction

A recurring theme in the development of child sexual exploitation (CSE) services in the United Kingdom (UK) – and in discussions of what constitutes high quality practice – is the way in which service users participate in decision-making, both about their individual lives and in relation to service design, policy and practice.

This issue of hearing and validating children's voices has attracted increasing concern in recent years following research and legal evidence, public inquiries and serious case reviews indicating that some children and young people's accounts of CSE have been ignored by adults in positions of responsibility (Coffey, 2014; Jay, 2014; Beckett and Warrington, 2015). The issue of engaging with children and young people's accounts and perspectives relates not only to recognition of such abuse, but also to how we best respond to it.

In recognition of these challenges, this chapter explores evidence about current practice in relation to the participation of children and young people in CSE services in the UK. This includes evidence about the way in which service responses are interpreted and experienced by young people, how 'participation' can be translated into the service user experience, and how such practice can be shared and developed. We draw on primary evidence collected during the Alexi Project (see www.alexiproject.org.uk for more information) and a range of other published literature.

We begin by examining historical and cultural strands that relate to the development of CSE services in the UK, and the social construction of participation within these. We then explore current evidence regarding participatory practice, considering how we can develop services that are accessible and acceptable to young people in the context of their experiences of CSE and embed and sustain participatory principles. We consider the value of such participatory practice and its relationship to the protection of children and young people, alongside the changes in organisational culture required to facilitate its realisation.

Definitions

It is important to begin by acknowledging that the term 'participation' – in relation to children and young people – is widely recognised as difficult to define, and subject to multiple interpretations (Brodie *et al.*, 2009; Percy-Smith and Thomas, 2010; Brodie *et al.*, 2016). Thomas (2007) explains that it can refer both to a process and an outcome, and that a distinction can be made between participation in collective decision-making and participation in decisions about children's individual lives. A variety of models have been developed through which to understand different types and levels of children's and young people's participation (Hart, 1992; Shier, 1997; Treseder, 1997), though these are not necessarily recognised or accepted by young people themselves (Horwath, Kalyva and Spyro, 2012; Charles and Haines, 2014). The difficulties in identifying what participation really is and what it means for practice is therefore a recurring theme of both research and practice discussion and one to which we will return.

That said, it is widely accepted that understanding of participation is inextricably linked to thinking about children's rights (Lansdown, 2010). Specifically, participation should be viewed in the context of Article 12 of the United Nations Convention on the Rights of the Child (UNCRC), ratified by the UK in 1991. This asserts the right of children to express their views freely in all matters affecting them, the views of the child being given due weight in accordance with the age and maturity of the child. It is important that this provision is viewed in the context of other civil rights, including rights to freedom of expression, religion, conscience, association and information and the right to privacy. In relation to CSE, it is worth noting the additional rights to protection: Articles 31 and 35 of the UNCRC stipulate that children have the right to be protected from all forms of sexual exploitation, sexual abuse and trafficking. Finally, it is worth noting that although 'participation' is not entirely synonymous with 'service-user involvement' the terms are often used interchangeably and share common principles, most notably a concern with addressing imbalances of power between those giving and receiving welfare support (Glasby and Beresford, 2008).

Some definition of 'CSE services' is also necessary. CSE is defined as per the recent Department for Education (DfE) guidance (DfE, 2017) as a form of child sexual abuse that is typified by exchange, with the child/young person and/or perpetrator receiving something in exchange for the sexual act (see Chapter 1). As noted elsewhere in this book, a range of services, both statutory and voluntary, are involved in responding to CSE, including, for example, the police, youth services, schools and health services. Specialist CSE services are viewed mostly as services with a specific focus on CSE and tend to have developed within the voluntary sector. These range from large, well-known charities which have played a leading role in campaigning for the recognition of the issue to small, local services, which may have evolved from sexual health or sex worker services (Scott and Skidmore, 2006; Harris *et al.*, 2015).

Policy and practice context

The emergence of CSE as an issue of public concern, requiring a targeted approach by local authorities, has been driven by a growing body of evidence, and intersected by legal changes and new government guidance and high-profile criminal cases (see Chapter 1; see also Melrose with Barrett, 2004; Pearce, 2009; Coffey, 2014; Jay, 2014). Government guidance in 2009 provided some impetus, albeit without accompanying resources, for the development of local policy on, and responses to, the issue. Subsequent research highlighted both the patchiness of service availability, but also the need for services to be developed that were acceptable to young people and included young people in decision-making about individual care and service design and development (Jago et al., 2011; Warrington, 2013a, 2013b; Beckett and Firmin, 2014).

Since then, criminal trials revealing the extent of CSE in towns such as Rotherham, Oxford, Peterborough and Derby and media coverage of the sexual abuse offences committed by Jimmy Savile, have highlighted ongoing gaps in service response. Central to this has been the failure of services to listen to, and believe, the accounts of individuals who have been abused (Coffey, 2014; Jay, 2014). The Jay Report into the exploitation of some 1,400 young people in Rotherham, for example, concluded that the failure of professionals to believe the accounts of young people, or respond to their pleas for help, was fundamental to the continued exploitation taking place (Jay, 2014). This message has been reiterated in other high-profile serious case reviews and official enquiries (see for example Coffey, 2014; Casey, 2015), and a myriad of research reports (Beckett, 2011; Beckett and Warrington, 2015 Beckett, Holmes and Walker, 2017).

Precedence for participation

Children and young people's participation in responses to CSE should be viewed and situated in wider practice and policy contexts. The concepts of participation and service user involvement in children's and young people's services are not new and have a well-established history in statutory services for children in care and services for disabled children (Sinclair, 2004; Wright et al., 2004; Leeson, 2007). Similarly youth work has a long history of promoting participation rights and is to an even greater extent based on principles of child or youth-led practice (Crimmens et al., 2004; Wade, 2004; Davies and Merton, 2009; Ord, 2016). In other services, such as health and schools, service user involvement has raised complex ethical questions, but is nonetheless recognised as necessary to appropriate and effective practice (Osler, 2000; Wyse, 2001; Day, 2008).

The need for participation within CSE

The history and widespread recognition of the importance of service user involvement, and its associated codification in governmental and other guidance relating to children, might lead to the conclusion that this is well-established in everyday welfare practice. However, research into safeguarding has tended to emphasise shortcomings in this regard, highlighting the sense of exclusion experienced by both children and their families in child protection and safeguarding processes and the failure to give their perspectives due consideration (Littlechild, 2000; Bell, 2002; Sanders and Mace, 2006; Gallagher et al., 2012). In this respect CSE is no different.

To expand, at a policy level the importance of children's and young people's participation with reference to CSE is explicitly recognised in government guidance and has been since 2009, with emphasis on the need for an approach that promotes a young person's involvement in decisions about their care and their opportunity to make choices (Beckett, Holmes and Walker, 2017; DfE, 2017; Shuker with Ackerley, 2017). As the new DfE (2017, p. 12) guidance highlights, 'all practitioners working with children and families should respond in ways that are child centred: recognising children and young people's rights to participate in decisions about them in line with their maturity, and focusing on the needs of the child'.

However, as highlighted above, recognised shortcomings in both the identification of, and response to, CSE has called into question the degree to which this commitment is being realised in practice. There is strong research and legal evidence that children's and young people's reports of CSE are not always taken sufficiently seriously by adults in positions of responsibility and that this significantly compromises professionals' ability to keep them safe (Jay, 2014). This has generated much media and public outrage, as well as extensive efforts to improve policy and practice through better listening (DfE, 2017; Scott and Botcherby with Ludvigsen, 2017).

The extent of participation

The evidence supports the view that children's and young people's participation rights must be recognised and responded to if professionals are to act in accordance with their responsibility to protect and promote the welfare of children and young people (Warrington, 2013a, 2013b; Hallett, 2017). But this recognition does not necessarily easily translate into practical change. Assertion of the principle that children and young people should be listened to, should be informed and have an active role in decision-making about their lives – and that their views and experiences should be the building blocks of effective service development – does not in itself result in changes to attitudes or current practice.

Participation may seem intuitively attractive. The philosophical arguments on which it is based are robust and seem to be borne out by the emerging body of empirical evidence (Brodie et al., 2016). But if participation is attractive, if it is positively received, if it is effective in the outcomes it delivers, if it is cost effective – then why is it not embedded in all practice with young people affected by CSE? There are examples of outstanding practice in supporting young people's participation in services at both individual and collective levels (see, for example, Ofsted, 2014; Smeaton, 2016). Such work has enabled young people to play an influential role in communicating what makes for effective practice, and letting other young people know what they should demand from their services, through a range of media including films, leaflets, training for professionals and other activities. However, the evidence base – admittedly also patchy – suggests that too often implementation is patchy and dependent on individual rather than wider organisational commitment (Research in Practice, 2015).

Definitional ambiguity

Returning to the question of definition is pertinent here. As noted earlier, how far 'participatory' policy and practice is implemented is also dependent on what 'participation' is taken to mean. Pragmatically, this can be taken as a spectrum, involving a range of activities and approaches. The danger of this position is that participation can then be viewed as optional, either in a particular form or activities undertaken by a specific person. A piecemeal approach to participation in CSE services is likely to lead either to charges of tokenism, or a piecemeal approach that is not in the best interests of the young person.

Professionals have differing views on the extent to which participatory approaches are embedded in their services. For some services, there is a strong sense that a philosophy of participation infuses decision-making. This is often rooted in the historical development of the service:

> The benefits to the organisation are that it's actually them being treated as equals, them not being judged as being inadequate and that actually they can participate as equal peers and have got something that's valid to say and have a lot of things to say, that are positive and negative, not just about our service but about things that are going on around and about other services and interactions with the police. [They] have got a huge amount to say that's so valid, into some of the national consultations, where people are doing things without even thinking about the consequences of it and not understanding what that's like when you're 13, 14, 15.
>
> *(service manager, the Alexi Project)*

> It's really important for it to be really open and for more than just a few young people to be involved. But one thing that I think like young people being involved with things like training and open mornings and interviews, particularly interviews because it shows the staff that are coming that this is what we are as an organisation and it says something so loudly without saying it, if that makes sense. You're kind of showing 'these are all values and this is what we want to do' in a real practical way.
>
> *(service manager, the Alexi Project)*

Such comments do not mean that managers believe they have 'succeeded' in embedding participation. Whilst some will view it as the 'glue' sticking the service together, it is more often acknowledged that working in a participatory way is difficult, and that this is to be expected in view of the complex nature of CSE. Even with strong commitments to equality and the rights of young people to shape actively the services they use, external constraints mean that compromises have to be made, and participatory ways of working continue to need to be fought for. At times this may feel that what was intended to be participatory has become tokenistic, though most will also acknowledge this is part of their learning.

Barriers to participatory practice

The historical overlooking of CSE cases has meant that the driver for much research, policy and practice development has been the fight for recognition of CSE and associated intervention and access to services, or the need to understand the vulnerability of particular groups.[1] Consequently less attention has been given to the nature of services or descriptions of practice that might inform improvement or debate, including children's and young people's participation and its role in safeguarding (Brodie *et al.*, 2016). This lack of attention to the issue of improving participatory practice is not unique to CSE. Yet it is one that cannot be ignored. Writing more generally on participation, Lansdown (2010, p. 11) argues that there is a need for a stronger focus on the application of learning about participation in order to ensure it is embedded as a 'sustainable right for all children, in all aspects of their lives'.

Victimhood and agency

The degree to which participatory practice is embedded in CSE services is also influenced by wider constructions of childhood and abuse. To expand, the development of children's services has been driven historically by perceptions of 'rescue' and state paternalism (Hayden, 1999), and this focus has enduring effects on approaches to safeguarding (Hickle and Hallett, 2016). CSE is no exception, and shares with other areas of child welfare a history of disparity of power between service users and those providing services.

There is an apparent tension between the need to demonstrate the victimhood of young people and a service response that recognises their agency (see Chapter 1; see also Pearce, 2009; Warrington, 2013b; Beckett, Holmes and Walker, 2017). Young people's choices – in terms of their behaviour and their willingness or not to engage with services – present challenges for services which have traditionally perceived their role as one of ensuring children's safety through investigation and intervention within the family.

Considering reasons for this tension, Melrose (2013, p. 21) argues that the discourse of CSE 'is produced by, and in turn reproduces, dominant conceptions of "childhood" and dominant ideologies of adolescent female sexuality which deny female sexual agency'. These conceptions of childhood include ideas of innocence and an absence of sexuality. They assume that children are situated within families and that they do not act outside these boundaries, with no recognition that children can act upon or influence their environments. Young people do not fit neatly within these constructs; a difficulty Melrose (2013) observes to be exacerbated by gendered assumptions around sexuality. The active protection of young people stands at odds with cultural suspicion of young women who are sexually active. Equally, discourses of (hyper)masculinity deny the possibility that young men can be abused and exploited. Within this, the nature of sexual abuse and violence also serves to oppress, resulting in fear and shame, feelings of self-blame and an absence of self-esteem (Coy, 2009; Dodsworth, 2014; Hallett, 2015; Warrington et al., 2017). Young people's agency within these narratives is therefore overlooked, denied or considered a problem rather than a resource.

Managing risk

Recognising that young people are victims of criminal abuse, and reconciling this with a relational approach, which recognises and respects young people's agency, is time consuming, and professionals may feel that the risks are too great. This is especially difficult in the context of current policy thinking relating to child protection, which has seen a move away from early help and family support to high-end, risk-averse practice (Parton, 2011; see also Thom, Sales and Pearce, 2007; Ayre and Preston-Shoot, 2010). These risks may appear even more difficult to manage in the context of austerity and the loss of early help and intervention, family support and youth services (Featherstone, Broadhurst and Holt, 2011; Featherstone et al., 2016).

Organisational structures and culture

There is considerable evidence witnessing to the intensity, professional expertise, time and resource required to embed relational and participatory approaches. This requires organisational commitment, which may not easily be made available. For example, the most recent report of the four UK Children's Commissioners on the implementation of the UNCRC (2015) describe the realisation of Article 12 in UK law and practice as 'highly variable' (paragraph 4:12). Issues include the failure of the Westminster government and devolved parliaments to incorporate the UNCRC into domestic law; the impact of budget cuts, which they argue has resulted in statutory services limiting their work to the delivery of statutory duties; and the lack of determined effort to ensure the voices of those who are more vulnerable or less heard to be engaged in decision-making.

Furthermore, participation in CSE services is only possible if services are available and accessible. Current evidence suggests that not all young people are guaranteed access to a specialist service, and that some young people will have to travel long distances to reach one (Brodie and Shuker, 2017). The question of service accessibility also relates to services that can provide information and forms of support that might prevent exploitation; the loss of youth services as a result of public sector cuts is notable in this respect.

The need for further evidence

There is an acceptance that research has yet to provide a full picture of the service user experience and the ways in which participatory working can be enhanced. This is particularly true of its application within the statutory sector (Lefevre *et al.*, 2017). The perspectives of those who have not engaged with services, or those who remain within statutory services, have on the whole not yet been researched (Brodie *et al.*, 2016). We also need further learning to disentangle the different elements that constitute participative working and understand how these principles relate to other conceptual or treatment models such as trauma-informed or relationship-based practice. It is also important that young people contribute directly to the assessment and measurement of participation.

Making participation happen

There is now a growing body of evidence attesting to the nature or quality of participative practice in terms of direct practice with young people affected by CSE (Warrington, 2016; Brodie *et al.*, 2016). This tends to be focused on the qualities of individual workers and the style of practice. Professionals are liked and valued when they show an ability to listen, to show understanding and care, are warm and friendly and use humour and are knowledgeable about the issues involved. It is similarly appreciated when they treat young people as individuals, keep them up to date with what is happening and allow them to make choices – and so work in what may be termed a 'participatory' way that recognises young people's competence and individual rights (Cossar *et al.*, 2013; Warrington, 2013a; Hallett, 2015). In turn, this permits the building of a relationship of trust, in which young people are more likely to talk about their experiences, or if this is not the case, to be better informed about what is happening to them and to consider ways in which harm can be managed or reduced (Hickle and Hallett, 2016; Lefevre *et al.*, 2017). Conversely, young people are reluctant or rejecting of professionals who are dismissive or judgemental or who display shock at what they are being told (Beckett and Warrington, 2015; Beckett *et al.*, 2016).

The importance of these personal qualities to effective engagement with young people are clearly important and are also recognised as essential by professionals working in statutory services (Lefevre *et al.*, 2017). The focus of this style of working is participative in the sense of enabling young people to play an active role in decision-making about their lives, and it is important to acknowledge that these qualities can be, and are, displayed by professionals working in a statutory setting. However, the capacity of services to make participation a matter not only of individual case work, but to facilitate the co-creation or co-production of service development, is much more dependent on the wider structures within which individuals work, as explored below.

Voluntary engagement

Young people identify a number of specific features of services that promote access to, and participation in, services (Warrington, 2013a; Gilligan, 2015). Voluntary engagement with services emerges as critical in this, but is significantly more likely to be associated with third-sector organisations (Pearce *et al.*, 2002; Melrose and Barrett, 2004). The quotes below illustrate the significance of this:

> The police referred me, but it was my choice – basically I got a visit by two project workers and I got a choice if I wanted to come or not.
>
> *(Mike, 16, in Warrington, 2013, p. 99)*

> With all my agencies that I've worked with I've never had a choice if I work with them or not, but I have here. Like if I don't want to come here I don't have to. Youth group – I have to, because I were on an order [from the courts]. I have to go there. I never had a choice with that one. Social services – I don't get a choice in the matter – if I didn't have to have them I wouldn't have them. It's just like loads of agencies I've never had a choice of going. . . If I don't ask for counselling even then they just go and make me anyway. . . But here, I like it so I come here all the time me.
>
> *(Phoebe, 17, in Warrington, 2013, p. 100)*

The option of whether to attend a service, and to withdraw, stands in contrast to the 'service offer' elsewhere. Symbolically, such choice denotes respect and recognition of the young person's autonomy, and sets the tone and pace of the work that then takes place (Warrington, 2013). This option may not be available to professionals working in some services, however desirable it may be to them.

Working practices

Alongside voluntary engagement young people emphasise the importance of time and control needed to feel comfortable in the service and to get to know professionals, but also a recognition of the time needed to come to terms with their exploitation, and to recover. This links with an understanding of the trauma associated with abuse and exploitation, and the other difficulties young people may be dealing with in their lives (Pearce, 2002; Beckett, 2011; Beckett and Warrington, 2014; Franklin, Raws and Smeaton, 2015).

> You went at your pace; it would never be that on a fixed session – you would have to talk; it was just like 'whenever you're ready'; it's like you decide.
>
> *(young person supported by SECOS, in Smeaton, 2016).*

Stability of personnel will also be an important element in this process. This is identified as especially important for young people whose cases of CSE are going through the criminal justice system, who say that support is often withdrawn when sentencing has taken place

(Beckett and Warrington, 2014). This presents challenges for services where there are high levels of turnover or where insufficient resource is available for longer term work.

Additionally, a commitment to young people's participation in CSE services will also require confidence in holding the risks associated with the young person's behaviour. Young people who have experienced CSE emphasise that they do not respond well to continual anxiety about risk and feel alienated by practice that continually emphasises this risk and seeks to manage it by limiting their behaviour (Shuker, 2014). Instead they argue for the value of practice that focuses on their strengths and abilities as individuals, fosters trust and autonomy and which help develop their self-confidence and self-esteem. This might include creative and arts-based activities. Again, this will require organisational support for the practice required to manage this, including confident management willing to hold risk and allowing staff sufficient autonomy to develop new activities, including group-based work.

Services that work in a participatory way with young people also seem to work differently with parents and carers, who often feel excluded from services and may have strong feelings of guilt about their child's abuse (D'Arcy et al., 2015; Department for Education, 2017; Shuker with Ackerley, 2017). Support that recognises the needs of parents and involves the provision of tailored interventions appears to result in greater emotional resilience and a greater ability to understand and respond appropriately to their child's behaviour. This is also valued by young people (D'Arcy et al., 2015; The Alexi Project, 2017).

Voluntary/statutory services

Young people have typically drawn a distinction between their experience of services with a specific focus on CSE and statutory child protection services. Young people view the voluntary sector as offering a distinctive type and quality of service, in contrast to statutory services which have often been experienced as intrusive and untrustworthy. These judgements are made in the context of extensive experience of other services (Coy, 2009; Warrington, 2013a; Hallett, 2015). This suspicion or rejection of statutory services can be a consequence of the shame and stigma associated with CSE, but it should also be considered in the wider context of individual, family and community experience, especially those associated with child protection and safeguarding and law enforcement. In one study of young people with experience of gang associated sexual violence, the majority said they would not report their experiences of sexual violence to the police (Beckett et al., 2013; Beckett et al., 2016). Young people and their families complain that their experiences have too often involved being passed from service to service, with a lack of adequate information or consistent personnel (D'Arcy et al., 2014; Beckett et al., 2016).

To this extent the experience of sexually exploited young people needs to be linked with other evidence from young people who are vulnerable or in various kinds of trouble, and who have experienced rejection or a lack of sympathy or humanity from statutory services (see, for example, Buckley, Carr and Whelan, 2011; Ghaffar, Manby and Race, 2011). Recognising this commonality is important in developing a more holistic view of young people's experience as service users and the way in which this may explain their engagement or not with services relating to their sexual exploitation.

This should not be taken to mean that professionals working in statutory services cannot be successful in working sympathetically with young people. At the individual level, there is evidence of approaches that are 'in tune' with young people, working at their pace and according to their needs, and allowing them to exercise autonomy and choice and experience a sense of control. This includes young people's experience of working with services which are often found to be alienating and hostile, such as the police (see, for example, Beckett and Warrington, 2015; Beckett *et al.*, 2016). Anecdotally, training professionals from the police, schools, health and other statutory services suggests that many are working with young people affected by CSE. Potentially, then, there is considerable space to extend discussion of what is meant by participatory approaches in working with sexually exploited young people.

Conclusion

Whilst we recognise that there is a need for further evidence regarding effective participatory practice, especially in the statutory sector (Lefevre *et al.*, 2017), the existing evidence base compellingly argues that participation represents not only a morally acceptable model for work with young people and families, but one that represents the best means to protection and longer-term recovery (Warrington, 2013a; Beckett and Warrington, 2015; Hallett, 2015; Beckett *et al.*, 2016; Warrington, 2016).

If the culture and techniques of practice with young people are to become more participative, then it is essential that the value of participative practice to outcomes for young people, their families, services and professionals is fully recognised. The importance of sufficient resourcing and supportive structures cannot be understated. The modelling of good practice, on the part of individual professionals and services, can also influence practice elsewhere. In turn, this requires a sharing of practice and discussion between practitioners about differences in approach, constraints and challenges in working with young people affected by CSE.

Discussion of young people's engagement in services can easily descend to the glib. Working with young people affected by CSE is a challenge, not least in light of the efforts of abusers to hold on to their victims. The evidence increasingly indicates, however, that it is only through effective engagement of young people that professionals can contribute to their empowerment, and in turn to their increased safety and well-being (Brodie *et al.*, 2016; Warrington, 2013a, 2013b; Lefevre *et al.*, 2017).

Note

1 For example, different ethnic groups (Gohir, 2013), young people with disabilities (Franklin, Raws and Smeaton, 2015) or children in care (Beckett, 2011).

References

The Alexi Project (2017) *The Alexia Project.* Available at: www.alexiproject.org.uk/ (Accessed: 14 August 2017).

Ayre, P. and Preston-Shoot, M. (eds) (2010) *Children's services at the crossroads: A critical evaluation of contemporary policy for practice.* Lyme Regis: Russell House Publishing.

Beckett, H. (2011) *'Not a world away': The sexual exploitation of children and young people in Northern Ireland.* Belfast: Barnardo's.

Beckett, H. with Brodie, I., Factor, F., Melrose, M., Pearce, J., Pitts, J., Shuker, L. and Warrington, C. (2013) *'It's wrong but you get used to it': A qualitative study of gang-associated sexual violence towards, and exploitation of, young people in England.* Luton: University of Bedfordshire.

Beckett, H., Holmes D. and Walker, J. (2017) *Child sexual exploitation: Definition and guide for professionals: Extended text.* Available at: www.beds.ac.uk/__data/assets/pdf_file/0009/536175/UOB-RIP-CSE-GuidanceFeb2017.pdf (Accessed: 8 August 2017).

Beckett, H. and Warrington, C. (2015) *Making justice work: Experiences of criminal justice for children and young people affected by sexual exploitation as victims and witnesses*. Luton: The University of Bedfordshire. Available at: www.beds.ac.uk/__data/assets/pdf_file/0011/461639/MakingJusticeWorkFullReport.pdf (Accessed: 25 July 2017).

Beckett, H., Warrington, C., Ackerley, E., and Allnock, D. (2016) *Children's voices research report: Children and young people's perspectives on the police's role in safeguarding: A report for Her Majesty's Inspectorate of Constabulary*. Luton: University of Bedfordshire.

Bell, M. (2002) 'Promoting children's rights through relationship'. *Child and Family Social Work*, 7, pp. 1–11.

Brodie, E., Cowling, E., Nissen, N. with Paine, A. E., Jochum, V. and Warburton, D. (2009) *Understanding participation: A literature review*. London: NCVO/IVR/Involve.

Brodie, I. with D'Arcy, K., Harris, J., Roker, D., Shuker, L. and Pearce, J. (2016) *The participation of young people in child sexual exploitation services: A scoping review of the literature*. Available at: www. alexiproject.org.uk/assets/documents/Alexi-Project-Participation-Scoping-Review.pdf (Accessed: 29 July 2017).

Brodie, I. and Shuker, L. (2017) *Principles for participatory work with young people affected by child sexual exploitation: The evidence base*. Luton: University of Bedfordshire.

Buckley, H., Carr, N. and Whelan, S. (2011) '"Like walking on eggshells": Service user views and expectations of the child protection system'. *Child & Family Social Work*, 16, pp. 101–110.

Casey, L. (2015) *Report of inspection of Rotherham metropolitan borough council*. London: Department for Education.

Charles, A. and Haines, K. (2014) 'Measuring young people's participation in decision-making'. *International Journal of Children's Rights*, 22, pp. 641–659.

Coffey, A. (2014) *Real voices: Child sexual exploitation in greater Manchester – An independent report by Ann Coffey, MP*. Manchester.

Cossar, J., Brandon, M., Bailey, S., Belderson, P., Biggart, L. and Sharpe, D. (2013) *'It takes a lot to build trust'. Recognition and telling: Developing earlier routes to help for children and young people*. London: Office of the Children's Commissioner for England.

Coy, M. (2009) '"Moved around like bags of rubbish that nobody wants": How multiple placement moves can make young women vulnerable to sexual exploitation'. *Child Abuse Review*, 18, pp. 254–266.

Crimmens, D., Factor, F., Jeffs, T., Pitts, J., Pugh, C., Spence, J. and Turner, P. (2004) *Reaching socially excluded young people: A national study of street-based youth work*. Lyme Regis: Russell House Publishing.

D'Arcy, K., Dhaliwal, S. and Thomas, R. with Brodie, I. and Pearce, J. (2015) *Families and communities against child sexual exploitation*. Luton: University of Bedfordshire.

Davies, B. and Merton, B. (2009) 'Squaring the circle? The state of youth work in some children and young people's services'. *Youth and Policy*, 103, pp. 5–24.

Day, C. (2008) 'Children's and young people's involvement and participation in mental health care'. *Child and Adolescent Mental Health*, 13, pp. 2–8.

Department for Education (DfE) (2017) *Child sexual exploitation: Definition and a guide for practitioners, local leaders and decision makers working to protect children from child sexual exploitation*. Available at: www. gov.uk/government/uploads/system/uploads/attachment_data/file/591903/CSE_Guidance_Core_Document_13.02.2017.pdf (Accessed: 8 August 2017).

Dodsworth, J. (2014) 'Sexual exploitation: Selling and swapping sex, victimhood and agency'. *Child Abuse Review*, 23, pp. 185–199.

Featherstone, B., Broadhurst, K. and Holt, K. (2011) 'Thinking systemically – thinking politically: Building strong partnerships with children and families in the context of rising inequality'. *British Journal of Social Work*, 42, pp. 618–633.

Featherstone, B., Gupta, A., Morris, K. M. and Warner, J. (2016) *Let's stop feeding the risk monster: Towards a social model of 'child protection'*. Available at: http://eprints.whiterose.ac.uk/98016/15/Morris%2C%20K%20-%20Lets%20stop%20feeding%20the%20risk%20monster%20-%20acceptance%202015-12-07.pdf (Accessed: 8 August 2017).

Franklin, A., Raws, P. and Smeaton, E. (2015) *Unprotected, overprotected: Meeting the needs of young people with learning disabilities who experience, or are at risk of, sexual exploitation*. Ilford: Barnardo's.

Gallagher, M., Smith, M., Hardy, M. and Wilkinson, H. (2012) 'Children and families involvement in social work decision-making'. *Children and Society*, 26, pp. 74–85.

Ghaffar, W., Manby, M. and Race, T. (2011) 'Exploring the experiences of parents and carers whose children have been subject to child protection plans'. *British Journal of Social Work*, 42, pp. 887–905.

Gilligan, P. (2015) 'What do young women say helps them to move on from child sexual exploitation?'. *Child Abuse Review*, early view.

Glasby, J. and Beresford, P. (2008) 'Who knows best? Evidence-based practice and the service user contribution'. *Critical Social Policy*, 26, pp. 268–284.

Gohir, S. (2013) *Unheard voices: The sexual exploitation of Asian girls and young women*. Birmingham: Asian Women's Network.

Hallett, S. (2015) '"An uncomfortable comfortableness": "Care", child protection and sexual exploitation'. *The British Journal of Social Work*, 46, pp. 2137–2152.

Hallett, S. (2017) *Making sense of child sexual exploitation: Exchange, abuse and young people*. Bristol: Policy Press.

Harris, J., Roker, D., D'Arcy, K. and Shuker, L. with Brodie, I. and Pearce, J. (2015) *Hub and spoke evaluation: Year 2 report*. Luton: University of Bedfordshire.

Hart, R. A. (1992) *Children's participation, from tokenism to citizenship*. Florence, Italy: UNICEF.

Hayden, C. (1999) *State child care: Looking after children? (Vol. 1)*. London: Jessica Kingsley Publishers.

Hickle, K. and Hallett, S. (2016) 'Mitigating harm: Considering harm reduction principles in work with sexually exploited young people'. *Children and Society*, 30, pp. 302–313.

Horwath, J., Kalyva, E. and Spyro, S. (2012) '"I want my experience to make a difference": Promoting participation in policy-making and service development by young people who experienced violence'. *Children and Youth Services Review*, 34, pp. 155–162.

Jago, S., Arocha, L., Brodie, I., Melrose, M., Pearce, J. and Warrington, C. (2011) *What's going on to safeguard children and young people from sexual exploitation? How local partnerships respond to child sexual exploitation*. Luton: University of Bedfordshire.

Jay, A. (2014) *Independent inquiry into child sexual exploitation in Rotherham: 1997–2013*. Rotherham: Rotherham Metropolitan Borough Council. Available at: www.rotherham.gov.uk/downloads/file/1407/independent_inquiry_cse_in_rotherham (Accessed: 25 July 2017).

Lansdown, G. (2010) 'The realisation of children's participation rights' in Percy-Smith, B. and Thomas, N. (eds) *A Handbook of Children and Young People's Participation*. London and New York: Routledge.

Leeson, C. (2007) 'My life in care: Experiences of non-participation in decision-making processes'. *Child & Family Social Work*, 12, pp. 268–277.

Lefevre, M., Hickle, K., Luckock, B. and Ruch, G. (2017) 'Building trust with children and young people at risk of child sexual exploitation: The professional challenge'. *British Journal of Social Work*, Advance Access, Published 14 February 2017, pp. 1–18.

Littlechild, B. (2000) 'Children's rights to be heard in child protection processes – law, policy and practice in England and Wales'. *Child Abuse Review*, 9, pp. 403–415.

Melrose, M. (2013) 'Young people and sexual exploitation: A critical discourse analysis', in Melrose, M. and Pearce, J. (eds) *Critical perspectives in child sexual exploitation and related trafficking (pp. 9–22)*. Basingstoke: Palgrave Macmillan.

Melrose, M. with Barrett, D. (2004) *Anchors in floating lives: Interventions with young people sexually abused through prostitution*. Lyme Regis: Russell House Publishing.

Ofsted (2014) *Involving children and young people in the services they receive: Street safe Lancashire*. London: Ofsted.

Ord, J. (2016) *Youth work process, product and practice: Creating an authentic curriculum in work with young people*. Lyme Regis: Russell House Publishing.

Osler, A. (2000) 'Children's rights, responsibilities and understandings of school discipline'. *Research Papers in Education*, 15, pp. 49–67.

Parton, N. (2011) 'Child protection and safeguarding in England: Changing and competing conceptions of risk and their implications for social work'. *British Journal of Social Work*, 41, pp. 854–875.

Pearce, J. (2009) *Young people and sexual exploitation: 'It's not hidden, you just aren't looking'*. London: Taylor & Francis.

Pearce, J. with Williams, M. and Galvin, C. (2002) *'It's someone taking a part of you': A study of young people and sexual exploitation*. London: National Children's Bureau.

Percy-Smith, B. and Thomas, N. (2010) 'Introduction', in Percy-Smith, B. and Thomas, N. (eds). *A handbook of children and young people's participation: Perspectives from theory and practice*. Available at: http://nmd.bg/wp-content/uploads/2013/02/Routledge-A_Handbook_for_Children_and_Young_Peoples_Participation.pdf (Accessed: 8 August 2017).

Research in Practice (2015) *Working effectively to address child sexual exploitation*. Dartington, UK: Research in Practice.

Sanders, R. and Mace, S. (2006) 'Agency policy and the participation of children and young people in the child protection process'. *Child Abuse Review*, 15(2), pp. 89–109.

Scott, S. and Skidmore, P. (2006) *Reducing the risk: Barnardo's support for sexually exploited young people. A two-year evaluation*. Ilford: Barnardo's.

Scott, S. and Botcherby, S. with Ludvigsen, A. (2017) *Wigan and Rochdale child sexual exploitation innovation project: Evaluation report*. London: Department for Education.

Shier, H. (1997) 'Pathways to participation: Openings, opportunities and obligations'. *Children and Society*, 15, pp. 107–117.

Shuker, L. (2014) *The Barnardo's safe accommodation project: Consultation with young people*. Luton: University of Bedfordshire.

Shuker, L. with Ackerley, E. (2017) *Empowering parents: Evaluation of parents as partners in safeguarding children and young people*. Luton: University of Bedfordshire.

Sinclair, R. (2004) 'Participation in practice: Making it meaningful, effective and sustainable'. *Children & Society*, 18, pp. 106–118.

Smeaton, E. (2016) *Going the extra mile: Learning from SECOS's child sexual exploitation service*. Ilford: Barnardo's.

Thom, B., Sales, R. and Pearce, J. (eds) (2007) *Growing up with risk*. Bristol: Policy Press.

Thomas, N. (2007) 'Towards a theory of children's participation'. *International Journal of Children's Rights*, 15, pp. 199–218.

Treseder, P. (1997) *Empowering children and young people: Training manual*. London: Save the Children and Children's Rights Office.

Wade, H. (2004) *Hear by right: Standards for the active involvement of young people – mapping the impact of organisational change*. London: Local Government Association/Leicester: National Youth Agency.

Warrington, C. (2013a) *'Helping me find my own way': Sexually exploited young people's involvement in decision-making about their care*. Professional Doctorate Thesis. Luton: University of Bedfordshire.

Warrington, C. (2013b) 'Partners in care? Sexually exploited young people's inclusion and exclusion from decision-making about safeguarding', in Melrose, M. and Pearce, J. (eds) *Critical perspectives in child sexual exploitation and related trafficking* (pp. 110–124). Basingstoke: Palgrave Macmillan.

Warrington, C. (2016) *Young person centred approaches in child sexual exploitation – promoting participation and building self-efficacy: Frontline tool*. Dartington, UK: Research in Practice. Available at: www.rip.org.uk/resources/publications/frontline-resources/young-personcentred-approaches-in-cse--promoting-participation-and-building-selfefficacy-frontline-tool-2017/ (Accessed: 8 August 2017).

Warrington, C. with Beckett, H., Ackerley, E., Walker, M. and Allnock, D. (2017) *Making noise: Children's voices for positive change after sexual abuse in the family environment*. Luton: University of Bedfordshire.

Wright, P., Turner, C., Clay, D. and Mills, H. (2004) *The participation of children and young people in developing social care. Participation Practice Guide 06*. London: Social Care Institute for Excellence.

Wyse, D. (2001) 'Felt tip pens and school councils: Children's participation rights in four English schools'. *Children & Society*, 15, pp. 209–218.

INDEX